To Alma~

Merry Christmas

from the yahoo! state

♥

lj-tex
2016

THE BEST OF
TYPICALLY TEXAS
COOKBOOK

FROM THE PUBLISHERS OF TEXAS CO-OP POWER

DESIGN AND PRODUCTION

Andy Doughty
Jane Sharpe
Grace Arsiaga

EDITORIAL

Karen Nejtek
Shannon Oelrich
Samantha Bryant
Chris Burrows
Christine Carlson
Suzanne Halko
Ellen Stader

Published by Texas Electric Cooperatives dba Texas Co-op Power
Copyright 2015, Texas Electric Cooperatives
Printed in United States of America
Library of Congress Control Number 2015955130
ISBN 0-9779560-1-2

TEXAS CO-OP POWER

1122 Colorado St., 24th Floor
Austin, Texas 78701
(512) 454-0311
www.texascooppower.com

First printing, November 2015
10 9 8 7 6 5 4 3 2 1

IMAGE CREDITS

ALL PHOTOS © SHUTTERSTOCK.COM | **FRONT COVER** BRENT HOFACKER | **SNACKS & DRINKS** MAGDANATKA | **BREADS** KATI MOLIN | **SOUPS & SALADS** ZORYANCHIK | **VEGETABLES & SIDES** SUPERCAT | **MAIN DISHES** LISOVSKAYA NATALIA | SHUTTERSTOCK.COM
DESSERTS | BRIAN OLIVER PHOTOGRAPHY | **SAUCES, SPREADS & MORE** CHRISTIAN JUNG | **BACK COVER** PINKYONE | **INDEX** STOCK CREATIONS | **ENDPAPER PATTERN** VENIMO | ISTOCK.COM

CONTENTS

FOREWORD

More than 40 years ago, Texas Electric Cooperatives published *Typically Texas Cookbook*—a book that captured the church social, potluck and dinnertime favorites of electric cooperative members living in rural and small-town Texas. The recipes and flavors were rich in heritage and exemplified "good home cooking."

After almost two decades of popularity, TEC presented a sequel, *The Second Typically Texas Cookbook.* The new volume continued the tradition of presenting recipes gathered from Texas electric cooperative members with an updated approach to ingredients that still produced simple and delicious flavors that warmed the heart.

More than 50,000 copies of *Typically Texas* cookbooks dwell in kitchens across Texas. With a whole new generation of cooks preparing family meals, it's time to share these recipes again.

The Best of Typically Texas Cookbook is what its title suggests— a collection of the best recipes from *Typically Texas Cookbook* and *The Second Typically Texas Cookbook*. This volume celebrates the legacy of Texas home cooks who have been making great food and bringing smiles to the dinner table for decades.

SNACKS
& DRINKS

Cheesy Olive Balls

MRS. J.W. DAY JR. | FLOYDADA, LIGHTHOUSE EC

½ cup butter, softened
1 cup flour
½ pound sharp cheese, grated
Stuffed green olives, well drained
Paprika

Mix butter, flour and cheese together. Roll into balls (a little larger than marble). Put on cookie sheet and mash with thumb. Cut olives into 3 pieces, and place 1 piece in the center of each bit of dough. Mold the dough up around the olive and chill 1 hour. Sprinkle with paprika. Preheat oven to 350 degrees. Bake 15 minutes or until done.

Cheese Roll

MRS. FRANK CARTER | MERKEL, TAYLOR EC

2 pounds processed cheese (Velveeta preferred)
8 ounces cream cheese
2 cups chopped pecans
1 teaspoon garlic powder
2 teaspoons crushed red pepper
Paprika or chili powder

Allow cheeses to soften to room temperature. Combine all ingredients except paprika in a bowl, mixing well. Form into rolls by hand. Roll in paprika or chili powder and keep in refrigerator for 24 hours before serving on party crackers.

Cheese Log

MRS. PAT ADCOX | SNYDER, MIDWEST EC

16 ounces cream cheese
1 pound sharp cheddar cheese, grated
Dash of garlic powder
Salt, to taste
2 cups finely chopped pecans
Chili powder

Have cream cheese at room temperature and cream well. Add grated cheddar cheese, garlic powder, salt and pecans. Make into a roll and roll in chili powder. Chill well and slice. Serve with crackers.

Cheese Snappies

MRS. HOLLAND HENDERSON | CORPUS CHRISTI, BANDERA EC

1 cup butter
2 cups flour
8 ounces extra sharp cheddar cheese, grated
1–3 teaspoons cayenne pepper
Salt, to taste
2 cups crispy rice cereal

Preheat oven to 350 degrees. Cut butter into flour until mixture resembles coarse meal. Mix in cheese, cayenne and salt. Add cereal and mix. Shape into small balls and place on ungreased cookie sheet. Flatten with fork. Bake 15 minutes.

Bean Dip

MRS. CONN J. TATUM | DAVILLA, BARTLETT EC

1 onion, chopped
½ cup bacon grease
2 cans (15 ounces each) refried beans
1 pound "rat" (mild cheddar) cheese, grated
1 small jar (8 ounces) picante sauce
Salt, pepper and garlic powder to taste

In a large skillet, sauté onion in bacon grease. Add refried beans and mix. Add cheese and simmer until melted. Add picante sauce, salt, pepper and garlic to taste.

Christmas Canapés

MRS. CARL NEWSOME | LUBBOCK, SOUTH PLAINS EC

½ cup mayonnaise
½ cup sour cream
1 packet Italian dressing mix
1 cup shredded Swiss cheese
1 cup finely chopped bell pepper
White and whole wheat bread slices
Pimientos

Mix together mayonnaise, sour cream and dressing mix. Add cheese and bell pepper. Using a Christmas cookie cutter, cut trees, stars and bells from slices of white and whole wheat bread. Spread 1 teaspoonful of mix on each slice of bread. Broil 2 minutes. Decorate with pimientos, making them into the shape of poinsettias.

Texas Crab Grass Canapés

AUDREY WANN | BAY CITY, JACKSON EC

1 package (10 ounces) frozen chopped spinach
½ cup finely chopped medium onion
½ cup butter
1 can or 1 cup crab meat, picked over
¾ cup grated Parmesan cheese
Melba toast

Cook and drain spinach well. Sauté onion in butter. Combine all ingredients. Serve on Melba toast, not crackers.

COOK'S NOTE: We go to Houston each New Year's Eve, and I think we are invited because of this recipe. They always assign us the hors d'oeuvres and say, "You'll bring the grass."

Welcome Wafers

MRS. GORDON SHOOK | PEARL, HAMILTON COUNTY EC

¾ cup butter, softened
½ cup grated cheddar cheese
⅓ cup crumbled blue cheese
½ clove garlic, grated
1 teaspoon parsley
1 teaspoon chives
2 cups flour

Cream together butter and cheeses. Mix with garlic, parsley and chives. Mix in flour. Shape into rolls. Chill for at least 1 hour. Preheat oven to 375 degrees. Slice rolls into wafers and place on cookie sheet. Bake 10 minutes.

Big Cheese Olives

ANNIE BELLE GIBBS | MONTGOMERY, MID-SOUTH ECA

11 ounces cream cheese
1 tablespoon mayonnaise or salad dressing
1½ teaspoons horseradish, or to taste
1 jar large stuffed olives (about 20)
2 or more cups finely chopped pecans

Mix cream cheese, mayonnaise and horseradish with an electric mixer. Using hands, shape cream cheese mixture around each olive. Mixture may need to be refrigerated briefly to be workable. Then, roll olives in chopped pecans. Refrigerate overnight; cut lengthwise to serve.

COOK'S NOTE: These are really worth the effort at Christmas and make a lovely serving platter of hors d'oeuvres.

Boursin Cheese

BARBARA A. KOVAL | LAKE KIOWA, COOKE COUNTY EC

8 ounces cream cheese, softened
⅓ cup sour cream
¼ cup unsalted butter, softened
1 tablespoon chives
1 tablespoon parsley
1 small clove garlic, grated
Salt and pepper, to taste

In blender or mixer, blend cream cheese, sour cream and butter. Add all other ingredients and mix well. Salt and pepper to taste. Put in a small mold and chill for at least 12 hours. Serve with crackers or cocktail-sized slices of pumpernickel.

Onion Crisp Snack

HELEN HOWARD | CLIFTON, MCLENNAN COUNTY EC

1 cup butter, softened
2 cups grated sharp cheddar cheese
1 packet onion soup mix
2 cups flour

Mix all ingredients together until they form a ball. Divide and form into rolls about the size of a quarter. Chill for 2–3 hours. Preheat oven to 350 degrees. Cut rolls into ¼-inch slices and put on cookie sheet. Bake 10-15 minutes.

Salami

LOIS NEUMANN FERGUSON | BIG FOOT, MEDINA EC

4 tablespoons curing salt
2½ teaspoons mustard seed
2½ teaspoons garlic powder
1½ teaspoons sausage seasoning
1 teaspoon hickory-smoked salt
5 pounds ground beef, or beef and venison

Mix spices and sprinkle over ground meat; mix thoroughly. Refrigerate 4 days. Knead once each day. Knead again and shape into 10 small rolls, 1½ inches in diameter. Bake at 150 degrees 8 hours.

Beef Jerky

MARTHA SITKA | HALLETTSVILLE, GUADALUPE VALLEY EC

2½ pounds round steak, sliced very thin
4 tablespoons liquid smoke flavoring
4 tablespoons soy sauce
1 teaspoon onion salt
1 teaspoon garlic salt
1 teaspoon black pepper

Mix all ingredients together. Make sure all meat is coated with the sauce. Put in a covered container in the refrigerator and marinate for 48 hours. Remove top oven rack and spray with cooking spray. Cover the bottom rack with foil to catch drippings. Lay the meat slices on top oven rack and return to oven. Cook at 125 degrees 4 hours. Cool and store in the refrigerator.

COOK'S NOTE: This is also good when made with venison.

Summer Sausage

DUSTIN GASKINS | KNOTT, CAP ROCK EC

2 pounds ground beef
1½ tablespoons curing salt
   (Morton's Tender Quick preferred)
1½ tablespoons liquid smoke flavoring
¼ teaspoon onion powder
1 teaspoon whole black pepper, crushed
¼ teaspoon dry mustard
¼ teaspoon garlic powder
1 cup water

Combine all ingredients. Mix thoroughly by hand and shape into 3 rolls. Wrap in plastic wrap. Chill at least 24 hours. After chilling, unwrap each roll and place on the rack of a broiler pan. Bake at 250 degrees 2 hours. Store wrapped in refrigerator.

COOK'S NOTE: I earned a blue ribbon with this recipe at the Howard County 4-H Food Show and also at the District 6 Food Show in Fort Stockton. I served my Summer Sausage with crackers at my grandmother's Christmas Eve party. Everyone enjoyed it.

Chicken Wings

ANN WOODLEY | PORTER, GATE CITY EC

20–25 chicken wings
1½ cups water
1½ cups soy sauce
1½ cups sugar
½ cup vegetable oil
½ cup pineapple juice
1½ teaspoons garlic powder
1½ teaspoons ground ginger

Cut off and discard tips of wings. Mix all other ingredients together. Reserve 1½ cups marinade. Pour remaining marinade over the wings in a large, shallow dish. Cover and refrigerate overnight. Pour marinade off. Place chicken wings in a shallow, foil-lined pan with reserved marinade over them. Bake at 350 degrees 1–1½ hours until glazed; turn occasionally during baking.

COOK'S NOTE: These are great appetizers for a before-dinner snack or a party. We have a grandson who can eat all of them in one sitting.

Dodie's Olive Balls

BERNIECE BAILEY | CHICO, WISE EC

2 cups grated cheese
½ cup butter, softened
1 cup flour
½ teaspoon salt
½ teaspoon pepper
48 small stuffed olives

Mix first 5 ingredients. Work dough around olives. Put in freezer until cold. Preheat oven to 400 degrees. Put on baking sheet with a lip and bake 10-15 minutes.

COOK'S NOTE: This recipe was given to me by a sister-in-law in 1943. It is a very good appetizer and can be frozen for several weeks before baking.

Mock Paté de Foie Gras

JOAN PLUMLEE | BURLINGTON, BELFALLS EC

1 pound chicken livers
2 tablespoons butter
2 tablespoons prepared horseradish
½ cup mayonnaise
1 teaspoon paprika
1 teaspoon salt
½ cup finely chopped onion
Parsley (optional)

Cook livers in butter until done. Process in food processor or put through food grinder. Mix with horseradish, mayonnaise, paprika, salt and onion. Store in crock or other covered container in refrigerator to blend flavors. Garnish with parsley, if desired, and serve with crackers or toasted bread fingers.

Ham and Cheese Appetizers

VETA FORD | TAHOKA, LYNTEGAR EC

2 cups baking mix (Bisquick preferred)
¾ cup finely chopped, fully cooked smoked ham
1 cup shredded Swiss or cheddar cheese,
    or ½ cup each
½ cup finely chopped onion
¼ cup sour cream
½ cup grated Parmesan cheese
2 tablespoons snipped parsley
½ teaspoon salt
2 cloves garlic, crushed
⅔ cup milk
1 egg

Preheat oven to 350 degrees. Grease a 9-by-13-inch pan. Mix all ingredients and spread in pan. Bake until golden brown, 25–30 minutes. Cut into 2-by-1½-inch rectangles. Makes 36 appetizers.

Ham Paté en Croute

MRS. ERNEST F. OSBORN | FRIONA, DEAF SMITH EC

½ cup butter or margarine, softened
2 cups ground smoked or boiled ham
1 tablespoon grated onion
1 teaspoon crushed garlic
3 tablespoons heavy cream
2 teaspoons prepared mustard
1 teaspoon dry mustard
2 tablespoons chopped parsley
2 tablespoons chopped chives
¼ teaspoon black pepper
2 teaspoons Worcestershire sauce
1 loaf French bread (about 8 inches long
    and 3 inches wide)

Beat butter at high speed with an electric mixer until light and fluffy. Gradually add ground ham. When ham-butter mixture is mixed, mix in remaining ingredients, except bread. Cover bowl with plastic wrap and chill until firm. While ham mixture is chilling, cut off ends of bread. Using a long slender knife, cut out and remove soft insides of bread, leaving a shell about ¼ inch thick. Stand bread upright on one end. Using a spoon, gently push ham mixture into hollow crust, packing it firmly and filling it completely. Replace ends of bread and wrap in aluminum foil; refrigerate for several hours or overnight. To serve, slice bread into about ¼-inch slices. One loaf will make about 30 slices, or will serve 6 people as a main course.

COOK'S NOTE: This recipe was served for brunch and guests always went back for seconds.

Armadillo Eggs

AUDREY WANN | BAY CITY, JACKSON EC

1 pound bulk pan sausage
1½ cups baking mix
⅓ cup self-rising flour
¼ pound Monterey jack cheese, cut into cubes
1 can (7 ounces) whole green chiles
1 box (5 ounces) seasoned coating mix
    (Shake 'n Bake preferred)

Mix sausage, baking mix and self-rising flour. Set aside. Slice green chiles and wrap them around the cheese cubes. Pat sausage mix around this and roll to resemble egg shape. Preheat oven to 375 degrees. Roll "eggs" in coating mix and place on a rack in a shallow pan. Bake 15-20 minutes. Serve hot.

Guacamole

LUNA CROCKER | MARIETTA, BOWIE-CASS EC

2 ripe avocados
2 tablespoons lemon juice
2 tablespoons grated onion
2 garlic cloves, crushed
½ teaspoon salt
¼ teaspoon pepper
4 tablespoons chopped green chiles
1 small tomato, chopped
Grated cheese, optional

Peel avocados and remove seeds. Chop coarsely and add lemon juice, onion, garlic, salt, pepper, chiles and tomato. Mash avocados and other ingredients (or put in blender) until smooth. Cover and chill. Grated cheese may be added, if desired. Serve on lettuce. Garnish with tomato wedges, or serve as a dip with corn chips or tortilla chips. Makes 2–4 servings.

Shrimp Mousse

HELEN MERKA | ROCKDALE, BARTLETT EC

16 ounces cream cheese
1 cup mayonnaise
2 cups sour cream
½ cup finely minced bell pepper
½ cup finely minced celery
¼ cup finely minced pimientos
¾ cup finely minced green onions
½ cup chili sauce
⅛ teaspoon hot sauce
1 teaspoon salt
1 tablespoon Worcestershire sauce
2 tablespoons unflavored gelatin granules
Juice of 2 lemons
¼ cup cold water
6 cups chopped, cooked and deveined shrimp
Watercress or parsley, for garnish

In a bowl, mix cream cheese, mayonnaise and sour cream until well blended. Add bell pepper, celery, pimiento, green onions, chili sauce, hot sauce, salt and Worcestershire; blend well. Dissolve gelatin in lemon juice and cold water. Heat over water in top of double boiler for 5–10 minutes. Cool, then gradually fold into the cheese mixture. Add shrimp and blend well. Pour into a 2-quart ring mold or shrimp mold. Refrigerate overnight. Unmold and garnish with watercress or parsley. Serve as hors d'oeuvres or as a main dish.

COOK'S NOTE: This makes a pretty plate for a luncheon by using individual molds. Excellent served with crackers.

Eggplant Caviar

MRS. NORMAN LAY | CHANDLER, NEW ERA EC

1 medium eggplant
1 medium onion, finely minced
1–2 cloves garlic, finely minced
1 teaspoon sugar
1 ripe tomato, peeled, seeded and finely chopped
3 tablespoons olive oil
2 tablespoons vinegar
Salt and pepper

Broil eggplant 5–6 inches from heat, turning often, 45 minutes, or until skin is blackened and blistered and very soft all the way through. Cool, peel and finely chop. In a bowl, blend with remaining ingredients. Cover and refrigerate at least 4 hours, or overnight. Serve with pita bread or rye crackers.

COOK'S NOTE: This recipe may also be served on a lettuce leaf as a first course.

Stuffed Mushrooms

DORA HILLIN | BEAUMONT, JASPER-NEWTON EC

1 pound medium mushrooms
Vegetable cooking spray
½ pound turkey sausage
¼ cup chopped green onions
1 clove garlic, minced
¼ cup soft bread crumbs
1 egg, beaten
2 tablespoons grated Parmesan cheese
½ teaspoon Italian seasoning

Clean mushrooms with a damp paper towel. Separate caps from stems, reserving whole caps. Finely chop stems. Coat a large nonstick skillet with vegetable cooking spray. Place over medium-high heat and add sausage, green onion, garlic and chopped stems. Cook until sausage is browned; drain, if necessary. Stir in bread crumbs, egg, Parmesan cheese and Italian seasoning. Preheat oven to 350 degrees. Stuff mushroom caps and place in baking dish. Bake 10 minutes. May be served as an entrée or hors d'oeuvre.

Spinach Roll-Ups

AUDRA WHITFILL | MEMPHIS, LIGHTHOUSE EC

2 packages (10 ounces each) frozen spinach,
    thawed and drained
1 cup sour cream
1 cup mayonnaise
1 packet ranch dressing mix
6 green onions, chopped
½ jar bacon bits
6–7 burrito-size flour tortillas

Dry spinach on paper towels. In a bowl, mix together sour cream, mayonnaise, dressing mix, onions and bacon bits. Stir in spinach. Spread approximately 3 heaping tablespoons of spinach mixture thinly on each tortilla, all the way to edges. Roll jellyroll fashion. Place seam side down on a cookie sheet. Cover and refrigerate overnight. Slice in desired sizes.

Tipsy Franks

BETTIE SHEFFIELD | HOCKLEY, SAN BERNARD EC

1 pound wieners, cut in ¼-inch pieces
½ cup bourbon
1¼ cups ketchup
½ cup brown sugar
1 tablespoon grated onion

Combine all ingredients in a saucepan and simmer on low heat, stirring occasionally, 5–10 minutes. Serve hot with toothpicks.

Jalapeño Cheese Ball

FERN LEE FINCK | KENDALIA, PEDERNALES EC

½ pound mild cheddar cheese, grated
18 ounces cream cheese, softened
2 cloves garlic, finely minced
2 large pickled jalapeños, finely chopped
3 tablespoons jalapeño pepper juice
½ cup chopped or minced black olives (optional)
1 cup chopped pecans

In a medium-size mixing bowl, combine cheeses, garlic, peppers, juice and olives, if desired. Mix well and shape into a ball. Roll ball in chopped pecans. Serve with crackers. Makes 16–20 servings.

Pineapple Cheese Ball

MRS. ANN ROGERS | WHITNEY, HILL COUNTY EC

16 ounces cream cheese
1 small can (8 ounces) crushed pineapple, drained
¼ cup chopped green bell pepper
¼ cup chopped green onions and tops
Seasoned salt, to taste
2 cups finely chopped pecans, divided use

In a bowl, mix first 5 ingredients together with 1 cup pecans. Form into a ball and roll in remaining cup of finely chopped pecans.

    COOK'S NOTE: Serve with your favorite crackers and enjoy the raves!

Spinach Balls

ELIZABETH HOWARD | BAY CITY, JACKSON EC

2 packages (10 ounces each) frozen chopped spinach
2 cups herb stuffing mix (Pepperidge Farm preferred)
1 cup finely chopped onion
6 eggs
¾ cup butter
½ cup grated Parmesan cheese
½ teaspoon thyme
1 tablespoon garlic salt
1 teaspoon pepper

Cook spinach and drain well. Put it in a large bowl and add remaining ingredients; mix well. Chill until workable. Form balls about 1 inch in diameter using a teaspoon. Freeze. When ready to use, thaw 15 minutes; while thawing, preheat oven to 350 degrees. Place balls on a baking sheet with a lip and bake 20-25 minutes. Makes 5 dozen.

COOK'S NOTE: This recipe may also be cooked without freezing. These are easy do-ahead hors d'oeuvres. Larger spinach balls can also be served as a vegetable.

Julie Johnson's Jalapeño Cheese Dip

MARTHA ROUSSEAU | WHITNEY, HILL COUNTY EC

1 medium onion, finely chopped
4–8 jalapeño peppers, to taste,
    seeded and finely chopped
1 pound cheddar cheese, grated
1 teaspoon garlic salt
2 cups mayonnaise

In a mixing bowl, combine all ingredients and beat 3 minutes, or until fluffy. This will make 1½ quarts of dip.

Cheese Spread Dip

MRS. PAT BOONE | TEXARKANA, BOWIE-CASS EC

½ pound processed cheese
¼ cup milk
½ cup sour cream
2 tablespoons finely chopped pimientos
2 tablespoons finely chopped onion
2 tablespoons finely chopped green pepper

In a saucepan, heat cheese over low heat, stirring until smooth. Add remaining ingredients, mix well, and chill. Serve with assorted vegetables. Makes 1½ cups.

Chili Con Queso

MARY ANN BRUNDIGE | MERCEDES, MAGIC VALLEY EC

3 large onions, chopped
3 tablespoons butter
4 cans (4 ounces each) chopped green chiles
3½ pounds American cheese, diced
5 tablespoons Worcestershire sauce
Dash of salt and pepper
Dash of hot sauce

Salt onions and cook slowly in butter in heavy iron skillet. Add peppers; simmer for a few minutes. Add cheese, stirring constantly. Add Worcestershire sauce, salt, pepper and hot sauce. Serve immediately on toasted crackers or with crisp fried tortillas. If cheese becomes stringy or too thick, thin with milk. Yields 20–25 servings.

Texas Cheese Dip

MRS. LLOYD D. GEORGE | HELOTES, BANDERA EC

1 pound ground beef
1 pound bulk sausage
2 pounds processed cheese (Velveeta preferred)
1½ cups picante sauce (mild, medium or hot, to taste)

In a large skillet, crumble beef and sausage, and cook until done. Drain on paper towels. Pour grease from skillet. Return meat to skillet. Add diced cheese and picante sauce. On low heat, let cheese melt; stir every now and then. Serve warm with corn chips.

COOK'S NOTE: This is a hearty dip I have been making for years.

Black-Eyed Pea Dip

HELEN MERKA | ROCKDALE, BARTLETT EC

¾ cup dry black-eyed peas
5 cups water
5 canned whole jalapeño peppers, seeded and chopped, or to taste (juice reserved)
⅓ cup chopped onion
1 clove garlic
1 cup butter or margarine
2 cups shredded sharp processed cheese
1 small can (4 ounces) chopped green chiles
1 tablespoon reserved jalapeño pepper juice

Wash peas and put in saucepan. Cover with water, bring to boil and cook 2 minutes. Remove from heat and let soak for 1 hour; drain. Combine peas and 5 cups water. Cook until tender, about 1 hour; drain. Combine peas, peppers, onion and garlic in food processor. Blend until smooth; set aside. Combine butter and cheese in top of double boiler and cook until melted. Add chiles, pepper liquid and pea mixture; stir well. Serve with corn chips. Makes 6 cups.

COOK'S NOTE: This is excellent for a New Year's Eve party.

Texas-Style Dip

JOANN LOWE | TEXARKANA, BOWIE-CASS EC

1 pound lean ground meat
1 cup picante sauce
8 ounces cream cheese, cut into cubes

In a skillet, brown ground meat, drain and return to pan. Add in picante sauce and cream cheese and simmer over medium-low heat 3–4 minutes, stirring to combine. Serve as a dip or use instead of melted cheese on nachos.

Hamburger Bean Dip

LOUISE CRAFT | EARTH, BAILEY COUNTY EC

1 can (15 ounces) refried beans
1 pound ground beef
1 onion, diced, divided use
1 small can (4 ounces) chopped green chiles
10 ounces shredded cheese
1 cup mild taco sauce
Sliced black olives

Preheat oven to 350 degrees. In a 9-by-13-inch glass baking dish, spread refried beans as a first layer. Brown beef, along with half of onion. Spread onto bean layer. Sprinkle green chiles, cheese and remainder of onion over top. Drizzle taco sauce over all. Bake 20–30 minutes. Garnish with black olives. Serve with tortilla chips.

Crab Dip

POPPY HULSEY | TULIA, SWISHER EC

1 cup sour cream
1 can (6 ounces) crab meat, drained and picked over
1 tablespoon grated onion
Salt, to taste
¼ cup mayonnaise
1 tablespoon capers
1 tablespoon lemon juice

Mix all ingredients well and allow to stand 1 hour before serving.

Artichoke Dip

MRS. JAKE C. WALKER | CARTHAGE, RUSK COUNTY EC

1 can water-packed artichoke hearts, undrained
1 cup grated Parmesan cheese
1 small can (4 ounces) chopped green chiles
1 cup mayonnaise

Preheat oven to 350 degrees. Pour all ingredients into blender and blend. Pour into a 9-by-13-inch glass pan. Bake 20–25 minutes, or until brown around the edges. Serve with crackers.

Texas Chili Dip

LUNA CROCKER | MARIETTA, BOWIE-CASS EC

2 pounds ground chuck
1 packet chili seasoning mix
1 can (10 ounces) diced tomatoes with green chiles
1 small can (8 ounces) tomato sauce
1 pound cheddar cheese, cut into small pieces
Corn chips or tostados

Cook meat with chili mix according to directions on packet. Heat together with remaining ingredients except corn chips/tostados until cheese is melted. Blend and serve hot with corn chips or tostados. Serves 12.

COOK'S NOTE: This works really well using a slow cooker to keep hot.

Mexican Pepper Dip

ANGELA BERRY | NAPLES, BOWIE-CASS EC

2 large tomatoes, peeled and chopped
4 green onions, chopped
1 can (7 ounces) fire-roasted green chiles, chopped
1 small can (2.25 ounces) ripe olives, chopped
3 tablespoons olive oil
1½ teaspoons vinegar
1 teaspoon garlic salt

Mix all ingredients, chill and serve with tortilla chips.

Tex-Mex Layered Dip

MRS. L.C. JENNINGS | LULING, HAMILTON COUNTY EC

1 can (15 ounces) refried beans
2 cups sour cream
1 packet taco seasoning mix
1 cup picante sauce
4 ripe avocados, mashed
2 teaspoons lemon or lime juice
2 medium tomatoes, chopped
1 bunch green onions with tops, thinly sliced
8 ounces cheddar cheese, grated
1 can (4 ounces) ripe olives, chopped
Tostados

Spread refried beans on bottom of 2-quart, glass salad bowl or decorative casserole. Mix sour cream and taco seasoning, and spread on top of bean layer. Add a layer of picante sauce. Next, mix mashed avocados with lemon and spread as a layer. Continue layering the next ingredients. Refrigerate covered, and serve with tostados.

Shrimp Con Queso

BILLIE ROLLINS | CORPUS CHRISTI, BANDERA EC

3 pounds shrimp, boiled, drained and peeled
1 cup chopped celery
1 cup chopped green onions with tops
1 cup diced bell pepper
2 tablespoons butter
½–1 can diced tomatoes with green chiles
    (5–10 ounces)
1 pound processed cheese, cut up
    (Velveeta preferred)
1 can (10.75 ounces) cream of celery soup
1 can (10.75 ounces) cream of mushroom soup

Chop shrimp; set aside. Sauté celery, onions and bell pepper in butter. Add remaining ingredients. Heat mixture over low heat just until cheese is barely melted. Add shrimp 5 minutes before serving.

COOK'S NOTE: A tossed salad and crunchy garlic bread go well with this. As a variation, leave the shrimp whole and serve hot over boiled rice.

Tex-Mex Wontons

CAROLINE KUTAC | SCHULENBURG, FAYETTE EC

½ pound ground beef
¼ cup chopped onion
2 tablespoons chopped green pepper
7–8 ounces refried beans
¼ cup shredded cheddar cheese
1 tablespoon ketchup
1½ teaspoons chili powder
¼ teaspoon ground cumin
4 dozen wonton skins
Vegetable oil, for deep frying

To make filling, cook ground beef, onion and green pepper in a large skillet until meat is brown and vegetables tender; drain fat. Stir beans, cheese, ketchup, chili powder and cumin into meat mixture; mix well. Place a wonton skin with 1 point toward you. Spoon a generous teaspoon of meat mixture onto center of skin. Fold bottom point of skin over filling; tuck point under filling. Fold side corners over, forming an envelope shape. Roll up toward remaining corner, moisten point and press to seal. Repeat with remaining wonton skins and filling. Fry, a few at a time, in deep hot oil (375 degrees), about 1 minute per side. Use a slotted spoon to remove wontons. Drain. Serve warm with picante sauce. These also freeze well.

Corn Dip

DORRIS EZZELL | LAKE DALLAS, WISE EC

1 can (11 ounces) Mexicorn, drained
½ cup chopped green onions
½ cup mayonnaise
½ cup sour cream
¾ cup grated cheddar cheese

Mix together and serve. Keeps well.

Cucumber Dip

FRANCES WHITSEL | DIME BOX, BLUEBONNET EC

3 cucumbers, peeled, seeded and grated
1 onion, grated
3 ounces cream cheese
2 heaping tablespoons mayonnaise
Salt, pepper, garlic and hot sauce, to taste

Mix all ingredients together and chill for 1 hour. Serve with chips.

Tortilla Pinwheels

GLORIA LEE | BOWIE, WISE EC

1 carton (8 ounces) sour cream
8 ounces cream cheese, softened
4 ounces diced green chiles, well drained
1 cup grated cheddar cheese
½ cup chopped green onion
4 ounces chopped black olives, well drained
Garlic powder, to taste
Seasoned salt, to taste
5 10-inch flour tortillas

Mix all ingredients except tortillas together thoroughly. Divide the filling and spread evenly over tortillas; roll up tortillas. Cover tightly with plastic wrap, twisting ends; refrigerate for several hours. Unwrap and cut in slices ½–¾ inch thick. Yields about 50 pinwheels. Serve with salsa.

COOK'S NOTE: These are so easy and look wonderful, and my family thinks they are delicious.

Oyster Cracker Snack

MRS. GONZELL HOGG | LAMESA, LYNTEGAR EC

½ teaspoon garlic salt
½ teaspoon dill weed
½ teaspoon lemon pepper
1 packet ranch dressing mix
1 cup vegetable oil
2 packages (9 ounces each) oyster crackers

Mix garlic salt, dill, lemon pepper and ranch dressing; then whisk in oil. Pour over crackers; stir until well coated. Place in airtight container. This recipe freezes well.

Cajun Party Mix

JUNE DONNELLY | DONIE, NAVASOTA VALLEY EC

¼ cup butter
1 tablespoon parsley flakes
1 teaspoon celery salt
1 teaspoon garlic powder
½ teaspoon cayenne pepper
4–8 drops hot sauce
2⅔ cups Wheat Chex cereal
2⅔ cups Corn Chex cereal
2⅔ cups Rice Chex cereal
1 can (6 ounces) French-fried onions, chopped

Preheat oven to 250 degrees. In open roasting pan, melt butter. Stir in parsley, celery salt, garlic, cayenne and hot sauce. Add cereals, stirring until well coated. Bake 45 minutes, stirring every 15 minutes. Add onions; mix well. Spread on paper towels to cool. Store in airtight container.

Toasted Pecans

MARVIN JOHNSON | MALAKOFF, NEW ERA EC

1 tablespoon vegetable oil
⅛ teaspoon red pepper
⅛ teaspoon garlic powder
¼ teaspoon salt
1 cup pecan halves

Preheat oven to 275 degrees. Combine first 4 ingredients in a small bowl and mix thoroughly. Add pecans and stir until well–coated. Spread pecans on a cookie sheet. Bake 20 minutes or until pecans are well toasted.

Barbecued Pecans

ANDREA THOMAS | CLARKSVILLE, LAMAR COUNTY EC

1 tablespoon sugar
2 tablespoons cider vinegar
½ teaspoon Worcestershire sauce
2 cups pecan halves
1 teaspoon butter or margarine, melted
½ teaspoon seasoned salt
¼ teaspoon chili powder

Preheat oven to 250 degrees. Mix sugar, vinegar and Worcestershire sauce in a quart jar; add pecans and shake to thoroughly coat nuts. Spread in shallow baking pan. Toast 1 hour, stirring every 15 minutes until lightly browned. Add butter, seasoned salt and chili powder, and toss to coat nuts. Continue baking until toasted. Cool and store in airtight container. Yields 2 cups.

Apple Cider Punch

MRS. B.A. LOVAASEN | TEMPLE, BARTLETT EC

4 cups apple cider
2 cups cranberry juice
1 cup orange juice
1 can (12 ounces) apricot nectar
1 cup sugar
2 sticks cinnamon
Orange slices
Whole cloves

Put all ingredients, except orange slices and cloves, in a pot over low heat and simmer 20 minutes. Decorate by floating orange slices with cloves in the punch. Serves 20–25 people.

Banana Punch

MRS. G.W. NELSON | SHALLOWATER, SOUTH PLAINS EC

6 cups water
4 cups sugar
1 large can (46 ounces) pineapple juice
1 can (12 ounces) frozen orange juice,
    diluted as directed on can
Juice of 2 lemons
5 bananas, pureed
1½ large bottles (2 liters each) ginger ale

In a pot, heat water and sugar, stirring until sugar is dissolved. Add juices and bananas; stir well. Cool and freeze. Set out of freezer 3 hours before serving, or until mushy. Put in punch bowl and pour chilled ginger ale over mixture; stir. Serves 50.

Cherry Punch

MRS. MAX MARBLE | HART, SWISHER COUNTY EC

2 packets cherry Kool-Aid, mix as directed
3 cups sugar
1 cup light corn syrup
1 large can (46 ounces) pineapple juice
1 large bottle (48 ounces) apple juice
1 quart tea, ready to serve

Mix all ingredients and chill.

COOK'S NOTE: This is ideal for parties, and children especially enjoy it. This may be frozen in cubes until ready to use, and the cubes can also serve as the ice for the punch bowl.

Jell-O Punch

MRS. V.R. LEVERETT | ABILENE, TAYLOR EC

3 large boxes (6 ounces each) Jell-O,
    your favorite flavor or a combination
4 large cans (46 ounces each) pineapple juice
2 bottles (32 ounces each) apricot juice
Juice of 2 dozen lemons
2 large bottles (2 liters each) ginger ale

Combine all juices and chill. Just before serving, add ginger ale.

COOK'S NOTE: Very refreshing and good for teas or receptions.

Lime Cooler

MRS. STAYTON T. FLOWERS SR. | VICTORIA, VICTORIA EC

1 quart lime sherbet, divided use
6 ounces frozen limeade concentrate
3 cups milk
Fresh mint, optional
Maraschino cherries, optional

Beat ½ quart of lime sherbet in a mixing bowl or blender. Add frozen limeade concentrate and milk. Pour into glasses, topping each with a scoop of remaining sherbet. Garnish with fresh mint or a cherry, if desired. Serve immediately.

Punch

MRS. REX LEE WILKES | BROWNFIELD, LYNTEGAR EC

2 cups sugar
3 quarts water
Juice of 12 lemons
Juice of 12 oranges
1 large can (46 ounces) pineapple juice
1 cup strong tea
2 large bottles (2 liters each) ginger ale

Boil sugar and water 8 minutes. Add juices and tea. Add ginger ale just before serving. Serves 50–65 people.

Frosted Strawberry Punch

MARTHA MATHIS | LUBBOCK, SOUTH PLAINS EC

1 cup sugar
½ cup water
1 packet unsweetened strawberry Kool-Aid
1 can (12 ounces) evaporated milk, thoroughly chilled
1 tablespoon lemon juice
1 bottle (1 liter) ginger ale, thoroughly chilled
1 package (10 ounces) frozen strawberries

In a saucepan, heat sugar, water and Kool-Aid until syrupy; cool. In a mixing bowl, whip evaporated milk and lemon juice until 3 times original volume. Fold in cooled Kool-Aid mixture and freeze. To serve, place frozen mixture in punch bowl or pitcher and add ginger ale and strawberries. Stir to create a slushy punch.

Instant Hot Chocolate

MRS. PAT ADCOX | SNYDER, MIDWEST EC

1 large carton (35.5 ounces) Nesquick chocolate flavored powder
1 box (16 ounces) powdered sugar
1 carton (16 ounces) powdered nondairy creamer
1 box (25 ounces) nonfat instant dry milk

Mix well in large bowl or pan. Use 2–3 tablespoons per cup boiling water.

Spiced Cocoa

RITCHIE SCHROEDER | LITTLEFIELD, LAMB COUNTY EC

2 tablespoons sugar
1 tablespoon unsweetened cocoa
¼ teaspoon pumpkin pie spice
¾ cup milk
Marshmallows

In a 10-ounce microwave-safe mug, combine the sugar, cocoa, spice and milk. Stir until smooth. Microwave on high 1½–2 minutes, until steaming. Stir. Garnish with marshmallows. Makes 1 serving.

Peppermint Eggnog

FLORENCE BAKER | GONZALES, GUADALUPE VALLEY EC

6 eggs, slightly beaten
4 cups milk
¼ cup sugar
½ teaspoon peppermint extract
¼ teaspoon salt
1 cup heavy whipping cream, whipped
14 peppermint candy canes

In a mixing bowl, mix eggs, milk, sugar, peppermint extract and salt together until well blended. Fold in whipped cream. Pour into bowl or pitcher. Cover and refrigerate several hours. To serve, ladle into punch cups and garnish with candy canes or crushed peppermint.

Cranberry Tea

GERRY HARDING | GONZALES, GUADALUPE VALLEY EC

1 quart cranberry juice
6 ounces frozen orange juice concentrate
6 ounces frozen lemonade concentrate
2 cups sugar
1 package red hots candies
1 stick cinnamon
12 whole cloves

Mix all ingredients together in a saucepan. Boil 7–8 minutes. Strain and store. Use 2 cups of water to 1 cup mixture. Heat and serve.

COOK'S NOTE: For a large party, use an electric coffee urn. This tea stays hot and is easy for guests to help themselves. Makes about 30 cups.

Iced Lemon Spritzer

ETHEL MIKESKA | FAYETTEVILLE, FAYETTE EC

3 quarts white grape juice
½ cup sugar
2 tablespoons grated lemon zest
½ cup fresh lemon juice
4 lemons, thinly sliced
Ice cubes
1 bottle (1 liter) club soda, chilled
Mint sprigs (optional)

In a large saucepan, heat the grape juice to boiling. Add sugar and lemon zest, juice and slices. Stir until well mixed. Pour into punch bowl or large jar. Refrigerate overnight. Just before serving, add ice cubes and chilled club soda. Garnish with sprigs of mint, if desired.

COOK'S NOTE: May substitute 6 cups apple juice in place of the white grape juice, if a sweeter beverage is desired.

Piña Colada Punch

VENESHA DEVON SCHROEDER | LITTLEFIELD, LAMB COUNTY EC

1 large can (46 ounces) pineapple juice, chilled
1 large can (20 ounces) crushed pineapple, undrained
1 can (15 ounces) cream of coconut
1 bottle (1 liter) club soda or 7UP, chilled

Mix ingredients together. Add ice. Serves 25–30.

Pineapple Apricot Punch

NELDA F. WILCOXEN | ABILENE, TAYLOR EC

1 can (12 ounces) frozen lemonade concentrate
1 can (46 ounces) pineapple juice, chilled
1 bottle (32 ounces) apricot nectar, chilled
1 bottle (1 liter) ginger ale, chilled

Dilute lemonade concentrate as indicated on can. Add the pineapple juice and apricot nectar. Stir well. When ready to serve, add the ginger ale.

Chocolate Mexicano

VICKI OCHOJSKI | HICO, ERATH COUNTY EC

6 cups milk
½ cup sugar
3 squares (1 ounce each) unsweetened baking chocolate, cut up
1 teaspoon ground cinnamon
¼ teaspoon salt
2 eggs, beaten
2 teaspoons vanilla extract
Cinnamon sticks

In a saucepan, combine milk, sugar, chocolate, ground cinnamon and salt. Heat and stir until chocolate melts and milk is very hot. Gradually stir 1 cup of the hot mixture into eggs; return to saucepan. Cook 2–3 minutes more over low heat. Remove from heat. Add vanilla; beat with rotary beater until very frothy. Pour into mugs; garnish with cinnamon sticks. Makes 6 servings.

Cafe de Ona

VICKI OCHOJSKI | HICO, ERATH COUNTY EC

8 cups water
½ cup packed dark brown sugar
1 4-inch stick cinnamon
2 whole cloves
½ cup regular-grind coffee

In a saucepan, combine water, brown sugar, cinnamon and cloves. Bring mixture to boil, stirring until sugar dissolves. Add coffee and simmer covered for 1 minute. Stir; let stand about 5 minutes or until grounds settle. Strain into mugs. Makes 8 servings.

Almond-Fruit Punch

MARY MATHIS | LUBBOCK, SOUTH PLAINS EC

2 large boxes (6 ounces each) Jell-O (cherry, lime
    or orange)
2 cups hot water
2 cups sugar
2 cups boiling water
1 can (46 ounces) pineapple juice
1 ounce almond extract
1 bottle (32 ounces) apple juice
Juice from 1 dozen lemons, or 1½ cups bottled lemon
    juice
2 cups water, or to taste

Dissolve Jell-O in 2 cups of hot water. Dissolve sugar in 2 cups boiling water. Mix; add other ingredients, except final 2 cups water. Add water to taste. Serve iced.

Surprising Buttermilk Cooler

MRS. M.C. KOVAL | LAKE KIOWA, COOKE COUNTY EC

4 scoops orange sherbet
2 tablespoons sugar
1 pint buttermilk

In a blender or with an electric mixer, blend orange sherbet, sugar and cold buttermilk. Serve icy cold. Yields approximately 3 cups.

COOK'S NOTE: Since biblical times, buttermilk has been a popular dairy product. Still, its full value was scientifically proven only within this century. Nutritionists rate it a low-calorie, nutrition-packed dairy product. People with sophisticated tastes rank buttermilk tops as a beverage, either "as is" or flavored because they enjoy its off-beat, tangy taste. Budgetwatchers like its real economy. Calorie-counters and those on low-fat diets welcome the variety that buttermilk makes possible in their meals.

Bloody Mary Mix

JO DIEGEL | LEAKEY, BANDERA EC

2 cups tomato juice
¼ cup lemon juice
½ teaspoon sugar
½ teaspoon dry mustard
2 tablespoons Worcestershire sauce
1 teaspoon celery salt
1 teaspoon onion salt or powder
1 teaspoon garlic powder
½ teaspoon hot sauce, or to taste
6 ounces vodka (optional)

Mix all ingredients together and serve over ice with a piece of celery. Makes 4 drinks.

Orange Julius

MRS. STAYTON T. FLOWERS SR. | VICTORIA, VICTORIA EC

6 ounces frozen orange juice
½ cup sugar
1 cup water
1 cup milk

Combine all ingredients in a blender. Fill rest of space in blender with chipped ice and blend until frothy.

Gin Slush

TRISHA BANKS | MIDLAND, CAP ROCK EC

2 cups sugar
9 cups water
1 can (12 ounces) frozen orange juice
1 can (12 ounces) frozen lemonade
2 cups gin
Lemon-lime soda

Bring water and sugar to a boil; simmer 15 minutes, then cool. This is an important step in making the slush. After the water and sugar mixture is completely cool, add the frozen juices and gin, then freeze. To serve, fill glasses half full and fill the rest with the soda. Fresh lemonade can be substituted for the frozen lemonade. Relax and enjoy.

Slush Drink

MRS. FRED M. VOGES | NEW BRAUNFELS, PEDERNALES EC

1 can (12 ounces) frozen orange juice
1 can (12 ounces) frozen lemonade
7 teaspoons instant tea
1 cup sugar
2½ cups rum, whiskey, gin or vodka
7 cups water
Ginger ale

Combine the first six ingredients in a large freezer-proof bowl and put in freezer. To serve, combine ½ cup slush with ½ cup ginger ale and sip with a straw.

Mardi Gras Punch

MARY STEFFEK | HALLETTSVILLE, SAN BERNARD EC

6 ounces frozen orange juice
6 ounces frozen lemonade
1 quart apple juice, chilled
2 quarts ginger ale, chilled
1 quart sherbet (raspberry, orange, lemon or lime)

In large punch bowl, mix together all juices. Just before serving, stir in ginger ale and sherbet scooped into balls. Yields 24 half-cup servings.

Fruit Punch for 50

MRS. HARRY E. RAU | GALVESTON, SAN BERNARD EC

Juice of 4 dozen oranges
4 cans (20 ounces each) pineapple slices
2 cans (46 ounces each) pineapple juice
Juice of 2 dozen lemons
2 jars maraschino cherries
2 quarts cold tea
6 cups sugar
4 quarts cold water

Mix fruit and juices; add to 2 quarts of cold tea. Add sugar and stir. Just before serving add 4 quarts of cold water.

BREADS

Angel Flake Biscuits

MRS. JAKE COLSTON | FLOYDADA, LIGHTHOUSE EC

5 cups flour
4 tablespoons sugar
1 teaspoon salt
1 teaspoon baking soda
3 teaspoons baking powder
1 cup shortening
1 package (¼ ounce) yeast
2 tablespoons lukewarm water (100–110 degrees)
2 cups buttermilk

Preheat oven to 400 degrees and lightly grease a baking sheet. Mix dry ingredients and cut in shortening. In a large bowl, dissolve yeast in warm water and mix in buttermilk. Add dry ingredients to yeast mixture. Roll dough to about ½ inch thick and cut with biscuit cutter. Bake 20 minutes.

COOK'S NOTE: Dough may be kept in refrigerator for future use.

Best-Ever Biscuits

MRS. ADOLPH BISKUP | BAY CITY, WHARTON COUNTY EC

2 cups self-rising flour
2 tablespoons mayonnaise
1 cup milk
Butter

Preheat oven to 450 degrees. In a bowl, mix flour, mayonnaise and milk. Turn out dough onto a floured board. Knead and roll out. Cut with biscuit cutter and place on a lightly greased or nonstick baking sheet. Bake 15–20 minutes, or until browned. Brush biscuits with butter.

Jiffy Rolls

MRS. DON C. SHACKELFORD | ANTELOPE, J-A-C EC

1¼ cups lukewarm water (100–110 degrees)
½ teaspoon salt
1 package (¼ ounce) yeast
1 box white cake mix (Jiffy preferred)
2½–3 cups flour

In a large bowl, combine water and salt. Before emptying cake mix from box, mix in yeast. Add cake mixture and flour to bowl with water and mix well. Cover and let stand 1 hour. Shape into rolls and let stand 2–3 hours. Bake at 425 degrees until golden brown.

Cheese Pepper Yeast Rolls

TERRIE SUGGS | LAMESA, LYNTEGAR EC

4 tablespoons yeast
2 cups lukewarm water (100–110 degrees)
½ cup sugar
½ cup vegetable oil
3 eggs
1 carton (8 ounces) sour cream
2 teaspoons salt
5 cups flour, divided use
2 cups sharp cheddar cheese, grated
2 jalapeño peppers, seeded and finely chopped

In a large bowl, dissolve yeast in warm water; add sugar and let the mixture set 10 minutes. Add oil, eggs, sour cream and salt. Add 2 cups flour and beat with mixer 2 minutes. Mix in cheese, peppers and remaining flour. Transfer dough onto a floured surface and knead 10 minutes. Put dough in a large, greased bowl, and let it rise in a warm place 40 minutes. Knead again 10 minutes. Make into rolls and set on a greased baking sheet. Let rise 40 minutes more, or until doubled in size. Bake at 375 degrees about 20 minutes. Yields 4 dozen rolls.

Betty's Potato Refrigerator Rolls

MRS. WAYNE TAYLOR | CLYDE, TAYLOR EC

1½ cups lukewarm water (100-110 degrees),
    or water left over from boiling potatoes
¾ cup sugar
1½ teaspoons salt
1 package (¼ ounce) yeast
2 eggs
⅔ cup shortening or bacon grease
1½ cups lukewarm mashed potatoes
7½ cups flour

In a large bowl, mix water, sugar, salt and yeast. Add eggs, shortening and potatoes. Mix in flour first with a spoon, then by hand. Knead until smooth. Place in a greased bowl and refrigerate at least 2 hours. Pinch off small amounts and shape into a ball or form of your choice and place rolls on a baking sheet. Let rise and bake at 400 degrees until brown.

COOK'S NOTE: Remainder of dough can be kept in refrigerator for several weeks. Be prepared for dough to rise in refrigerator. When rolls are desired, just pinch off the amount needed, form into rolls, let rise and bake. This is an excellent roll for all occasions and makes delicious cinnamon rolls.

Savory Breakfast Roll

MILDRED L. PIETZSCH | ROSCOE, LONE WOLF EC

2 cans (10-count each) biscuits
½ pound bacon or sausage, cooked and crumbled
⅓ cup butter, melted
¼ cup chopped onion
¼ cup chopped bell pepper
¼ cup Parmesan cheese or other cheese

Preheat oven to 350 degrees. Cut biscuits into quarters. Mix all ingredients and put into a greased Bundt pan or 9-by-13-inch dish. Bake 20–25 minutes.

Parkerhouse Rolls

MRS. MAX MARBLE | HART, SWISHER EC

1 package (¼ ounce) yeast
2 cups lukewarm milk (100–110 degrees)
1 teaspoon salt
½ cup sugar
4 tablespoons shortening
1 egg, beaten
5½ cups flour
Melted butter, to taste

In a large bowl, mix yeast and milk. Add salt, sugar, shortening and egg; mix well. Gradually add flour without overworking dough. Cover with cloth. Let rise until doubled in size. Knead and roll out until ¼ inch thick. Spread melted butter on half of dough and fold over remaining dough. Cut with biscuit cutter and place on a baking sheet. Let rise until doubled again. Bake at 400 degrees until golden brown.

Sopapillas

BETTY KIDWELL | MOUNT PLEASANT, BOWIE-CASS EC

2 cups flour
½ teaspoon salt
3 teaspoons baking powder
1 tablespoon shortening
¾ cup lukewarm water

In a bowl, sift dry ingredients; cut in shortening. Add water gradually, stirring with a fork. Mixture will be a little crumbly. Turn dough out onto a lightly floured surface and knead lightly until smooth. Divide dough in half; let stand 10 minutes. Roll dough out to ⅛ inch thickness. Cut into 3-inch squares. Stretch squares slightly before dropping into hot deep fat, 4 or 5 at a time. Cook for about 30 seconds on each side. Drain. Serve warm with honey.

Mexican Cornbread

PAT HENDERSON | FRANKSTON, NEW ERA EC

1 tablespoon shortening
2 cups yellow cornmeal
1 cup flour
2 teaspoons baking powder
1 teaspoon salt
1 tablespoon sugar
2 jalapeño peppers, seeded and finely chopped
1 cup grated cheddar cheese
2 eggs
1 small can (8 ounces) cream-style corn

Preheat oven to 425 degrees. In a 9-by-13-inch pan, preheat 1 tablespoon shortening. In a bowl, mix next 5 ingredients. Add peppers, cheese, eggs and corn, stirring well. Pour batter into hot pan with preheated shortening. Bake 1 hour, or until brown on top and knife inserted in top comes out clean.

Keri's Blue Ribbon Mexican Cornbread

KERI REYNOLDS | GOLDTHWAITE, HAMILTON COUNTY EC

1 cup yellow cornmeal
½ cup flour
½ teaspoon baking soda
¾ teaspoon salt
1 can (14.75 ounces) cream-style corn
½ cup vegetable oil or bacon grease
1 cup milk
2 eggs, well beaten
1 pound ground meat, browned and drained
1 medium onion, chopped
8–12 ounces cheddar cheese, grated
1 jalapeño pepper, chopped

Preheat oven to 350 degrees. In a large bowl, mix cornmeal, flour, soda and salt. Add corn, oil, milk and eggs, stirring well. Heat a greased 10-inch skillet until hot. Pour half of batter into the skillet. Layer meat, onion, cheese and pepper. Pour remaining batter on top and bake 50 minutes.

Blue Corn Sticks

MOLLIE L. GARDNER | HAMILTON, HAMILTON COUNTY EC

1 cup flour
1¼ cups blue cornmeal
2 tablespoons sugar
½ teaspoon salt
1 teaspoon baking powder
Butter or oil, for sautéing
3 garlic cloves, minced
3 serrano chiles, stemmed, seeded and minced
2 eggs
6 tablespoons butter, melted and cooled
6 tablespoons shortening, melted and cooled
1 cup buttermilk, room temperature
Dash of baking soda
3 tablespoons chopped cilantro

Preheat oven to 400 degrees. In a large bowl, sift together flour, cornmeal, sugar, salt and baking powder. Set aside. In the butter or oil, sauté the garlic and chiles over medium heat for 1–2 minutes. Set aside. In a separate bowl, beat eggs lightly and add melted butter and shortening. Stir in the buttermilk and baking soda. Pour buttermilk mixture into dry ingredients and beat just until smooth; do not over-mix. Fold in chiles, garlic and cilantro. Pour batter into a lightly buttered, cast-iron corn-stick pan. Bake in center of oven until cornbread is golden brown, about 15–17 minutes.

COOK'S NOTE: Yellow cornmeal can be substituted.

Hush Puppies

MRS. A.J. PINN | COLUMBUS, SAN BERNARD EC

2 cups cornmeal, unsifted
1 cup flour, sifted
1½ tablespoons baking powder
1 tablespoon salt
1 teaspoon pepper
1½ cups buttermilk
2 eggs
Finely chopped onions and bell peppers, to taste

In a bowl, mix all ingredients well. Fry in fish grease (oil that has been used to fry fish) at 380 degrees until brown.

Corn Patch Spoon Bread

MRS. A.J. SCHAMERHORN | LUFKIN, SAM HOUSTON EC

¾ cup cornmeal
1 teaspoon salt
¼ teaspoon baking soda
3 teaspoons baking powder
1 cup boiling water
1 can (14.75 ounces) cream-style corn
2 eggs
1 cup milk
2 tablespoons butter, melted

Preheat oven to 350 degrees. In a heatproof bowl, combine first 4 ingredients and stir in boiling water, mixing thoroughly. Add corn, eggs, milk and butter. Place in a very hot, buttered skillet and bake 30 minutes, or until brown on top.

Broccoli Cornbread

HELEN HAYNES | ANSON, STAMFORD EC

¾ cup butter, melted
2 boxes (8.5 ounces each) cornbread mix
    (Jiffy preferred)
4 eggs
1 carton (16 ounces) cottage cheese
1 package (10 ounces) frozen chopped broccoli,
    thawed
1 medium onion, chopped

Preheat oven to 350 degrees. Combine all ingredients in a large bowl and pour into a buttered 9-by-13-inch baking dish. Bake 40 minutes.

COOK'S NOTE: This will be pretty moist in center. I have been a member of the Texas Extension Homemakers Association for 40 years. I enjoy cooking very much.

Apricot Nut Bread

MRS. T.I. ELIOTT | SUNDOWN, LYNTEGAR EC

1 cup chopped dried apricots
1¼ cup sugar, divided use
2 tablespoons shortening
1 egg, well beaten
½ cup orange juice
2 cups sifted flour
2 teaspoons baking powder
½ teaspoon baking soda
1 teaspoon salt
1 cup chopped nuts

Soak apricots in warm water 20 minutes. Preheat oven to 350 degrees. In a mixing bowl, cream together 1 cup sugar, shortening and egg. Stir in remaining sugar and orange juice. Add dry ingredients; blend well. Drain apricots; stir apricots and nuts into batter. Bake in a greased and floured loaf pan 65 minutes.

Carrot Bread

LUCILE BUZEK | MOULTEN, FAYETTE EC

2 cups vegetable oil
3 cups sugar
6 eggs
4½ cups flour
3 teaspoons baking soda
1½ teaspoons cinnamon
3 cups grated carrots

Preheat oven to 350 degrees. Combine all ingredients and mix well. Pour into 3 well-greased and floured loaf pans. Bake 45 minutes or until done.

Onion Shortcake

JILL TRALFANSTEDT | AUSTIN, TEXAS ELECTRIC COOPERATIVES

1 onion, chopped
¼ cup butter
1 package (6 ounces) Mexican cornbread mix
1 egg
1⅓ cup milk
1 can (14.75 ounces) whole kernel corn, drained
2 drops hot pepper sauce
1 carton (8 ounces) sour cream
¼ teaspoon salt
¼ teaspoon dill weed
1 cup grated cheddar cheese, divided use

Preheat oven to 425 degrees. Sauté onion in butter and set aside. In a bowl, combine cornbread mix, egg, milk, corn and hot pepper sauce. Pour into buttered 8-by-8-inch pan. To the sautéed onions, add sour cream, salt, dill weed and half the cheese. Mix and spread over the batter. Sprinkle with remaining cheese. Bake 25–30 minutes.

Dilly Bread

MRS. G.F. JARRELL | GRAHAM, FORT BELKNAP EC

1 package (¼ ounce) yeast
¼ cup lukewarm water (100–110 degrees)
1 cup cottage cheese, slightly heated
2 tablespoons sugar
1 egg
1 tablespoon instant minced onion
2 teaspoons dill seed
1 teaspoon salt
¼ teaspoon baking soda
1 tablespoon butter
2¼–2½ cups flour
Butter and milk, to taste, if desired

Dissolve yeast in warm water. In a large bowl, mix yeast with all other ingredients, adding flour last, enough to make a stiff dough. Beat well and cover. Let dough rise until it doubles in size, about 1 hour. Stir mixture down and turn into a well-greased loaf pan. Let dough rise to double in size again, about 30 minutes. Bake at 350 degrees 45 minutes. If desired, brush top crust with a mixture of butter and milk while bread is still warm.

Fruit Bread

MRS. BENNIE ELDRED | MONTGOMERY, MID-SOUTH EC

2½ cups sugar
1½ cups mashed ripe bananas
3 eggs, well beaten
1 small can (8 ounces) crushed pineapple
1 jar (10 ounces) maraschino cherries,
    drained and chopped
¾ cup vegetable oil
2½ cups flour
¼ teaspoon salt
¾ teaspoon baking soda
1 teaspoon vanilla extract
1 cup chopped pecans

Preheat oven to 300 degrees. In a large bowl, mix sugar, bananas, eggs, pineapple and cherries. Add oil. In a small bowl, combine flour, salt and soda, then stir into first mixture. Fold in nuts and vanilla. Grease a Bundt pan and dust lightly with flour. Put dough in the pan, spreading evenly. Bake 1 hour and 45 minutes. Cool on a wire rack.

COOK'S NOTE: Will keep well but may be frozen.

Fluffy Gingerbread

MRS. TOM MCKINNEY | ATLANTA, BOWIE-CASS EC

1 cup flour
¾ teaspoon baking soda
¼ teaspoon salt
½ teaspoon ginger
½ teaspoon cinnamon
¼ teaspoon ground cloves
½ cup shortening or butter
¼ cup sugar
1 egg, well beaten
⅓ cup dark corn syrup
½ cup boiling water

Preheat oven to 350 degrees. Into a bowl, sift flour; add soda, salt and spices. In a mixing bowl, cream butter or shortening until light. Add sugar gradually, beating after each addition. Add egg, beating well again. Alternate adding dry ingredients and syrup, beating after each addition. Add boiling water and stir in well. Pour into a greased 9-by-9-inch pan and bake 20–25 minutes.

Oatmeal Bread

MRS. H.R. DABBS | POST, LYNTEGAR EC

1 cup old-fashioned rolled oats
¾ cup brown sugar
1 tablespoon salt
2 cups boiling water
2 packages (¼ ounce each) yeast
½ cup lukewarm water (100–110 degrees)
2 eggs, beaten
1 cup vegetable oil
6 cups flour

In a heatproof bowl, mix oats, sugar and salt. Pour boiling water over this. Let cool until lukewarm. Dissolve yeast in lukewarm water, then add it to the oatmeal mixture along with the eggs and oil. Put flour in large bowl; make a well and pour in wet mixture, mixing well. Put in well-greased bowl and let rise until double. Work down on floured board. Divide into 3 loaves or make into rolls. Let rise and bake at 350 degrees 45 minutes.

Quick Orange Nut Bread

MRS. GEORGE E. LANGSTON | GILMER, UPSHUR-RURAL EC

2 cups sifted flour
1 cup sugar
1 teaspoon baking powder
½ teaspoon baking soda
½ teaspoon salt
¾ teaspoon ground allspice
1 egg
2 tablespoons grated orange zest
⅔ cup orange juice
3 tablespoons butter, melted
1 cup chopped walnuts

Preheat oven to 350 degrees. Sift first 6 ingredients together into a large bowl. In a smaller bowl, beat egg thoroughly and combine with orange zest, juice and melted butter. Add liquid to flour mixture and blend well. Fold in nuts. Bake in well-greased loaf pan 50 minutes and cool.

Peanut Bread

MILDRED CLUTE | MARQUEZ, ROBERTSON EC

1¾ cups sifted flour
1 teaspoon baking soda
1 teaspoon salt
1 cup packed brown sugar
⅓ cup peanut butter
1 egg, beaten
1 cup buttermilk

Preheat oven to 350 degrees. Resift flour 3 times with soda and salt. In a mixing bowl, blend sugar into peanut butter and stir in egg. Beat until smooth. To this, add flour mixture and buttermilk alternately, beating until smooth after each addition. Turn into a buttered loaf pan and bake 1 hour or until browned.

Pineapple Nut Bread

MRS. KENT O. WATTS | LULING, GUADALUPE VALLEY EC

2¼ cups sifted flour
¾ cup sugar
1½ teaspoons salt
3 teaspoons baking powder
½ teaspoon baking soda
1 cup shredded whole bran or shredded whole wheat
¾ cup chopped walnuts
1½ cups crushed pineapple, undrained
1 egg, beaten
3 tablespoons shortening, melted

Preheat oven to 350 degrees. Into a large bowl, sift dry ingredients together 3 times. Stir in remaining ingredients, mixing only enough to dampen all the flour. Pour into a greased loaf pan. Bake 1 hour and 15 minutes.

COOK'S NOTE: This bread keeps moist 7–10 days and slices best when a day old.

Zucchini Bread

MRS. VERNON D. COOPER | WINTERS, COLEMAN COUNTY EC

1 cup vegetable oil
2 cups sugar
3 eggs
1 tablespoon vanilla extract
2 cups shredded, unpeeled zucchini
3 cups flour
1 teaspoon salt
2 teaspoons baking soda
½ teaspoon baking powder
1 tablespoon cinnamon
1 cup pecans, chopped

Preheat oven to 325 degrees. In a large bowl, mix oil, sugar, eggs and vanilla. Add zucchini and mix well. In a separate bowl, sift together dry ingredients, then add to the sugar mixture, mixing well. Fold in pecans. Pour into 2 loaf pans, greased and floured. Bake 1 hour. Store in refrigerator or freeze.

COOK'S NOTE: My family refers to this as "cake," and they like it with ice cream or whipped topping.

Cherry Nut Bread

RUTH YATES | MCLEOD, BOWIE-CASS EC

2 cups sugar
1 cup butter
3 eggs
2½ cups flour
2 teaspoons baking powder
Pinch of salt
1 jar (10 ounces) maraschino cherries, drained and chopped
2 tablespoons cherry juice
1 cup chopped pecans

Preheat oven to 325 degrees. In a mixing bowl, cream sugar and butter. Add eggs 1 at a time, mixing after each, and mix well. In a separate bowl, combine flour, baking powder and salt. Add to sugar mixture, along with cherries, cherry juice and pecans. Stir until ingredients are moistened. Pour batter into 2 greased loaf pans. Bake 1 hour.

COOK'S NOTE: Can be made into smaller loaves and given as gifts.

Strawberry Bread

MRS. CLINT FARRIS | GEORGETOWN, PEDERNALES EC

3 cups flour
1 teaspoon baking soda
1 teaspoon salt
1 tablespoon cinnamon
2 cups sugar
4 eggs
1½ cups vegetable oil
2 packages (10 ounces each) frozen strawberries
1 cup chopped pecans

Preheat oven to 350 degrees. In a large bowl, mix together dry ingredients. In a separate bowl, combine eggs, oil, strawberries and nuts. Make a well in center of dry ingredients and add liquids. Stir until well moistened. Spray pans with cooking spray. Bake in a Bundt pan 1 hour and 10 minutes; loaf pans 50 minutes; or muffin tins 15–20 minutes.

COOK'S NOTE: Very often, I bake this in miniature muffin tins. It makes good party snacks, and small children like that size, too.

Peach Bread

MRS. JACK PEEK | AVERY, LAMAR COUNTY EC

2 cups flour
⅔ cup sugar
2 teaspoons baking powder
½ teaspoon baking soda
½ teaspoon salt
½ teaspoon ground cloves
2 eggs, lightly beaten
2 tablespoons butter, melted
1 can (15 ounces) sliced peaches, chopped, reserve juice
GLAZE:
½ cup powdered sugar
4 teaspoons reserved peach juice

Preheat oven to 350 degrees. In a mixing bowl, combine first 6 ingredients. Add eggs and butter. Fold in peaches. Mix 2 minutes at medium speed. Pour into greased and floured 9-by-13-inch pan. Bake 60 minutes, or until brown. For Glaze, blend sugar and peach juice together until well mixed. Pour Glaze over cooled bread.

Clara's Beer Bread

EDYTH BARTON | CHANDLER, NEW ERA EC

1 can (12 ounces) beer
3 cups self-rising flour
2 tablespoons sugar
Melted butter

Bring all ingredients to room temperature. Preheat oven to 350 degrees. Run a little hot water over the top of the can of beer. Then put the flour, sugar and beer in a bowl and mix. Beat by hand 25 strokes, then pour into a greased loaf pan and bake 1 hour and 15 minutes. Brush with butter when done. Cool on a rack.

Sweet Potato Bread

VERNIE SMITH | WEATHERFORD, TRI-COUNTY EC

3 cups sugar
1 cup vegetable oil
3 eggs
1 teaspoon vanilla extract
2 cups mashed sweet potatoes
1 cup chopped walnuts or pecans
3 cups sifted flour
½ teaspoon salt
½ teaspoon baking soda
1 teaspoon baking powder
1 teaspoon cinnamon
1 teaspoon ground nutmeg
1 teaspoon ground allspice

Preheat oven to 350 degrees. In a large bowl, mix sugar, oil, eggs, vanilla, mashed sweet potatoes and nuts. In a small bowl, mix flour, salt, baking soda and powder, and spices. Pour flour mixture into sugar mixture and mix well. Pour batter into 3 1-pound coffee cans to ⅔ full. Bake 1 hour and 15 minutes. Let cool, then turn out.

COOK'S NOTE: The sweet potato bread can be frozen. It increases in taste with age. I have kept it in freezer for up to two years, and it is always good. I like to serve it with any kind of greens.

Molasses Wheat Bread

KATHY SCHULLE | DRIFTWOOD, PEDERNALES EC

¼ cup honey
¼ cup molasses
1 package (¼ ounce) yeast
1¾ cups lukewarm water (100–110 degrees)
⅔ cup nonfat dry milk
2 eggs, beaten
2 tablespoons vegetable oil
2 teaspoons salt
½ cup wheat germ
½ cup quick-cooking or old-fashioned rolled oats
½ cup whole bran cereal
2 cups whole wheat flour
1 cup high-gluten flour or all-purpose flour
2½–3¼ cups all-purpose flour

In a large bowl, combine honey, molasses and yeast in warm water. Cover; let stand until foamy (10 minutes). Stir in dry milk, eggs, oil and salt. Blend in wheat germ, oats and cereal. Beat in whole wheat and high-gluten flours. Stir in enough all-purpose flour to make a moderately stiff dough; knead on floured surface 5–8 minutes. Cover; let rise until double. Halve the dough; let rest 10 minutes. Shape into 2 loaves and place in 2 greased loaf pans. Cover; let rise until nearly doubled. Bake at 350 degrees 40 minutes.

Pumpkin Bread

MARY HALFMANN | BALLINGER, COLEMAN COUNTY EC

3½ cups flour
2 teaspoons baking soda
1 teaspoon salt
1 teaspoon cinnamon
1 teaspoon ground nutmeg
3 cups sugar
1 cup vegetable oil
4 eggs, beaten
⅔ cup water
2 cups pumpkin, cooked

Preheat oven to 325 degrees. Sift all dry ingredients into large bowl. Add the rest of the ingredients and mix well. Put into lightly greased Bundt pan or 2 loaf pans. Bake 1 hour.

COOK'S NOTE: For variation, 1 cup nuts or 1 cup raisins may be added. Bread can be served immediately or "seasoned" for several days if wrapped in plastic wrap. Freezes well.

Crumb Coffee Cake

MRS. EARL BUENGER | CUERO, DE WITT COUNTY EC

2½ cups flour
1 cup sugar
1 cup brown sugar
⅞ cup vegetable oil
1 egg, beaten
1 teaspoon baking soda
1 cup sweetened flaked coconut
½ cup chopped pecans
1 cup buttermilk
1 teaspoon cinnamon
2 teaspoons vanilla extract

Preheat oven to 350 degrees. In a large bowl, mix first 4 ingredients until crumbly. Pull out 1 cup for topping; set aside. Mix remaining ingredients with crumb mixture and pour batter into a 9-by-13-inch pan. Sprinkle reserved crumb mixture over the top of cake and bake 35–40 minutes.

Pear Coffee Ring

CHRIS COKER | NAPLES, BOWIE-CASS EC

¾ cup sugar
⅓ cup chopped nuts
1 teaspoon cinnamon
2 cans (10-count each) biscuits
¼ cup butter, melted
2 pears, cored and sliced into 20 pieces
   (⅛–¼ inch thick)
½ cup powdered sugar
1¼ teaspoons vanilla extract
2–3 teaspoons milk

Preheat oven to 375 degrees. Grease a 9-inch round pan. In a bowl, combine sugar, nuts and cinnamon. Separate biscuits into 20 pieces. Dip biscuits in melted butter, then in sugar mixture. Arrange standing in pan, overlapping. Place a pear slice between each biscuit. Bake 25–30 minutes, or until golden brown. Cool 5 minutes. If you have any sugar mixture left, sprinkle on top and return to oven 3 minutes. Remove, cool 2 minutes and invert onto serving plate. Combine powdered sugar, vanilla and milk; beat until smooth. Drizzle over coffee cake.

COOK'S NOTE: In pear season, I make lots of these, wrap them well and freeze. Good for quick use or to use as gifts. One apple can be substituted for the two pears.

Quick Coffee Cake

MRS. O.L. BLANTON | KAUFMAN, KAUFMAN COUNTY EC

1 package frozen rolls
½ cup pecans, chopped, divided use
¾ cup sugar
1 package pudding mix (not instant)
1 teaspoon cinnamon
½ cup butter

Put frozen rolls in a greased Bundt pan. Sprinkle with ¼ cup pecans. Mix sugar, pudding mix and cinnamon; sprinkle half of the mixture over the frozen rolls. Add remaining pecans and remaining pudding mixture. Dot with butter. Put in oven overnight. The next morning, turn on oven to 300 degrees and bake 30 minutes, or until brown.

Streusel-Filled Coffee Cake

MRS. HARRY E. RAU | GALVESTON, SAN BERNARD EC

FILLING:

¾ cup brown or white sugar

3 tablespoons flour

3 teaspoons cinnamon

2 tablespoons butter, melted

¾ cup chopped pecans

COFFEE CAKE:

1½ cups flour

3 teaspoons baking powder

¼ teaspoon salt

¾ cup sugar

¼ cup shortening

1 egg, beaten

1 teaspoon vanilla extract

½ cup milk

1 cup raisins, if desired

Preheat oven to 375 degrees. To make Filling, combine sugar, flour and cinnamon in a bowl. Add melted butter and mix well; add nuts. To make Coffee Cake, mix all dry ingredients together in a large bowl; add shortening, mixing with fingers until batter has the consistency of cornmeal. Add egg, vanilla and milk, beating just enough to mix. Mixture will be lumpy. Put half the batter into a square pan lined with waxed paper. Sprinkle with half of Filling. Add the rest of the batter, then sprinkle remainder of Filling on top. Bake 25–30 minutes.

Date Nut Muffins

MRS. BENNIE ELDRED | MONTGOMERY, MID-SOUTH EC

4 eggs

1 cup sugar

1 cup flour

½ teaspoon baking soda

½ package pitted dates (½ of 8-ounce package)

1 cup chopped nuts

1 teaspoon vanilla extract

Preheat oven to 325 degrees. In a bowl, cream together eggs, sugar, flour and soda. Add dates, nuts and vanilla. Cook in greased muffin pans, filling ½–¾ full, until done.

Tea Muffins

MAE BOMAR | SILVERTON, LIGHTHOUSE EC

1¼ cups butter

1 cup sugar

4 eggs

½ cup molasses

1 cup buttermilk

4 cups flour

½ teaspoon cinnamon

½ teaspoon ground ginger

¼ cup raisins

⅔ cup chopped nuts

Preheat oven to 425 degrees. In a mixing bowl, cream together butter, sugar, eggs and molasses. Add other ingredients. Pour into muffin pans and bake 20 minutes.

COOK'S NOTE: Place batter in a tightly covered jar and put in refrigerator; it will keep for some time and can be used a small amount at a time.

Blueberry Muffins

MAE LANGLEY | ARGYLE, DENTON COUNTY EC

½ cup shortening

1 cup sugar

2 egg yolks, beaten

1½ cups flour

1 teaspoon baking powder

½ teaspoon salt

1 cup milk

2 egg whites

1 teaspoon vanilla extract

1½ cups blueberries, tossed with flour

Preheat oven to 350 degrees. In a mixing bowl, cream shortening and sugar; then add egg yolks. In a separate bowl, combine next 3 ingredients, then add to creamed mixture, alternating with milk. In another bowl, beat egg whites until stiff. Fold in egg whites, vanilla and blueberries. Bake in muffin tins 20–25 minutes.

COOK'S NOTE: This recipe was sent to me by my cousin, Myrtle Keddy, in Nova Scotia.

Oat Bran Banana Muffins

GLENNA CLIVER | MURCHISON, NEW ERA EC

1¼ cups oat bran flour
1¼ cups flour
¼ teaspoon baking soda
1¾ teaspoons baking powder
½ teaspoon salt
2 bananas, mashed
2 teaspoons lemon juice
⅔ cup butter
⅔ cup sugar
2 eggs, beaten
¼ cup honey
1 teaspoon vanilla
¼ cup buttermilk
½ cup raisins

Preheat oven to 400 degrees. Sift flours, baking soda and powder, and salt into a bowl. Mix bananas with lemon juice; set aside. In a mixing bowl, cream butter with sugar; add eggs, then banana mixture, honey and vanilla. Add buttermilk, alternately, with dry ingredients. Fold in raisins. Pour into greased muffin cups, filling ¾ full. Bake 25–30 minutes.

Quick Banana Muffins

SANDRA MAYO | SPUR, DICKENS EC

2 cups biscuit mix
⅓ cup brown sugar
1 egg, beaten
3 tablespoons vegetable oil
1¼ cups mashed ripe bananas
½ cup chopped pecans, walnuts or peanuts

Preheat oven to 400 degrees. In a large bowl, combine biscuit mix and brown sugar. Stir in remaining ingredients until the batter is moistened; do not over-beat. Grease bottoms of 12 muffin cups. Divide batter evenly among cups. Bake about 15 minutes, or until golden brown.

Pineapple Cornmeal Muffins

LEA FREEMAN | GATESVILLE, HAMILTON COUNTY EC

¾ cup yellow cornmeal
1 cup sifted flour
3 teaspoons baking powder
2½ tablespoons sugar
¼ teaspoon salt
1 egg
⅔ cup pineapple juice
3 tablespoons shortening, melted
½ cup crushed pineapple, drained

Preheat oven to 400 degrees. Sift dry ingredients into a bowl. Beat egg and pineapple juice in a larger bowl. Stir in flour mixture. Stir in shortening and pineapple until just mixed. Fill greased muffin pans ⅔ full. Bake 20–25 minutes until lightly browned.

COOK'S NOTE: This recipe has been in our family for over 40 years. I don't remember where it came from, but it is a favorite of the whole family.

German Drop Donuts

MRS. GEORGE O. FISHER | PAIGE, BLUEBONNET EC

2 cups flour
3 teaspoons baking powder
½ teaspoon baking soda
½ teaspoon salt
1 cup buttermilk or sour milk
1 egg
⅓ cup sugar

Sift all dry ingredients together into a large bowl, then add buttermilk and egg; mix well. Drop by the tablespoon in deep fat and fry until brown. Drain on paper towels; then roll in sugar. Serve warm.

Donuts

MRS. ELDRED A. BROWN | FRIONA, DEAF SMITH EC

1 package (¼ ounce) yeast
¼ cup lukewarm water (100–110 degrees)
1 cup milk
½ cup shortening
¼ cup sugar
1 teaspoon salt
1 cup flour
2 eggs, beaten
2½ cups flour
1 teaspoon vanilla extract
GLAZE:
1 box (16 ounces) powdered sugar
⅓ cup hot water

Dissolve yeast in water; set aside. In a saucepan, scald milk with shortening, sugar and salt. Let cool. In a large bowl, combine flour, eggs and yeast mixture; add cooled mixture to this and mix until smooth. Add flour and vanilla; mix until smooth; let set 1 hour. Turn out on floured board and flatten to ½ inch thickness. Cut with donut cutter. Let stand 30 minutes. Fry in deep fat. Turn only once; drain. To make Glaze, mix powdered sugar and water. After frying, dip donuts into Glaze and lay on rack set over pan to drain.

Zion Lutheran Donuts

ARLETA STILL | WILLS POINT, KAUFMAN COUNTY EC

3 cups sugar
2 tablespoons shortening, melted
4 eggs, beaten
2 teaspoons vanilla extract
4 cups buttermilk
4 teaspoons baking powder
4 teaspoons baking soda
7–9 cups sifted flour, divided use
2 teaspoons salt
1 teaspoon ground nutmeg

In a mixing bowl, cream sugar and shortening; then add eggs, vanilla and buttermilk. In a large bowl, combine baking powder and soda, 7 cups flour, salt and nutmeg. Add dry ingredients to wet, adding more flour to the mixture to make a very stiff dough. Roll and cut with a donut cutter. Fry in deep fat. Makes 8 dozen donuts. Top with glaze or sugar.

Apple Pancakes

JUANITA OXFORD | AZLE, TRI-COUNTY EC

3 apples
Butter
2 tablespoons sugar, plus more for frying apples
¾ cup flour
½ teaspoon salt
1 teaspoon baking powder
2 eggs
⅔ cup milk
⅓ cup water
½ teaspoon lemon zest
Powdered sugar

Peel, core and finely chop apples. In a skillet over medium heat, fry apples in butter with a little sugar sprinkled over the top. Mix all other ingredients together in a bowl. To make pancakes, put batter in circles in a buttered skillet or griddle over medium-high heat, spooning some of the apple on top of the batter, then adding another layer of batter. Cook, flip over and cook on other side. Serve with powdered sugar sprinkled over them.

Kreppel

MRS. C.W. VOELKEL | NORDHEIM, DE WITT COUNTY EC

4 eggs
1 cup sugar
1 cup milk
Pinch of salt
2 tablespoons shortening, melted
1 teaspoon baking powder
Flour

In a mixing bowl, beat eggs, then add sugar, milk, salt and shortening. Add baking powder and enough flour to make a soft, springy dough for rolling. Roll out into rectangle and cut strips measuring about 2-by-5 inches. Cut a slit through center and pull 1 end of dough through. Fry in hot fat as for donuts.

COOK'S NOTE: As children, my sister and I enjoyed these on cold wintry days, dipping them in preserves or just sugared.

Yogurt Pancakes

RITA SCHUETZE | KERRVILLE, BANDERA EC

½ cup flour
¾ teaspoon baking powder
¼ teaspoon baking soda
¼ teaspoon salt
1 tablespoon sugar
½ cup yogurt, plain or fruit
1 egg
1 tablespoon vegetable oil

In a bowl, blend dry ingredients. Add yogurt, egg and oil. Mix well. Cook as usual.

Giant Popovers

DOROTHY BISHOP | KIRBYVILLE, JASPER-NEWTON EC

6 eggs
6 tablespoons butter, melted
2 cups milk
2 cups flour
1 teaspoon salt

Preheat oven to 375 degrees. In a large bowl, beat eggs until frothy, then add butter, and beat until blended. Add milk, flour and salt. Beat until well blended. Fill greased muffin tins ¾ full. Bake 50 minutes. Quickly cut slits to let steam out. Bake 10 minutes longer. Serve hot with honey, syrup or jelly.

Feather Dumplings

MRS. JOHN C. POLANSKY | WEST, HILL COUNTY EC

1 cup sifted cake flour
1¼ teaspoons baking powder
½ teaspoon salt
⅓ cup milk
2 teaspoons shortening, melted

Sift together cake flour and baking powder into a bowl. Add the salt and sift again. Add the milk and melted shortening. Stir quickly and lightly until a soft dough is formed.

COOK'S NOTE: Use in any recipe that calls for dumplings.

SOUPS
& SALADS

Mexican Soup

MRS. J.E. GIBBONS | SHERMAN, GRAYSON-COLLIN EC

1 pound ground beef
1 medium onion, chopped
4 medium potatoes, cubed
2½ cups water, divided use
1 can (14.5 ounces) stewed tomatoes, undrained
2 teaspoons cumin
¼ teaspoon garlic salt
⅛ teaspoon pepper
2 teaspoons chili powder
1 teaspoon salt

Cook ground beef and onion until brown, stirring to crumble meat; drain drippings. Combine potatoes and 1½ cups water in a large Dutch oven. Bring to boil. Reduce heat, cover and simmer for 15 minutes. Add tomatoes, remaining water and seasonings; bring to boil. Add meat mixture, reduce heat and cover. Simmer 30 minutes. Yields 7 cups.

Gazpacho

MRS. J.E. GIBBONS | SHERMAN, GRAYSON-COLLIN EC

2 cups finely chopped tomatoes
1 cup finely chopped celery
1 cup finely chopped green pepper
1 cup finely chopped cucumber
1 cup sliced green onion
1 small can (4 ounces) chopped green chiles
2 small cans (8 ounces each) tomato sauce
½–1 cup water
¼ cup vinegar
¼ cup vegetable oil
3–4 teaspoons salt
2 teaspoons Worcestershire sauce
Dash of pepper

Combine vegetables and chiles in a large bowl. Combine remaining ingredients; beat well. Pour over vegetables and toss lightly. Cover and chill 6–8 hours. Stir gently before serving. Makes 6–8 servings.

Split Pea Soup

WILMA SLEZAK | TROUP, CHEROKEE COUNTY EC

1 cup dry split peas, soaked overnight
6 cups water
½ medium onion
1 carrot, peeled and sliced
1 rib celery, chopped
1 bay leaf
1 teaspoon salt
Pepper, to taste
1 tablespoon butter
1 heaping tablespoon flour

In a large pot, combine the first 8 ingredients and bring to a boil. Simmer for 3–4 hours, or until peas are soft. (If using a pressure cooker, cook for half an hour.) In a frying pan, make a roux by heating the butter then adding the flour and blending well. As soon as the roux starts to thicken, add 1 cup of the soup stock. Continue blending for about 5 minutes and then add the roux to the soup. Heat soup until well blended. Adjust seasonings. Serve with croutons. Serves 6–8. This soup keeps well and can be frozen.

COOK'S NOTE: For three generations, our Christmas Eve meal always began with Split Pea Soup.

No Peek Stew

MRS. BENNIE ELDRED | MONTGOMERY, MID-SOUTH EC

2 pounds lean chuck, cut in 2-inch cubes
1 envelope onion soup mix
1 can (10.75 ounces) cream of mushroom soup
1 cup ginger ale or water
1 small can (4 ounces) sliced mushrooms

Put ingredients in a 2½-quart casserole and cover. Bake at 300 degrees 3 hours. DO NOT PEEK. Let stand 30 minutes before serving. Can be served with cooked rice or noodles. Makes 6 servings.

German Shepherd's Soup (Hirtensuppe)

ANN STURROCK | SAN ANTONIO, PEDERNALES EC

2 tablespoons bacon grease or shortening
1 pound lean stewing beef, cut into ½-inch cubes
1 large onion, diced
1 teaspoon salt
1 teaspoon caraway seeds
1 clove garlic, crushed
Dash of paprika
3 tablespoons flour
2 tablespoons vinegar
2 quarts hot beef broth
3 medium potatoes, peeled and cubed
Croutons, for garnish
Dill, for garnish

Heat bacon grease in a 3-quart saucepan and sauté beef cubes in it. Add onions and cook until golden brown. Add salt, caraway seeds, garlic and paprika. Sprinkle with flour; stir and cook over low heat until flour is browned. Sprinkle with vinegar. Stir thoroughly, continuing to cook on low heat. Add broth and simmer about 45 minutes. Add potatoes and cook very slowly for 1 hour. Serve with croutons and sprinkle with dill.

Best-Ever Cheese Soup

TERRIE SUGGS | LAMESA, LYNTEGAR EC

2 carrots, grated
2 celery stalks, diced
½ cup butter
2 cans (14.5 ounces each) chicken broth
3 cans (10.75 ounces each) cream of potato soup
½ pound jalapeño cheese, grated
½ pound longhorn cheese, grated
3 heaping tablespoons sour cream
Salt and pepper, to taste

Sauté vegetables in butter on low heat. Set aside. Heat next 4 ingredients in a saucepan, stirring frequently. Add sautéed vegetables and heat thoroughly. Remove from heat. Add sour cream, salt and pepper. Serve hot.

Taco Soup

DOROTHY CHAMBERLAND | WHITNEY, HILL COUNTY EC

2 pounds ground beef
1 medium onion
1 medium can (7 ounces) whole green chiles
½ teaspoon salt
1 teaspoon pepper
1 packet taco seasoning
1 can (15 ounces) pinto beans
2 cups water
1 packet ranch dressing mix
1 can (15 ounces) hominy, drained
3 cans (14.5 ounces each) stewed tomatoes
1 can (15 ounces) kidney beans

Brown ground meat; drain. Chop onions and chiles. Mix with rest of ingredients and heat thoroughly.

Tortilla Soup

GINGER TEST | NOVICE, COLEMAN COUNTY EC

1 small onion, chopped
1 small can (4 ounces) green chiles, chopped
2 garlic cloves, chopped
2 tablespoons vegetable oil
1 teaspoon ground cumin
1 teaspoon salt
1 teaspoon chili powder
⅛ teaspoon coarsely ground pepper
2 teaspoons Worcestershire sauce
1 tablespoon steak sauce
1 cup peeled and chopped tomatoes
1 can (14.5 ounces) chicken broth
1 can (14.5 ounces) beef broth
1½ cups water
1½ cups tomato juice
3 corn tortillas, cut in ½-inch strips
¼ cup grated cheddar cheese

Sauté onion, green chiles and garlic in oil. Add remaining ingredients, except tortillas and cheese. Simmer covered for 1 hour. Add tortillas and garnish with cheese. Cook 10 more minutes.

COOK'S NOTE: From a Ruidoso, New Mexico, restaurant. Better made a day ahead and then reheated.

Caldillo (Mexican Stew)

MARTHALYN SMITH | PALESTINE, NEW ERA EC

1½ pounds cubed beef
1½ cups chopped onion
Vegetable oil
1–3 cups chopped tomatoes
2 cans (7 ounces each) whole green chiles,
    sliced into strips
½ cup beef broth
½ cup chicken broth
2 teaspoons salt
2 teaspoons pepper
2 cloves garlic, chopped
2 teaspoons ground cumin
2 pounds potatoes, cubed

Sauté beef and onions in oil. Add tomatoes, chili strips, broths and seasonings. Cook over low heat until meat is tender. Add cubed potatoes during last 30 minutes. Serves 6.

Quick Vegetable Beef Soup

KATHY ROBISON | MARLIN, NAVASOTA VALLEY EC

1 round steak
Salt and pepper, to taste
Water
1–2 beef bouillon cubes
1 small can (8 ounces) tomato sauce
1 large can (28 ounces) stewed tomatoes
1 large can (29 ounces) mixed vegetables, drained
    (Veg-All Homestyle Large Cut Vegetables
    preferred)
1 small can (8.75 ounces) sweet corn, drained

Cube round steak; sprinkle with salt and pepper. In large Dutch oven over medium heat, brown the round steak (no oil needed); do not drain. In same Dutch oven, add enough water to fill pot halfway. Add bouillon cubes, tomato sauce and tomatoes. Cook over medium heat 45 minutes. Add vegetables and continue to simmer until veggies are hot.

Earnest's Carne Guisada (American Version Mexican Stew)

MRS. EARNEST ARMSTRONG | HEBBRONVILLE, MEDINA EC

2 pounds round steak, trimmed
    and cut in I-inch cubes
2 teaspoons vegetable oil
I large onion, chopped
½ teaspoon cumin seeds
Whole black peppercorns
3 cloves garlic, chopped
4–5 chile pequins (small hot green or red peppers)
1 small can (8 ounces) tomato sauce
Water
1 teaspoon salt
1 tablespoon flour

In a heavy iron skillet or Dutch oven, lightly brown the meat in oil. Add onion and stir. Put cumin seeds, black pepper, garlic and chiles in a mortar and crush. Add about a tablespoon of water to the mortar and pour into the meat and onion mixture. Add the tomato sauce, then fill the can twice with water and add to mixture. Add salt. Cover and cook slowly for about 1½ hours. Mix the flour with a small amount of water and add to the stew to thicken. Serve over a baked potato or fluffy rice. Good served with a tossed salad and tortillas or hot French bread.

COOK'S NOTE: Most cowboys have a version of "Cowboy Stew," and this one is my husband's. Most people put some form of pasta in their stew, but Earnest does not. Our children love it, and we often serve it to guests, especially in the winter because it is rather HOT!

Creamy Broccoli Soup

MRS. CLINTON MARTIN | HONDO, MEDINA EC

6 cups water
1 package (16 ounces) frozen chopped broccoli
¾ cup finely chopped onion
2 teaspoons salt
2 teaspoons pepper
1 teaspoon garlic powder
8 ounces American cheese, shredded
1 cup milk
1 cup heavy whipping cream
¼ cup butter
½ cup water
⅓ cup flour

Bring water to boil. Add broccoli and onions; boil 10 minutes. Add salt, pepper, garlic powder and cheese; stir until cheese melts. Add milk, cream and butter. Stir and heat to boiling. Add ½ cup cold water to flour in a small bowl and mix well. Slowly add to hot mixture, stirring quickly. Cook and stir until soup is the consistency of heavy cream. Serves 8.

Egg Drop Soup

FRANCES ROBERTSON | KOSSE, NAVASOTA VALLEY EC

2 tablespoons plus 1⅓ cups water, divided use
1 can (14.5 ounces) chicken broth
1 teaspoon soy sauce
1 tablespoon cornstarch
1 egg, beaten
1 tablespoon sherry
Green onions, thinly sliced

Combine 2 tablespoons water with cornstarch, stirring well and set aside. Add remaining water, broth and soy sauce to medium saucepan; bring to boil. Add cornstarch mixture to broth. Boil 1 minute over medium heat, stirring occasionally. Combine egg and sherry and slowly pour egg mixture into boiling soup, stirring constantly. Ladle soup into bowls. Sprinkle with onion.

Texas Rattlesnake Chili

MRS. JACK PEEK | AVERY, LAMAR COUNTY EC

2 tablespoons vegetable oil
½ cup chopped onion
½ cup chopped green pepper
1 pound lean ground beef
1 cup cubed snake meat
1 teaspoon cayenne pepper
3 tablespoons chili powder
2 teaspoons salt
8 cups or 4 cans (14.5 ounces each) diced tomatoes, undrained
⅔ cup tomato paste
2 cups water
2 cups Texas-shaped pasta, uncooked

In a 5-quart saucepan, heat oil and sauté onion and green pepper until tender, but not browned. Add beef and snake meat. Brown and cook until done, about 5 minutes. Stir in cayenne pepper, chili powder, salt, tomatoes and tomato paste. Bring to a boil, reduce heat and simmer. Before serving, add water and return to boil. Stir in uncooked pasta and continue boiling. Stir now and then 10 minutes, or until pasta is tender.

Cauliflower Soup

ELLEN MARTINDALE | LUEDERS, STAMFORD EC

3 cups chicken broth
½ cup chopped onion
6 potatoes, diced in small pieces
1 medium head cauliflower, chopped
1 pint half-and-half

Combine first 4 ingredients in saucepan and cook until vegetables are tender. Add half-and-half and serve immediately.

Bootlegger Stew

MINNIE N. MOORE | SPICEWOOD, PEDERNALES EC

Leftover grilled steak
1 medium onion, chopped
1 potato, finely chopped
1 tablespoon butter
2 ounces canned chopped green chiles
1 can (14.5 ounces) stewed tomatoes
Dash of garlic powder (optional)
½–¾ cup burgundy wine

Cut steak into 1-inch pieces. Sauté steak, onion and potato in butter. Add chiles, tomatoes, garlic powder, if desired, and wine. Cover and simmer until potato is done.

COOK'S NOTE: When we grill steaks, we always grill an extra for Bootlegger Stew.

Bud's Venison Chili

O.O. HARE JR. | HOUSTON, RUSK COUNTY EC

3 pounds ground venison
¼ cup olive oil
1 quart water, or more if needed
½ cup chili powder
3 teaspoons salt
12 cloves garlic, chopped
1 teaspoon ground cumin
1 teaspoon oregano
1 teaspoon cayenne pepper
1 tablespoon sugar
1 tablespoon paprika
3 tablespoons flour
½ cup cornmeal

Place meat in hot oil in large pot. Sear until slightly gray. Do not brown! Add water and simmer 2 hours. Add 1 quart more water, if needed (we usually do). Add all seasonings and cook 30 minutes more. Mix flour and cornmeal together, add water to make paste and add to chili. Cook 5–10 minutes longer. Makes 2 quarts.

COOK'S NOTE: Even better the next day.

Green Chile Stew

RAYAN DOSHER | MULESHOE, BAILEY COUNTY EC

2 pounds lean beef stew meat
1 small can (4 ounces) chopped green chiles
2 cans (14.5 ounces each) stewed tomatoes, sliced
1 large onion, diced
1 clove garlic
1 teaspoon chili powder
½ teaspoon ground cumin
Salt and pepper, to taste
Water
2–3 medium potatoes
Warm flour tortillas

Add all ingredients, except potatoes and tortillas, together in a pot. Let cook on low heat all day. One hour or so before serving, turn heat to high setting and add potatoes. Let cook until tender. Serve with flour tortillas.

COOK'S NOTE: For a quicker version of this dish, add all ingredients, except potatoes, together in a pressure cooker. Let pressure build, then turn heat down and let pressure cook slowly about 20–30 minutes. Check meat, and if tender, add potatoes and let cook without pressure until tender.

Potato Cheese Soup

JOANN KNOX | WEATHERFORD, TRI-COUNTY EC

3 stalks celery, thinly sliced
1 small onion, chopped
3 carrots, grated
¼ cup butter
2 cans (14.5 ounces each) chicken broth
3 cans (10.75 ounces each) potato soup
½ cup milk
8 ounces Velveeta, cubed
8 ounces sour cream
Parsley

Sauté vegetables in butter until tender. Add next 4 ingredients and heat slowly. Add sour cream just before serving and sprinkle with parsley. Serves 8.

Venison Stew

MARTHALYN SMITH | PALESTINE, NEW ERA EC

3 pounds venison, cut into 1-inch cubes
Flour for dredging
3 tablespoons vegetable oil
2 cups dry red wine
1¼ cups vinegar or lemon juice
6 peppercorns, crushed
1 teaspoon salt
2 bay leaves
2 whole cloves
1–3 cloves garlic, crushed
½ teaspoon thyme
¼ teaspoon tarragon
1 cup beef broth
2 carrots, sliced
2 large onions, sliced

Dredge venison in flour. Fry in oil until lightly browned. Combine red wine, vinegar, peppercorns, salt, bay leaves, cloves, garlic, thyme, tarragon and broth. Add to venison in a stew pot. Add carrots and onions. Bring to a boil. Reduce heat and simmer 1½–2½ hours, or until meat is fork-tender. Serves 6.

Hamburger Soup

MARY POPLAWSKI | ENNIS, NAVARRO COUNTY EC

1 small onion, chopped
1 tablespoon oil
1 pound ground beef
46 ounces V-8 vegetable juice
1 can (10.75 ounces) cream of mushroom soup
¼ teaspoon salt
1 package frozen mixed vegetables

Sauté onion in a small amount of oil. Add ground beef and brown. Combine ground beef mixture with remaining ingredients and cook until vegetables are done.

Blue Ribbon Chili

DOROTHY BISHOP | KIRBYVILLE, JASPER-NEWTON EC

1½ medium onions, chopped
1 medium bell pepper, chopped
1 large rib celery, chopped
1 small clove garlic, minced
1 jalapeño pepper, chopped
3 tablespoons vegetable oil
4 pounds ground round beef
8 tablespoons chili powder
1 tablespoon ground cumin
¼ teaspoon hot sauce, or to taste
2 teaspoons garlic salt
Salt and pepper, to taste
1 can (12 ounces) beer or water
1¼ cups water
1 can (14.5 ounces) stewed tomatoes
1 small can (8 ounces) tomato sauce
1 small can (6 ounces) tomato paste
1 small can (4 ounces) chopped green chiles
1 bay leaf

Sauté first 5 ingredients in oil until onion is transparent. Add ground beef. Cook until beef loses its redness. Combine chili powder, cumin, hot sauce, garlic salt, and salt and pepper with beer, if using or 12 ounces of water. Let stand 1–2 minutes. Add beer-spice mixture, water, all tomato products, green chiles and bay leaf to meat mixture. Simmer covered 3 hours. Makes 10 servings.

Chicken Rice Soup

WANDA ROBINSON | MULESHOE, BAILEY COUNTY EC

1 can (14.5 ounces) whole tomatoes, undrained
1 small onion
3 cups cubed cooked chicken or turkey
2 cups cooked brown rice
1 package (12 ounces) frozen whole kernel corn,
  thawed
2 cans (14.5 ounces each) chicken broth
¼–½ cup picante sauce, to taste (Pace preferred)
¼ teaspoon ground cumin
½ teaspoon salt
½ teaspoon chili powder
Green onion, sliced or chopped for garnish
Fresh cilantro, for garnish

Combine tomatoes and onion in blender or food processor; blend until smooth. Pour into large saucepan or Dutch oven. Add chicken, rice, corn, broth, picante sauce, cumin, salt and chili powder; bring to a boil. Reduce heat; simmer 10 minutes. Ladle into soup bowls; top with green onions and cilantro. Serve with additional picante sauce.

Plaza III Steak Soup

REBA COZART | ROUND ROCK, COLEMAN COUNTY EC

½ cup butter
1 cup flour
½ gallon water
1 large onion
3 large carrots
3 ribs celery
1 can (10.75 ounces) tomato puree
6 beef bouillon cubes
1 teaspoon black pepper
Large sirloin or round steak, enough for 3 cups cubed
Salt to taste

In large pot, brown butter and flour together to make a roux. Add water and cook to boiling. Stir until smooth. In a food processor, chop the onion, carrots and celery. Add to soup mixture along with tomato puree, beef bouillon and black pepper. Broil steak and cut into cubes (need 3 cups). Add to soup, along with meat drippings. Simmer for 1 hour. Add salt to taste.

Turkey Wild Rice Soup

PAT WOOLEVER | GRANBURY, ERATH COUNTY EC

3 cans (14.5 ounces each) chicken broth
2 cups water
½ cup wild rice
½ cup chopped onion
¾ cup flour
½ cup butter
½ teaspoon salt
¼ teaspoon poultry seasoning
⅛ teaspoon pepper
2 cups half-and-half
1½ cups cubed chicken or turkey
8 slices bacon, crisply cooked and crumbled
1 tablespoon chopped pimiento
Parsley, for garnish

In a saucepan, combine broth and water. Add wild rice and onion; simmer 35–40 minutes until rice is tender. Lightly spoon flour into measuring cup; level off. In medium saucepan, melt butter; stir in flour, salt, poultry seasoning and pepper. Cook over low heat, stirring constantly, until mixture is smooth and bubbly. Add half-and-half; cook 2 minutes until mixture thickens slightly, stirring constantly. Slowly add half-and-half mixture to rice mixture, stirring constantly. Add remaining ingredients; heat thoroughly, without boiling. Garnish with additional bacon and parsley. Makes 8 servings.

Chicken and Noodle Stew

MRS. J.W. HOWARD | HASKELL, STAMFORD EC

1½ cups cooked chicken
4 cups chicken broth
⅔ cup evaporated milk
½ cup chopped celery
½ cup chopped onion
½ cup chopped pimiento
1 teaspoon salt
½ teaspoon poultry seasoning
⅛ teaspoon pepper
6 ounces noodles
2 tablespoons flour
¼ cup cold water

In a large Dutch oven, place chicken, broth and milk. Bring to a boil. Add chopped celery, onion, pimiento, salt, poultry seasoning and pepper. Bring to a boil and add noodles, stirring so they don't stick together. Boil uncovered 10–15 minutes, or until noodles are tender. Combine flour and water; pour into stew. Stir continuously until thick and bubbly. Serves 6.

Chicken and Dumplings

MRS. JOHN R. MAHAN | FRANKLIN, NAVASOTA VALLEY EC

1 whole chicken
6 tablespoons butter
1 teaspoon salt
1 teaspoon baking powder
½ cup hot water
Flour
1 cup milk
Salt and pepper, to taste

Boil chicken in water until done; cool, reserving broth. Remove meat from bones and return meat to broth. Reheat to boiling. Put butter, salt and baking powder in mixing bowl. Add hot water. Stir until butter is melted and other ingredients dissolve. Add flour until dough is stiff. Roll out thin on floured board. Cut into strips and add to boiling chicken broth. After dumplings cook, turn heat to low and stir in milk. Add salt and pepper, to taste.

Chili

BEULAH WOOD | LULING, GUADALUPE VALLEY EC

3 pounds coarse ground chuck beef
2–3 medium onions, chopped
1 bell pepper, chopped
1–2 cloves garlic, minced
½ teaspoon oregano
¼ teaspoon cumin seed
2 small cans (6 ounces each) tomato paste
1 quart water
Salt and pepper
3 tablespoons chili powder
Pinto beans, cooked or canned

Brown chuck in a Dutch oven; drain, if desired. Add onions, bell pepper, garlic, oregano and cumin seed to meat. Add tomato paste and water. Salt liberally and add in black pepper and chili powder. Simmer 1½ hours before adding pinto beans. Once beans are added, simmer another half hour.

COOK'S NOTE: Place remainder after the meal in the refrigerator, and the second day it will taste better, still better the third and absolutely superb the fourth. You can't even begin to imagine the delights in store for you 1 week later.

Sausage Bean Chowder

MARIE FLOURNOY | BAGWELL, LAMAR COUNTY EC

2 pounds ground sausage
4 cups water
2 cans (15 ounces each) pinto beans
2 cans (14.5 ounces each) stewed tomatoes
1 onion, chopped
2 potatoes, peeled and diced
1 bay leaf
½ teaspoon salt
½ teaspoon pepper
½ teaspoon garlic salt

Brown sausage and drain. Add all ingredients in large pan and simmer for 1 hour.

COOK'S NOTE: If you want it hot and spicy, use hot sausage and diced tomatoes and green chiles instead of stewed.

Cream of Artichoke Soup

DR. ELEANOR CROWDER | AUSTIN, PEDERNALES EC

2 tablespoons instant chicken bouillon
1 quart boiling water
2 jars (6.5 ounces each) marinated artichokes
1 teaspoon Beau Monde seasoning
1 teaspoon salt
⅛ teaspoon black pepper
1 cup half-and-half
2 teaspoons arrowroot, or 1 tablespoon flour
1 tablespoon cold water
1 teaspoon chervil

Dissolve bouillon in boiling water. Set aside. Drain artichoke hearts and place them in blender. Add enough chicken broth to purée artichokes; pour into a large saucepan. Add remaining chicken broth to pan. Season with Beau Monde seasoning, salt and pepper. Add half-and-half. Dissolve arrowroot in water (more water is needed if flour is used). Stir into soup. Heat soup, stirring constantly until it begins to boil and is slightly thickened. Sprinkle with chervil and serve. May also be served chilled. Serves 6.

German-Style Cream of Potato Soup

VIRGINIA J. HOOD | MURCHISON, NEW ERA EC

4 large potatoes, peeled and diced
1 large onion, minced
Salt, to taste
¾–1 pound bacon, cut in ½-inch pieces
3 tablespoons flour
2 large cans (12 ounces each) evaporated milk
Black pepper, to taste

Add potatoes, onion and salt to a pot. Cover with water and cook until tender. In a skillet, fry bacon until crisp. Then add flour and brown lightly. Add bacon-flour mixture to cooked and drained potatoes. Add evaporated milk and black pepper. Stir and simmer about 10 minutes.

Crab Gumbo

MRS. J.F. MOORE | HOUSTON, JACKSON EC

¼ cup diced bacon
¾ cup chopped onion
¼ cup chopped green onion
Hot peppers, to taste
1 clove garlic
1 cup finely chopped okra
2 tablespoons flour
¾ cup chopped tomatoes
2 cups canned chicken and rice soup
1 cup finely chopped celery
1 teaspoon parsley
1 teaspoon Worcestershire sauce
½ bay leaf
1 pound lump crab meat, picked over
Cooked shrimp (optional)
Salt and pepper, to taste
½ tablespoon gumbo filé
1 cup cooked rice

Fry bacon in heavy iron pot. Remove bacon and save. Sauté onions, pepper, garlic and okra in bacon fat, until onions are tender, not brown. Add flour, stir in and cook over low heat until mixture becomes light tan. Stir in tomato and simmer 3 minutes. Add bacon and chicken soup, plus water (4 soup cans). Add celery, parsley, Worcestershire sauce and bay leaf. Add crab and some cooked shrimp, if desired. Simmer 2 hours. Season to taste with salt and pepper. Add water as needed. Remove from heat and stir in gumbo filé and rice. Serve with French bread.

West Texas Shrimp Gumbo

MR. CHARLES E. HUBBARD | ROCHELLE, MCCULLOCH EC

¼ cup olive oil
3 tablespoons flour
3–4 cloves garlic, finely diced
1 large onion, chopped
1 green bell pepper, finely chopped
¾ cup finely chopped celery
2½ quarts water, approximately
3 beef bouillon cubes
4 tablespoons Worcestershire sauce
⅛ teaspoon ground cloves
½ teaspoon black pepper
1 tablespoon red pepper
¼ teaspoon basil
2 tablespoons salt
½ teaspoon cracked California bay leaves
1 teaspoon gumbo filé
1 small can (8 ounces) tomato sauce
2 cans (14.5 ounces each) diced tomatoes
2 packages (16 ounces each) frozen okra,
    or 3 cans (14.5 ounces each) okra
3 pounds shrimp, boiled, peeled and deveined
Cooked rice

Heat oil in heavy kettle, then stir in flour. Cook over low heat until mixture turns brown, stirring continually. Add garlic, onion, bell pepper and celery, then sauté. Add remaining ingredients, except rice, and simmer another 45 minutes or so. Serve over rice. Makes 10 large servings.

Mexican Salad

DORIS SYMM | GATESVILLE, MCLENNAN COUNTY EC

1 pound ground beef
1 packet taco seasoning
1 can (10 ounces) diced tomatoes and green chiles
¾ head of lettuce, chopped
2 medium tomatoes, chopped
1 bunch green onions, chopped
¼–½ pound colby or cheddar cheese, grated
1 small package tortilla chips, crushed

Brown meat and drain. Add taco seasoning and canned tomatoes and cook until liquid is gone. Make salad with lettuce, tomatoes, green onions, cheese and chips. Add meat mixture and mix well. Serve cold or heat in oven until warm.

Cranberry Salad

MRS. ELIZABETH CAUDLE | ATLANTA, BOWIE-CASS EC

1 quart cranberries
2 cups sugar
1 can (20 ounces) crushed pineapple, undrained
1 small package (10 ounces) miniature marshmallows
1 apple, finely chopped
1 small box (3 ounces) raspberry Jell-O
1 tablespoon unflavored gelatin granules
1 cup boiling water
Juice of 1 lemon
Juice of 1 orange

Grind cranberries; cover with 2 cups of sugar. Let stand overnight. Next morning, stir in pineapple, marshmallows and apple. Dissolve raspberry Jell-O and gelatin in boiling water. Add cranberry mixture. Add lemon and orange juices. Mix well and pour in mold. Chill until firm.

COOK'S NOTE: This is the cranberry salad we had in my family when I was small (in the 1920s and '30s) for the holidays of Thanksgiving and Christmas. We looked forward to this treat.

Cranberry Salad

MRS. W.W. GURLEY | TAHOKA, LYNTEGAR EC

2 cups raw cranberries, ground
1 cup sugar
1 cup heavy whipping cream
1 package (10 ounces) large marshmallows,
    cut into bits
1 cup drained, crushed pineapple
½ cup chopped nuts

In a bowl, combine cranberries and sugar. Let
stand 2 hours. In a separate bowl, whip cream and
add marshmallows. Let stand 2 hours. Combine
the mixtures and add pineapple and nuts. Let
stand overnight.

24-Hour Fruit Salad

MRS. H.R. DABBS | POST, LYNTEGAR EC

4 tablespoons sugar
4 tablespoons vinegar
3 bananas, sliced just before using
1 small can (8 ounces) crushed pineapple, undrained
1 can (20 ounces) fruit cocktail, drained
1 cup miniature marshmallows
½ pint heavy whipping cream

Cook sugar and vinegar until thickened; cool. Whip
whipping cream. In a large bowl, combine fruit
with sugar mixture. Fold in whipped cream. Put in
refrigerator overnight.

Fancy-Five-Salad

MRS. J.D. GIBSON | COLORADO CITY, LONE WOLF EC

1 cup drained, canned mandarin oranges
1 cup pineapple chunks
1 cup sweetened flaked coconut
1 cup miniature marshmallows
1 cup sour cream
Snipped chives and maraschino cherries, for garnish

Mix first five ingredients and refrigerate 12 hours.
Serve on greens. Garnish with chives and a cherry.
Yields 6 servings.

Green Christmas Salad

LORETTA ROBERTS | WELCH, LYNTEGAR EC

1 small box (3 ounces) lime Jell-O
1 can (20 ounces) crushed pineapple, drained,
    juice reserved
1 package (8 ounces) cream cheese,
    room temperature
¾ cup chopped pecans
1 cup sweetened flaked coconut

Mix Jell-O as directed on package subsituting the
pineapple juice for up to the needed 1 cup of water.
When firm, place in a bowl and whip with a mixer.
Add cream cheese and beat until smooth. Add
crushed pineapple, pecans and coconut, and chill
until very firm.

COOK'S NOTE: We always place in a pink
Depression-glass bowl for the family Christmas
dinner. Very pretty and sooo good.

Pie Filling Salad

MRS. A.R. POTTS | DIKE, FARMERS EC

1 can (14 ounces) sweetened condensed milk
1 large container (16 ounces) whipped topping
1 can (21 ounces) cherry pie filling
1 cup chopped pecans
1 cup sweetened flaked coconut
1 cup miniature marshmallows
1 cup crushed pineapple

In large bowl, mix condensed milk and whipped
topping. Add rest of ingredients. Mix well and chill
overnight.

COOK'S NOTE: I love this salad with my holiday
meals.

Custard Apple Salad

MRS. ANTON A. BUJNOCH SR. | HALLETTSVILLE, GUADALUPE VALLEY EC

2 eggs
2 tablespoons sugar
2 teaspoons vinegar
3 teaspoons butter
Dash of pepper
1 tablespoon prepared mustard
½ cup cream or evaporated milk
4–6 apples, pared, sliced and cooked

Beat eggs, add remaining ingredients and cook in a saucepan over low heat, stirring until it begins to thicken (like heavy cream). Remove from heat; cool. Mix in cream or evaporated milk. Pour over apples.

COOK'S NOTE: This recipe my mother used over 60 years ago when I was a little girl. I now have six children and 13 grandchildren, and all enjoy eating this dish.

Champagne Salad

RUTH M. TSCHIRHART | LAKEHILLS, BANDERA EC

1 package (8 ounces) cream cheese
¾ cup sugar
2 bananas, sliced
1 package (10 ounces) frozen strawberries,
    thawed, juice reserved
1 can (20 ounces) crushed pineapple
1 medium container (12 ounces) whipped topping
½ cup chopped pecans

Mix cream cheese and sugar in mixer. Add juice from strawberries. Fold in bananas, pineapple and strawberries. Fold in whipped topping and pecans. Turn into 9-by-13-inch pan and freeze.

Cool Fresh Fruit Salad

BETTYE KATE SMITH | LITTLEFIELD, LAMB COUNTY EC

½ cup sugar
3 tablespoons cornstarch
1½ cups orange juice
¼ cup lemon juice
1 teaspoon lemon zest (optional)
1 cup each of any 5–6 fresh fruits, chopped

In a saucepan, mix together sugar and cornstarch. Stir in orange juice. Bring to a boil over medium heat. Boil 1 minute, stirring constantly. Remove from heat and add lemon juice (and zest, if desired). Cool completely, then mix with fresh fruit.

COOK'S NOTE: I like to use strawberries, melon balls, nectarines, green grapes and bananas. Do not substitute frozen fruit.

Date Salad

MRS. L.T. HARGROVE | BOWIE, WISE EC

1 package (8 ounces) cream cheese, softened
1 small container (8 ounces) whipped topping
1 package (8 ounces) chopped dates
1 small can (8 ounces) crushed pineapple, drained
1 cup chopped pecans
½ teaspoon vanilla extract

In a bowl, mix softened cream cheese until fluffy and stir in whipped topping. Add rest of ingredients and chill before serving.

Grape Salad

MRS. KENT O. WATTS | LULING, GUADALUPE VALLEY EC

1 package (8 ounces) cream cheese
½ cup pineapple juice
1 large can (20 ounces) crushed pineapple, drained
4 cups seedless white grapes
⅔ cup chopped nuts
6 ounces miniature marshmallows

In a bowl, cream together cream cheese and pine-apple juice. Fold in the rest of the ingredients. Mix well and refrigerate several hours. Serve on lettuce leaves. Serves 6–8.

COOK'S NOTE: This is very good served at salad luncheons. Holds up very well.

Heavenly Hash Salad

GLADYS JONES | FLOYDADA, LIGHTHOUSE EC

1 can (20 ounces) crushed pineapple, drained
½ cup sugar, or more to taste
1–2 cups miniature marshmallows, to taste
1 cup coarsely chopped pecans
8 maraschino cherries, each cut into 4 pieces
2 cups heavy whipping cream

Mix everything, except cream, and refrigerate at least 12 hours. Whip cream and sweeten as desired. Fold whipped cream into fruit mixture.

COOK'S NOTE: Use real whipping cream; whipped topping won't work!

Grandma's Red Bean Salad

J.C. FRANKLIN | MIDLAND, CAP ROCK EC

2 cans (14.5 ounces each) red beans, drained well
1 cup finely chopped celery
½ cup finely chopped dill pickles
1 cup finely chopped onion
2 hard-boiled eggs, finely chopped
2 heaping tablespoons salad dressing or mayonnaise
1 teaspoon salt

Mix all ingredients well, scraping bowl thoroughly. Chill ½ hour. Serves 8–10 people.

Seven-Layer Salad

BETTY RUNYAN | SOUTHLAKE, TRI-COUNTY EC

½ head iceberg lettuce, torn into bite-size pieces
2 bunches green onions with tops, chopped
5 ribs celery, chopped
1 package (10 ounces) frozen green peas,
    cooked and cooled
3 carrots, sliced
2 cups mayonnaise
2 cups grated cheddar cheese
6 strips of bacon, crumbled
Croutons

To present this salad, serve in a clear glass bowl. Layer vegetables in order, topped with mayonnaise, so all sides are sealed. Spread grated cheese on top. When ready to serve, sprinkle croutons on top.

COOK'S NOTE: This salad is best when made a day ahead. Enjoy!

Pork 'n Bean Salad

PEGGY BAIN | LUBBOCK, SOUTH PLAINS EC

1 medium head of lettuce, torn into bite-size pieces
2 cups diced boiled ham
2 medium tomatoes, diced
1 medium can (15 ounces) pork and beans
1 medium onion, diced
2 cups diced cheddar cheese
1–1½ cups mayonnaise
Salt and pepper, to taste
Garlic salt, to taste

Mix all ingredients together and refrigerate until ready to use.

COOK'S NOTE: The longer it marinates, the better it is, because the flavors blend together. This makes a big salad. You may adjust ingredients as you prefer. We like ours real creamy, so we use more mayonnaise. Delicious with barbecue!

Super Broccoli Salad

GEORGIA BUNKER | CHANDLER, NEW ERA EC

4 cups broccoli florets (raw or blanched)
8 strips bacon, cooked until crisp and chopped
¼ cup finely chopped onion
¼ cup raisins
¼ cup chopped walnuts or pecans, toasted if desired
¾ cup mayonnaise
¼ cup sugar
2 tablespoons vinegar

Combine broccoli, bacon, onion, raisins and walnuts in large salad bowl. To make dressing, combine mayonnaise, sugar and vinegar in small jar; shake well. Pour dressing over broccoli mixture immediately before serving and toss well.

COOK'S NOTE: I take this to our monthly covered-dish dinners, and there is never a bite left, and someone is always requesting the recipe. Even the grandchildren, 4½ and 2½, love it.

Carrot-Apple Salad

MRS. ALBERT R. YOUNG | AXTELL, NAVASOTA VALLEY EC

4 cups shredded carrots
2 apples, peeled, cored and cut into small chunks
1 can (20 ounces) pineapple chunks, drained
¼ cup raisins, optional
½ cup sour cream
½ cup mayonnaise
¼–⅓ cup sugar, to taste

Mix carrots, apples, pineapples and raisins. To make dressing, combine sour cream, mayonnaise and sugar. Mix well and pour over carrot mixture. Keeps well in refrigerator.

Avocado Salad

MARVIN L. CAMPBELL JR. | FORT WORTH, TRI-COUNTY EC

2 large apples, sliced
4 carrots, grated
1 avocado, sliced
Mayonnaise, to moisten

Mix apples, carrots and avocado with mayonnaise. Serve on a bed of lettuce.

Cauliflower Salad

CAROLYN CUNNINGHAM | LOCKNEY, LIGHTHOUSE EC

3 heaping tablespoons salad dressing
    (Miracle Whip preferred)
2 heaping tablespoons sour cream
1 tablespoon ranch dressing mix
1 head cauliflower, cut into florets
½ bell pepper, chopped
¾ cup chopped celery
½ cup chopped cucumber

Mix salad dressing, sour cream and ranch dressing and pour over chopped vegetables. Toss together until vegetables are moistened.

Cornbread Salad

LOIS M. SKAGGS | SNYDER, MIDWEST EC

1 package (6 ounces) cornbread mix,
    prepared as directed
Salt and pepper, to taste
1 medium onion, chopped
2 tomatoes, chopped
1 green pepper, chopped
⅓ cup diced celery
8 slices bacon, cooked and crumbled
Salad dressing or mayonaise

Crumble cornbread; add salt and pepper, onion, tomatoes, green pepper, celery and bacon. Add only enough dressing to moisten.

COOK'S NOTE: This is a favorite salad at the cafeteria in the hospital where I work. It is good with most everything, but is especially good with beans and all vegetables.

Corn Salad

BRENDA HUSE | GRANBURY, JOHNSON COUNTY EC

1 can (15 ounces) yellow corn
1 can (11 ounces) shoe peg corn
3 ribs celery, chopped
½ cup chopped bell pepper
1 small jar (2 ounces) pimientos
½ cup chopped green onion
¾ cup vegetable oil
¼ cup vinegar
½ cup sugar
Salt, to taste

In a bowl, mix first 6 ingredients together. In a separate bowl, whisk together vegetable oil, vinegar, sugar and salt. Pour dressing over corn mixture and let stand 24 hours before serving.

Shredded Surprise

MRS. MAC GASKINS | KNOTT, CAP ROCK EC

½ cup sugar
½ cup vegetable oil
½ cup vinegar
1 teaspoon salt
1 teaspoon black pepper
1 teaspoon celery seed
1 medium head cabbage, coarsely shredded
1 medium sweet bell pepper, seeded and diced

In a saucepan, heat sugar, oil and vinegar to boiling. Add spices, then pour over vegetables while hot; toss. Store covered in refrigerator overnight. Makes 12 generous servings.

Black-Eyed Pea Salad

NORMA HADDOCK | MCGREGOR, MCLENNAN COUNTY EC

3 tablespoons chopped onion
½ teaspoon red pepper
2 tablespoons white vinegar
3 tablespoons red wine vinegar
3 tablespoons vegetable oil
¼ teaspoon salt
1 tablespoon sugar (optional)
4 cans (15 ounces each) black-eyed peas, drained

In a small bowl, whisk all ingredients together, except peas, until sugar is dissolved. Pour over black-eyed peas in a larger bowl, and refrigerate. Will keep in refrigerator several days.

Potato Salad

WYNOMA JOHNSON | MALAKOFF, NEW ERA EC

5 medium potatoes
5 hard-boiled eggs
½ cup sweet pickle relish
1 small onion, chopped
1 small jar (2 ounces) pimiento
1 tablespoon dried parsley
½ teaspoon celery seed, or ¼ cup chopped celery
½ cup mayonnaise
1 teaspoon prepared mustard
½ teaspoon salt
¼ teaspoon pepper
½ teaspoon sugar
¼ cup vinegar or sweet pickle juice

Boil potatoes until done (firm, but not mushy). Cut potatoes into ½-inch cubes. Cut eggs into ½-inch or larger pieces. Mix all ingredients, except for potatoes and eggs, in a large bowl. Adjust seasonings before adding potatoes and eggs.

COOK'S NOTE: For variety, add a dash of hot sauce to dressing before adding the potatoes and eggs. Serves 5. If using sweet pickle juice, eliminate sugar.

Super German Sauerkraut Salad

OLIVIA DEE | WIMBERLEY, PEDERNALES EC

½ cup vinegar
½ cup sugar
1 can (14.5 ounces) sauerkraut, drained
½ cup chopped green pepper
½ cup chopped onion
½ cup pimientos
½ cup chopped celery

In a saucepan, mix vinegar and sugar; boil a few minutes. Put rest of ingredients in a bowl and pour vinegar mixture over all; toss. Let sit overnight in refrigerator.

COOK'S NOTE: This recipe came from Germany.

Marinated Vegetable Salad

MRS. JOSEPHINE ROBUCK | DALLAS, NEW ERA EC

¾ cup vinegar
½ cup vegetable oil
1 cup sugar
¼ teaspoon salt
1 teaspoon pepper
1 can (14.5 ounces) French-style green beans
1 can (15 ounces) young sweet peas
1 can (11 ounces) shoe peg corn
1 small jar (2 ounces) chopped pimientos
1 green pepper, diced
1 cup diced celery
1 bunch green onions, chopped

Whisk together vinegar, oil, sugar, salt and pepper in a bowl. Drain all canned vegetables and combine in a bowl with fresh vegetables; add vinegar mixture. Toss gently and refrigerate at least 12 hours. Serves 12.

Delicious Seafood Salad

GENIA BAIZE | COPPERAS COVE, HAMILTON COUNTY EC

½ cup mayonnaise
½ cup chopped celery
1 teaspoon grated onion
½ teaspoon Worcestershire sauce
1 teaspoon lemon juice
¾ teaspoon salt
⅛ teaspoon pepper
8 ounces frozen shrimp, cooked, peeled and drained
8 ounces frozen crab meat, cooked and drained
2 hard-boiled eggs, chopped
Paprika, for garnish

Mix together the first 7 ingredients in a large mixing bowl to make the dressing. Rinse shrimp and crab meat. Cut crab meat into bite-size pieces. Add shrimp and crab meat to the dressing mixture. Add chopped boiled eggs and toss gently. Refrigerate until ready to serve. Serve on lettuce leaves and garnish with paprika, if desired. Serves 6.

COOK'S NOTE: This is a great summer or holiday salad!

Mom's Shrimp Salad

MARY ANN SCHIEFELBEIN | FLORESVILLE, KARNES EC

1 cup large shrimp, cooked and chopped
1 cup celery, chopped
3 hard-boiled eggs, chopped
½ cup mayonnaise
Salt and pepper, to taste
Lettuce, tomato and olives, for garnish

Combine all ingredients. Serve on lettuce leaves or stuff large tomato. When serving on lettuce leaf, garnish with tomato wedges and olives. Serves 4–5.

COOK'S NOTE: You can also add 2 tablespoons of chopped pickles or 2 large avocados, diced and sprinkled with the juice of ½ lemon.

Tuna Crunch Salad

MRS. B.A. LOVAASEN | TEMPLE, BARTLETT EC

1 can (5 ounces) tuna, drained
¼ cup chopped sweet pickles
1 tablespoon minced onion
1–2 tablespoons lemon juice
¾ cup salad dressing or mayonnaise
1½ cups shredded cabbage
1¼ cups crushed potato chips or corn chips,
    divided use

Combine first 5 ingredients. Chill, cover until ready to serve. To serve, add cabbage and toss; then, add 1 cup chips and toss. Heap in bowl and sprinkle with remaining chips.

Mediterranean Tuna Salad

MINNIE N. MOORE | SPICEWOOD, PEDERNALES EC

1 can (5 ounces) tuna, drained and flaked
2 tablespoons finely chopped onion
2 stalks celery, finely chopped
1 tablespoon red wine vinegar
¾ teaspoon dried basil, crumbled
1 teaspoon Dijon mustard
¼ cup olive oil

Place tuna in serving bowl. Mix in onion and celery; set aside. In a small bowl, combine vinegar, basil and mustard; whisk in oil. Pour dressing over tuna. Toss to blend. Serves 2. Serve on lettuce leaves, or use as sandwich filling.

Salmon Salad

MRS. EDWIN MOELLER | ROWENA, COLEMAN COUNTY EC

1 egg, beaten
½ cup heavy cream
1 cup vinegar
2 tablespoons sugar
1 can (14.75 ounces) salmon, bones removed, mashed
4 cups boiled and diced potatoes
1 medium onion, finely chopped
½ cup chopped dill or sour pickles
Salt and pepper to taste

In a saucepan, boil egg, cream, vinegar and sugar until thick and creamy; cool and then add to salmon, potatoes, onions and pickles. Add salt and pepper to taste. Cover and set in refrigerator until ready to serve.

Salad for Barbecue

LLOYD D. GEORGE | HELOTES, BANDERA EC

2 large tomatoes, cut into wedges
1 green pepper, sliced into rings
1 large onion, sliced into rings and separated
2 cucumbers, sliced crosswise
2 carrots, sliced crosswise
1 teaspoon cider vinegar
1 teaspoon salt
½ teaspoon black pepper
1 tablespoon sugar
½ teaspoon paprika

Place all vegetables into salad bowl and cover with vinegar. Add salt, pepper, sugar and paprika. Let stand in refrigerator about 4 hours before serving.

Three Bean Salad

MRS. F.A. SULTEMEIER | JOHNSON CITY, PEDERNALES EC

½ cup vegetable oil
¾ cup sugar
⅔ cup vinegar
1 teaspoon salt
½ teaspoon pepper
1 medium onion, chopped
1 bell pepper, chopped
1 small jar (2 ounces) pimientos, chopped, optional
1 can (14.5 ounces) green beans
1 can (14.5 ounces) wax beans
1 can (15 ounces) kidney beans

In a bowl, whisk together oil, sugar, vinegar, salt and pepper. Mix in vegetables and beans. Refrigerate overnight. Serve cold. Yields 12 servings.

Texas Apple Surprise

LORI NEVERS | BOERNE, BANDERA EC

1 small head cabbage
6 small Red Delicious apples
Juice of 1 lemon
⅔ cup mayonnaise
½–⅔ cup sugar
⅓ teaspoon salt
¼ cup raisins, if desired

Shred cabbage. Do not peel apples; use a grater and press hard. Use all of the juice of the lemon and pour over apples right away (prevents apples from turning dark). Mix all ingredients very well in a large bowl.
   COOK'S NOTE: The red from the apple peel adds a little color. Delicious with pork or veal cutlets.

Spinach Salad

MRS. G.F. JARRELL | GRAHAM, FORT BELKNAP EC

4–5 cups chopped tender spinach
1 hard-boiled egg, chopped
2 slices bacon, fried crisp and chopped
2–3 green onions, chopped
2 tablespoons vegetable oil
1 teaspoon vinegar
Salt and pepper to taste
2 tablespoons salad dressing, or more to taste
   (Miracle Whip preferred)

In a large bowl, mix all ingredients; add enough salad dressing to moisten.

Layered Spinach Salad

BRENDA HUSE | GRANBURY, JOHNSON COUNTY EC

Fresh spinach, chopped
Lettuce, chopped
Green onions, chopped
Celery, sliced
1 can (5 ounces) sliced water chestnuts, drained
1 package (12 ounces) frozen peas, thawed
1 carton (8 ounces) sour cream
1 cup mayonnaise
1 tablespoon lemon juice
1 tablespoon Worcestershire sauce
Dash of hot sauce
½ teaspoon garlic powder
½ teaspoon onion powder
1 cup grated cheddar cheese

Layer first 6 ingredients in a deep bowl. Mix next 7 ingredients together for dressing and spread on top of peas. Sprinkle cheese on top. Refrigerate until ready to serve; then toss at the table.

Cracker Salad

ALIDA WILLIAMS | HOUSTON, BLUEBONNET EC

1 stack saltine crackers, crushed
1 cup chopped onion
1 cup chopped sweet pickles
1 medium bell pepper, chopped
1 jar (2 ounces) pimientos, drained and chopped
5 hard-boiled eggs, chopped
1 teaspoon salad dressing

In a large bowl, mix all ingredients. Serve or refrigerate. Serves 8.

Chicken Salad Balls

VIRGINIA J. HOOD | MURCHISON, NEW ERA EC

1½ cups chicken, cooked and chopped
1 tablespoon chopped onion
Dash of hot sauce
2 tablespoons chopped pimiento
1 cup chopped pecans
½ cup salad dressing or mayonnaise
Potato chips

Combine all ingredients except potato chips, mixing well; chill several hours. Shape into 1-inch balls. Roll in crushed potato chips. Serve cold.

Chicken Salad

ROSIE ROSS | TAYLOR, BARTLETT EC

2 cups cooked shredded chicken, cold
1 cup chopped celery
1 tablespoon lemon juice
Salt and pepper to taste
¾ cup mayonnaise
2 hard-boiled eggs, chopped

Mix chicken, celery, lemon juice, salt and pepper. Add mayonnaise, mix well. Fold in chopped eggs, blending well. Serve as a sandwich filling or on a bed of crisp lettuce leaves.

Oleta's Macaroni Salad

MRS. OLETA M. SMITH | O'DONNELL, LYNTEGAR EC

1 package (12 ounces) seashell pasta or macaroni
1 tablespoon seasoned salt
1 teaspoon plain salt
2 large onions, chopped
9 hard-boiled eggs, sliced
2 cups chopped celery
½ cup chopped pimientos
1 cup sliced green pepper
1 bag (10 ounces) frozen young sweet peas, thawed
1½ cups mayonnaise

Boil macaroni in salted water until tender. Drain; blanch with cold water and drain again. Add other ingredients except mayonnaise. Toss lightly. Then mix in mayonnaise. Cover and chill for several hours before serving.

Macaroni Salad

CAROLYN CUNNINGHAM | FLOYDADA, LIGHTHOUSE EC

1 package (12 ounces) elbow macaroni
1 jar corn relish
1 jar (4 ounces) pimiento, chopped and drained
1 tablespoon parsley (optional)
2 teaspoons grated onion
1½ teaspoons salt
1 cup mayonnaise
½ cup sour cream

Cook, rinse and drain macaroni. In a large bowl, mix all ingredients in order given, except mayonnaise and sour cream. Mix these in small bowl and pour over all; mix well. Refrigerate several hours or overnight before serving.

VEGETABLES
& SIDES

Asparagus Bake

WAYNE RUEDE | BANDERA, BANDERA EC

2 cans (15 ounces) asparagus, drained, reserve juice
24 buttery crackers, crumbled (Ritz preferred)
1 can (10.75 ounces) cream of mushroom soup
Milk
2 hard-boiled eggs, chopped
Salt, pepper and paprika, to taste

Preheat oven to 350 degrees. Butter a baking dish. Arrange the asparagus over a thin layer of cracker crumbs in the baking dish. Place additional cracker crumbs on top of the asparagus. Beat soup, a little milk and asparagus juice until smooth. Pour on top of asparagus and cracker crumbs. Sprinkle the eggs on top, along with the salt, pepper and paprika. Bake 30 minutes.

Green Beans and Potatoes

TERESA GREGUREK | HEARNE, NAVASOTA VALLEY EC

1–2 pounds fresh green beans
4–8 small red potatoes
3–4 slices bacon, cut into small pieces
1 small onion, chopped
1 tablespoon olive oil
1 can (14.5 ounces) stewed tomatoes
1 teaspoon garlic salt
¼ teaspoon salt
1 teaspoon dill weed
1 teaspoon chili powder
1¼ teaspoons pepper

Wash green beans and trim off ends. Wash potatoes. Add green beans and potatoes to a large pot. Add just enough water to cover vegetables. Cook over low heat about 30 minutes, until beans and potatoes are tender. Meanwhile, sauté bacon and onions in olive oil in a skillet. Add stewed tomatoes to bacon and onion mixture. Add seasonings. Simmer 5 minutes. Add tomato mixture to green bean mixture, simmering for 10 minutes. Serve.

Green Bean Casserole

ROY O'BRIEN | FRIONA, DEAF SMITH EC

2 cans (14.5 ounces each) French-cut green beans or
    2 packages (16 ounces each) frozen green beans
1 can (5 ounces) water chestnuts, sliced
½ can bean sprouts, drained (7.5 ounces total)
2 small cans (4 ounces each) sliced mushrooms, drained
1–2 cans (6 ounces each) French-fried onions
1 medium onion, chopped
1 can (10.75 ounces) cream of mushroom soup
½ cup water

Preheat oven to 300 degrees. In a 2-quart casserole dish, arrange half of the first 5 ingredients in layers. Repeat layers; top with chopped onions. Mix soup with water and pour over layers. Bake 15–20 minutes.

Dill Green Beans

PENNY NICHOLS | PICKTON, FARMERS EC

2 cans (14.5 ounces each) cut green beans
1 tablespoon bacon grease
½ teaspoon dill seed
6 tablespoons butter
6 tablespoons flour
1 cup liquid from beans
1 cup milk
3 tablespoons grated onion
¾ cup grated cheese
¼ teaspoon hot sauce
2 tablespoons Accent or salt, to taste
Pepper, to taste
Buttered breadcrumbs

Put green beans, bacon grease and dill seed in a pan with water just to cover; boil 30 minutes. Set aside several hours or refrigerate overnight. Drain beans, saving liquid, and place in a shallow dish. Melt butter in a saucepan; add flour and stir until smooth. Add other ingredients, and salt and pepper to taste. Stir on low heat until mixture thickens. Pour over beans. Top with buttered breadcrumbs.

Beer Beans

DEBI STUDEBAKER | BECKVILLE, RUSK COUNTY EC

2 pounds ground beef, browned and crumbled
4 cans (15 ounces each) ranch-style beans
2 small cans (4 ounces each) mushroom slices
1 cup green olives with pimientos, chopped
2 cans (10 ounces each) diced tomatoes
    and green chiles
2 cans (12 ounces each) beer

Combine all ingredients in a large pan. Cover and simmer 3 hours.

COOK'S NOTE: Great with cornbread.

Cuban Black Beans

GWEN ELLIOTT | HUNTSVILLE, MID-SOUTH EC

1 pound dried black beans
1 large onion, chopped
1 green pepper, chopped
3 cloves garlic, minced
1 celery stalk, chopped
3 slices bacon, cut up
5 cups water
1 large can (12 ounces) tomato paste
1 tablespoon vinegar
1 teaspoon salt
1 teaspoon sugar
1 teaspoon pepper
1 jalapeño, seeded and chopped
Hot cooked rice
Shredded cheddar cheese
Chopped tomatoes
Chopped green onion

Sort and wash beans. Place in a large Dutch oven. Cover with water 2 inches above beans. Soak 8 hours or overnight; drain in a colander. Sauté onion, green pepper, garlic, celery and bacon until tender in the Dutch oven. Add beans back in with remaining ingredients through jalapeño. Cover and simmer 1½ hours, or until beans are tender. Serve over rice. Garnish with cheese, tomatoes and green onion. Makes about 8 servings.

Baked Beans

DORLENE HIGGINSON | CIBOLO, GUADALUPE VALLEY EC

3 cans (15 ounces each) great northern beans
1 cup chili sauce
¼ cup brown sugar
2 tablespoons molasses
⅔ cup chopped onion
¼ teaspoon mustard
6 slices bacon

Preheat oven to 300 degrees. Combine all ingredients. Pour into baking dish. Bake 1½–2 hours. Stir once or twice during baking.

COOK'S NOTE: If beans become too dry, add a small amount of water.

Baked Squash Pudding

MRS. WALTER MAHLOW | RAYMONDVILLE, MAGIC VALLEY EC

1 cup sugar, divided use
2 cups cooked squash, drained
2 eggs, beaten
2 tablespoons cornstarch
½ cup plus 2 tablespoons milk, divided use
½ teaspoon salt
½ teaspoon vanilla extract
Cinnamon
Sugar

Preheat oven to 350 degrees. Pour ¼ cup sugar over squash in bowl and add eggs. Dissolve cornstarch in 2 tablespoons milk and pour into squash mixture. Add remaining sugar and milk, salt and vanilla; mix well. Pour into casserole dish. Sprinkle with cinnamon and sugar. Bake 45 minutes.

Texas Lima Bean Casserole

MRS. PAUL E. GARNER | MICO, BANDERA EC

2½ cups cooked lima beans, drained
1 teaspoon dry mustard
1 cup sour cream
3 tablespoons brown sugar
1 tablespoon blackstrap molasses
¼ cup butter

Preheat oven to 350 degrees. Combine all ingredients and bake 45 minutes.

COOK'S NOTE: Serve with pork sausage links or ham.

Harvard Beets

SHIRLEY SMITH | GOLIAD, DEWITT COUNTY EC

¼ cup sugar
1 tablespoon cornstarch
½ teaspoon salt
White pepper, to taste
1 can (15 ounces) sliced beets, drained,
    liquid reserved
¼ cup vinegar
¼ cup frozen orange juice concentrate
1 teaspoon grated orange zest (optional)

Combine sugar, cornstarch, salt and pepper into a 1-quart pan. Measure reserved beet liquid and add enough water to make ¾ cup. Stir into sugar mixture along with vinegar and orange juice concentrate. Cover and cook 5–7 minutes, or until mixture is glossy and slightly thickened, stirring twice. Add sliced beets and heat until beets are hot. Sprinkle orange zest over top before serving.

COOK'S NOTE: Serve warm or chilled. Keeps well in the refrigerator.

Tejas Frijo-Ole

IRMA AGUILAR | DOOLE, MCCULLOCH EC

3 cups dry pinto beans, cleaned and well rinsed
5 quarts boiling water
1½ tablespoons salt
1 teaspoon pepper
2 tablespoons chili powder
1 jalapeño pepper, cut into wedges
¼ cup sliced onion
3 fresh garlic cloves
½ teaspoon ground cumin
2 tablespoons finely chopped cilantro
3 tablespoons ketchup
2 tablespoons vegetable oil
1 can (12 ounces) beer

In an uncovered 8-quart saucepan, add beans to boiling water and cook on high heat 45 minutes. Lower heat. Add all ingredients except beer. Cover and simmer 30 minutes. Uncover and add beer. Cover and simmer on low heat 1 hour. Makes 12–16 servings.

Baked Broccoli

EMILY EVANS ROBERSON | HICO, ERATH COUNTY EC

1 egg
⅔ cup mayonnaise
1 can (10.75 ounces) cream of mushroom soup
1 large package (19 ounces) frozen broccoli, cooked,
    well drained and finely chopped
1 cup grated Swiss cheese
1 medium onion, chopped
½ cup seasoned breadcrumbs, finely crumbled
2 tablespoons butter
Paprika

Preheat oven to 350 degrees. In a bowl, beat egg; add mayonnaise and soup. Mix well. Stir in broccoli, cheese and onion. Pour into a 9-by-13-inch pan; sprinkle with breadcrumbs and dot with butter. Sprinkle with paprika. Bake 30 minutes.

Broccoli and Rice Casserole

DOLORES MILLER | CLIFTON, ERATH COUNTY EC

1 cup rice
2½ cups water
1 large package (16 ounces) frozen chopped broccoli
1 small onion, chopped
1 clove garlic, minced
2 tablespoons butter
12 ounces Mexican or jalapeño processed cheese, cubed or shredded
½ can (10.75 ounces) cream of mushroom soup
½ can (10.75 ounces) cream of chicken soup
Salt and pepper, to taste

Bring water to boil in saucepan. Add rice and cook until done. Prepare broccoli according to package directions and drain. Sauté onion and garlic in a small amount of butter. Preheat oven to 350 degrees. Stir together the cooked rice, broccoli and onion, and pour into a casserole dish. Mix together the cheese, soups, salt and pepper. Pour over the rice and broccoli mixture. Stir ingredients together. Bake 20–30 minutes, or until bubbly.

Broccoli Soufflé

MRS. W.C. DAVIS | KOPPERL, JOHNSON COUNTY EC

1 tablespoon chopped onion, or more, to taste
Butter
3 eggs, beaten
½ cup milk
½ cup cream
1½ cups chopped cooked broccoli
1 teaspoon salt
⅛ teaspoon black pepper
⅛ teaspoon paprika

Preheat oven to 350 degrees. In a skillet, brown the onion in butter, then combine with remainder of ingredients in a 1-quart greased casserole dish. Set the casserole pan in water. Bake 45 minutes.

Broccoli Casserole

MARGARET BEARD | SPRINGTOWN, TRI-COUNTY EC

1 large package (16 ounces) frozen chopped broccoli, thawed
½ cup chopped onion
½ cup chopped green pepper
½ cup chopped celery
½ cup quick-cooking rice, uncooked
1 can (10.75 ounces) cream of chicken soup
1 small can (5 ounces) evaporated milk
1 teaspoon salt
1 teaspoon pepper
1 cup grated sharp cheese

Preheat oven to 350 degrees. Mix all ingredients except cheese. Bake in covered greased casserole dish 35 minutes. Remove from heat and top with cheese. Return to oven until cheese melts.

Baked Cajun Cabbage

MRS. WALDO LUEDEKER | NEW ULM, SAN BERNARD EC

1 large head cabbage, cut into bite-size pieces
½ cup butter
4 tablespoons flour
1 onion, chopped
1 cup chopped celery
1 cup chopped bell pepper
Salt
Cayenne pepper
1½ cups milk
½ pound cheddar cheese, grated
1 cup green onion, chopped
¼ cup seasoned Italian breadcrumbs

Place cabbage in a large pot with water to cover. Boil about 10 minutes, uncovered, until tender-crisp. Drain and set aside. Combine butter and flour in a saucepan, blending well over medium heat. Add onions, celery, bell pepper, salt and cayenne pepper, to taste. Sauté 10 minutes. Add milk, blending well over low heat until creamy. Add cheese; stir until smooth. Preheat oven to 350 degrees. Place cabbage in a 2-quart casserole dish; top with seasoned cheese sauce. Sprinkle with chopped green onions and breadcrumbs. Bake about 30 minutes. Yields 6 servings.

Fried Cabbage

NANCY POLANSKY | WEST, HILL COUNTY EC

1½ pounds cabbage
3 strips bacon
¼ cup vinegar
1 teaspoon sugar
Salt and pepper, to taste

Shred cabbage medium-fine and set aside. Fry bacon until crisp, keep pan with drippings. Blot bacon on paper towel and break into pieces. Add cabbage to bacon drippings and sauté, stirring constantly. Add vinegar, sugar, salt and pepper. Serve immediately with bacon sprinkled on top. Makes 6 servings.

Marinated Carrots

EDITH YOUNG | GRANBURY, JOHNSON COUNTY EC

2 pounds carrots, cleaned, cut diagonally
    in ¾-inch pieces
1 medium onion, sliced thin
1 green pepper, diced
1 cup sugar
1 teaspoon dry mustard
½ cup vegetable oil
¾ cup vinegar
1 can (10.75 ounces) tomato soup

Partially cook carrots, cool, and place in bowl with onion and green pepper. Mix together sugar, mustard, oil, vinegar and tomato soup. Pour over the carrots. Cover and refrigerate overnight.

COOK'S NOTE: Use leftover mixture as salad dressing.

Carrot Copper Pennies

MRS. LEE BEHANNON | CORPUS CHRISTI, JASPER-NEWTON EC

2 pounds carrots
1 small green pepper, cut into rings
1 medium onion, cut into rings
1 can (10.75 ounces) tomato soup
½ cup vegetable oil
1 cup sugar
¾ cup vinegar
1 teaspoon prepared mustard
1 teaspoon Worcestershire sauce
Salt and pepper, to taste

Slice and boil carrots in salted water until crisp-tender. When ready, remove from hot water; dunk in cold water with ice cubes to stop cooking. In a dish, alternate layers of carrots, peppers and onion. Make marinade of remaining ingredients, heating well until completely blended. Pour mixture over vegetables and refrigerate, covered.

COOK'S NOTE: The secret is to keep carrots crisp. Can be prepared several days before using.

Au Gratin Cauliflower

MRS. WAYNE RUEDE | BANDERA, BANDERA EC

1 head cauliflower, cut into flowerets
2 tablespoons butter
2 tablespoons flour
Salt and pepper, to taste
1 cup milk
1½ cups grated Swiss cheese

Cook cauliflower in slightly salted water until tender; drain. In a saucepan, melt the butter; whisk in the flour, salt and pepper. Add the milk. Cook over low heat until smooth and thick. Preheat oven to 350 degrees. Put cauliflower in a baking dish. Pour white sauce on top. Top with cheese. Bake 20–25 minutes.

Mexican Corn

GERALDINE HALL | FORT WORTH, ERATH COUNTY EC

2 tablespoons vegetable oil
1 cup chopped onion
1 cup chopped bell pepper
1 small clove garlic, mashed
3½ cups fresh corn
Salt, to taste
½ teaspoon ground cumin
¼ teaspoon sugar
Cayenne pepper, to taste
3 tomatoes, peeled and diced

Heat oil in a large skillet. Sauté onion, bell pepper and garlic until tender. Stir in corn and cook about 10 minutes. Add all seasonings and tomatoes. After about 5 minutes, taste, adjust seasonings if necessary, and cook 10 minutes longer.

Baked Corn

ANNA STURROCK | SAN ANTONIO, PEDERNALES EC

½ cup minced onion
½ green pepper, chopped
¼ cup plus 2 tablespoons butter, divided use
1 egg, beaten
2 tablespoons sugar
⅔ cup milk
Salt and pepper, to taste
2 tablespoons chopped pimientos
1 can (14.75 ounces) cream-style corn, drained
1 can (14.75 ounces) whole kernel corn, drained
1 cup cracker crumbs
1 cup grated sharp cheese

Sauté onion and pepper in 2 tablespoons butter. In a bowl, combine egg, sugar, milk, salt, pepper, pimientos and corn; stir in sautéed onions and pepper. Pour into well-buttered 2-quart casserole dish. Melt ¼ cup butter and mix with cracker crumbs and cheese in a bowl. Spread on top of casserole. Bake 1 hour. Serves 8–10.

Corn Casserole

RITA CLARK | GAINESVILLE, COOKE COUNTY EC

2 cans (14.75 ounces each) whole kernel corn,
    drained
1 can (14.75 ounces) French-cut green beans, drained
1 can (10.75 ounces) cream of celery soup
½ cup chopped onion
½ cup chopped green pepper
1 cup sour cream
1 cup shredded sharp cheddar cheese
½ cup butter, melted
1 stack buttery crackers, crushed (Ritz preferred)

Preheat oven to 350 degrees. In a bowl, mix together first 7 ingredients. Pour into a 9-by-13-inch baking dish. Stir butter and cracker crumbs together. Spread on casserole and bake 1 hour.

Corn Fritters

MRS. BILL HAIRE | HOUSTON, JASPER-NEWTON EC

1 cup sifted flour
1 teaspoon baking powder
½ teaspoon salt
2 tablespoons sugar
1 egg
⅓ cup milk
1 tablespoon vegetable oil
1 can (14.75 ounces) whole kernel corn, drained

Resift flour with next 3 ingredients into a bowl. In a separate bowl, beat egg; add milk and oil; then add flour mixture and beat until smooth. Fold in drained corn. Let stand 5–10 minutes before frying. Drop by the spoonful into hot oil; fry until browned; drain on paper towels.

Hominy Casserole

KATHRENE DELLIS | GOLDTHWAITE, HAMILTON COUNTY EC

1 can (15.5 ounces) white hominy, drained
1 can (15.5 ounces) yellow hominy, drained
1 cup sour cream
1 small can (4 ounces) chopped green chiles
1 small can (5 ounces) water chestnuts, drained
4 green onions, chopped
½ cup cream of mushroom soup
Garlic, to taste
1 cup grated cheese

Preheat oven to 350 degrees. Combine all ingredients except cheese and pour into a buttered casserole dish. Bake uncovered 30 minutes. Sprinkle cheese on top and bake uncovered 30 more minutes.

Cheese Grits Casserole

BOBBIE DYER | LOMETA, HAMILTON COUNTY EC

6 cups water
1½ cups quick-cooking grits
½ cup butter
3 eggs, beaten
1 teaspoon salt
2 teaspoons seasoned salt
1 teaspoon hot sauce
Pepper, to taste
3 jalapeños, chopped
1 pound cheese, grated

In a pot, bring water to a boil. Stir in grits. Cook 2 minutes; grits will be thin. Add butter, beaten eggs, salts, hot sauce, pepper and jalapeños. Stir in grated cheese. Preheat oven to 300 degrees. Pour into lightly greased, shallow baking dish. Bake 45 minutes.

Fried Stuffed Eggplant

MRS. OSCAR REED | IREDELL, ERATH COUNTY EC

1 large or 2 medium eggplants
½ pound ground meat
1 green pepper, chopped
2 medium onions, chopped
3 tablespoons shortening
1 cup cooked rice
Salt and pepper, to taste

Cut ends from eggplant but do not peel. Scoop out center. Chop center and fry with meat, pepper and onion in hot fat. Mix in rice. Season mixture and pack firmly into eggplant; let cool. Cut slices about 1¼ inches thick, coat with flour and fry slowly in fat until eggplant is tender.

COOK'S NOTE: If gravy is desired, thicken fat with flour, add tomato juice or hot water and flavor with a bit of chili sauce.

Baked Eggplant

THELMA NEW | HAWLEY, TAYLOR EC

3 young eggplants, peeled and chopped
1 small onion, chopped
6 tablespoons cream cheese
1 can (10.75) cream of mushroom soup
Salt and pepper, to taste
Butter

Preheat oven to 350 degrees. Combine all ingredients except butter and pour into a casserole dish; dot with butter. Cover and bake 20–25 minutes.

Mama's Eggplant Fritters

PAULETTE MALAMUD | GEORGETOWN, PEDERNALES EC

1 medium eggplant
6 cups water
1 teaspoon salt
1 cup sugar
1 egg, beaten
4–6 tablespoons artificial vanilla flavoring
2½ cups flour
4 teaspoons baking powder

Peel eggplant and dice into 1-inch cubes. Boil in a pan with water and salt until dark green and soft; drain. Place in bowl and add sugar; allow to cool 10–15 minutes. Add egg and mix thoroughly; then add vanilla. Sift in flour and baking powder into the eggplant mixture to make a batter. (You may need a little more or less flour, depending on the size of the eggplant.) Drop teaspoons of batter into a deep-fat fryer until golden brown on both sides. These must be fried in a deep fryer, or they will be greasy and heavy. Yields 24–36 fritters.

COOK'S NOTE: Do not use vanilla extract, only artificial vanilla flavoring, because extract tastes bitter in this recipe.

Okra Pilaf

MARTHA SITKA | HALLETTSVILLE, GUADALUPE VALLEY EC

4 slices bacon, chopped
1 medium onion, chopped
½ medium green pepper, chopped
⅓ cup uncooked rice
2 cups sliced okra
1 can (14.5 ounces) stewed tomatoes
Salt and pepper, to taste

Fry bacon until crisp, remove from pan and set aside. Add onion and green pepper to drippings. Cook over medium heat, stirring often until tender, about 5 minutes. Add rice, okra and tomatoes. Cook, continuing to stir often, until liquid from tomatoes is absorbed and rice is tender, about 25 minutes. Stir in reserved bacon and season with salt and pepper. Serves 4–6.

Texas Okra Patties

DEBBIE MASTERSON | DAWSON, NAVARRO COUNTY EC

1 pound okra, washed and chopped
½ cup chopped onion
1 teaspoon salt
¼ teaspoon pepper
½ cup water
1 egg, beaten
1 teaspoon baking powder
2 cups cornmeal

In a bowl, combine okra, onion, salt, pepper, water and egg. Separately, mix together baking powder and cornmeal, then stir into okra mixture. Drop by the tablespoonful into hot oil and brown over medium heat. Drain on paper towels. Makes 8 or more patties.

COOK'S NOTE: Great when you have an abundance of okra from your garden!

Cheesed Onion Bake

MRS. KENT O. WATTS | LULING, GUADALUPE VALLEY EC

6 cups thinly sliced onion rings
   (about 6 medium onions)
¼ cup butter
¼ cup flour
2 cups milk
½ teaspoon salt
2 cups grated sharp cheese

Place onion rings in ungreased casserole dish. Melt butter in saucepan; blend in flour. Gradually stir in milk. Cook, stirring constantly, until thick. Preheat oven to 350 degrees. Stir salt and cheese into milk mixture until cheese is melted. Pour over onions. Bake uncovered 1 hour or until onions are tender. Serves 6.

Crispy Golden Onion Rings

MRS. SAVELL L. SHARP | MERIDIAN, ERATH COUNTY EC

1 cup flour
1 teaspoon baking powder
¼ teaspoon salt
1 egg
1 cup milk
1 tablespoon vegetable oil
Pinch of sugar (optional)
3 large onions
Shortening
Salt

Into a small bowl, sift together flour, baking powder and salt. In a deep bowl, beat egg. Add milk and vegetable oil. Stir in dry ingredients and beat until smooth. Add pinch of sugar, if desired. Slice onions about ¼ inch thick and separate into rings. Dip a few at a time into the batter, completely coating each ring. Fry in shortening about 3 inches deep heated to 375 degrees. Fry until golden brown, turning once. Lift out and drain on paper towel. Sprinkle with salt. Serves 4.

COOK'S NOTE: My family considers this a real treat.

Marvelous Macaroni

JO HART PATRICK | CLARENDON, LIGHTHOUSE EC

¼ cup chopped onion
¼ cup pimientos, chopped
1 tablespoon butter
2 cups shredded cheese
1 can (10.75 ounces) cream of mushroom soup
½ cup mayonnaise
1 can (4 ounces) sliced mushrooms
1 package (10 ounces) shell pasta, cooked

Preheat oven to 350 degrees. In a large saucepan, sauté onion and pimiento in butter. Add the remaining ingredients and mix well. Pour the macaroni mixture into a casserole dish. Bake 30 minutes. Serves 6.

Sweet-and-Sour Black-Eyed Peas

ALVINA ARMBRECHT | WINTERS, COLEMAN COUNTY EC

3 cups fresh shelled black-eyed peas
1 small onion, chopped
1 teaspoon salt
¼ teaspoon black pepper
2 tablespoons bacon drippings
2 tablespoons sugar
2 tablespoons vinegar
Chopped bacon

Cook the black-eyed peas in water until nearly done. Then add remaining ingredients.

COOK'S NOTE: Canned black-eyed peas can be used.

Christmas Potatoes

ELIZABETH SCHIEVELBEIN | SEGUIN, GUADALUPE VALLEY EC

8 cups potatoes, peeled and cut into ¼-inch slices
2 large onions, thinly sliced
1¼ teaspoons salt, divided use
Water
¼ cup butter
3 tablespoons flour
2 cups milk
¼ teaspoon white pepper
½ cup chopped fresh parsley
1 small jar (2 ounces) pimientos,
    drained and chopped
Fresh parsley sprigs (optional)

Preheat oven to 375 degrees. Combine potato slices, onions and ½ teaspoon salt in a Dutch oven; add water to cover. Bring to a boil, cover, reduce heat and cook 5 minutes. Drain and set aside. Melt butter in a heavy saucepan over low heat; add flour, stirring until smooth. Cook 1 minute, stirring constantly. Gradually add milk and cook over medium heat, stirring constantly, until mixture is thick and bubbly. Stir in ¾ teaspoon salt, white pepper, chopped parsley and pimiento. Spoon potato mixture into a lightly greased, 8-by-12-inch baking dish and pour sauce over top. Bake 40–50 minutes. If desired, garnish with fresh parsley. Serves 8.

COOK'S NOTE: This dish appeals to the eye and goes with your holiday menu.

Potatoes Supreme

NAOMI GIVENS | ROPESVILLE, SOUTH PLAINS EC

2 cups grated cheddar cheese
¼ cup plus 2 teaspoons butter, divided use
6 medium potatoes, peeled, boiled and grated
1½ cups sour cream
⅓ cup green onion, chopped
1 teaspoon salt
¼ teaspoon black pepper
Paprika, to taste

Preheat oven to 350 degrees. Melt cheese and ¼ cup butter. Stir in potatoes, sour cream, onion, salt and pepper. Pour into a greased casserole dish. Dot with 2 teaspoons butter and sprinkle with paprika. Bake uncovered 30 minutes.

Make-Ahead Mashed Potatoes for a Crowd

KAY SMITH | FLOYDADA, LIGHTHOUSE EC

5 pounds potatoes, peeled, cooked and mashed
2 cups sour cream
¾ cup cream cheese
Salt and pepper, to taste
Milk or cream

Combine all ingredients except milk or cream; mix well, adding milk or cream to desired consistency. Turn into casserole dishes. Refrigerate until ready to use. To bake, preheat oven to 350 degrees and then bake 30 minutes.

COOK'S NOTE: May be covered and stored in a refrigerator for a week.

Potato Casserole

CALLIE EUDY FINLEY | CLARKSVILLE, LAMAR COUNTY EC

1 package (30 ounces) frozen hash browns, thawed
1 can (10.75 ounces) cream of chicken soup
2 cups sour cream
1 cup grated cheddar cheese
½ cup chopped onions
1 tablespoon salt
½ teaspoon pepper
¼ cup butter, melted
2 cups cornflakes, crushed

Preheat oven to 300 degrees. Thaw potatoes. Mix all ingredients, except butter and cornflakes. Put the potato mixture into a 2½- or 3-quart casserole dish. Combine butter and cornflakes. Spread the cornflake mixture on top of the potato mixture. Bake 1 hour.

Old-Fashioned Potato Cakes

MRS. HARRY E. RAU | GALVESTON, SAN BERNARD EC

2 eggs
3 large white or Irish potatoes, grated
1 tablespoon flour
1 teaspoon salt
1 teaspoon baking powder
1 small onion, grated
Ground black pepper, to taste
Butter or shortening

Beat eggs lightly; add potatoes. Mix in flour, salt and baking powder; add grated onion and pepper. Fry in hot buttered pan or in deep fat until brown on both sides.

COOK'S NOTE: Serve with applesauce, crisp bacon or syrup. Extra good.

Cranberry Yams

TAMMY PLUNKETT | VAN VLECK, JACKSON EC

½ cup flour
½ cup packed brown sugar
½ cup old-fashioned rolled oats
1 teaspoon cinnamon
⅓ cup butter
2 cans (15 ounces each) yams, drained
2 cups fresh cranberries
1½ cups miniature marshmallows

Preheat oven to 350 degrees. Combine flour, brown sugar, oats and cinnamon in a bowl. Cut in butter until crumbly. Combine 1 cup oat mixture with yams and cranberries, tossing to mix. Pour the mixture into a casserole dish; sprinkle with remaining oat mixture. Bake 35 minutes. Top with marshmallows. Broil until lightly browned.

Sweet Potato and Apple Casserole

MARALEE A. WILLHELM | MALAKOFF, NEW ERA EC

3 medium sweet potatoes, peeled and thinly sliced
2 large apples, peeled and sliced
2 cups miniature marshmallows
¼ cup sugar
1 teaspoon salt
1 teaspoon cinnamon
2 teaspoons cornstarch
½ cup water
4 teaspoons butter

Preheat oven to 350 degrees. Spread half of the sweet potatoes in bottom of a 3-quart casserole dish. Top with half of the apples and marshmallows. Combine the sugar, salt and cinnamon. Sprinkle some over casserole. Repeat layers with remaining potatoes, apples and sugar mixture. Dissolve cornstarch in water; pour over casserole. Dot with butter. Cover and bake 1 hour. Yields 6–8 servings.

Sweet Potato Casserole

MRS. HERMAN HYDE | MABANK, KAUFMAN COUNTY EC

3 cups mashed sweet potatoes
¾ cup butter, divided use
4 cups evaporated milk
1½ cups sugar
2 eggs
½ teaspoon cinnamon
½ teaspoon ground nutmeg
½ teaspoon vanilla extract
1 cup finely crushed cornflakes
½ cup nuts
½ cup brown sugar

Preheat oven to 425 degrees. Mix sweet potatoes, half of butter, milk, sugar, eggs, cinnamon, nutmeg and vanilla. Pour the potato mixture into a greased baking dish. Bake 15 minutes. Melt the remaining butter and mix with cornflakes, nuts and brown sugar. Spread on top of the potatoes. Reduce oven temperature to 400 degrees. Return casserole to oven and bake 15 minutes.

Baked Spinach Casserole

ELLEN MARTINDALE | LUEDERS, STAMFORD EC

1 package (10 ounces) frozen chopped spinach
4 cups cottage cheese
½ cup grated Swiss or mozzarella cheese
½ cup grated cheddar cheese
½ cup butter, cut in chunks
6–8 eggs
6–8 tablespoons flour

Cook spinach according to the package directions; drain and cool. Preheat oven to 350 degrees. In a bowl, mix together the 3 cheeses. Add butter and cooled spinach; mix well. In a separate bowl, beat eggs. Add flour and mix well. Pour egg mixture into cheese mixture and mix well. Pour into an ungreased 9-by-13-inch pan. Bake 1 hour, or until golden brown on top.

Crustless Spinach Quiche

MRS. LESLIE R. MONTAG | VICTORIA, VICTORIA EC

1 large onion, chopped
1 tablespoon vegetable oil
1 package (10 ounces) frozen chopped spinach,
    thawed and pressed dry
5 eggs, beaten
3 cups grated Muenster cheese
¼ teaspoon salt
⅛ teaspoon black pepper
¼ cup chopped green chiles (optional)

Sauté onion in oil in a large skillet. Add spinach and cook until excess moisture evaporates; cool. Preheat oven to 350 degrees. In a bowl, combine eggs, cheese, salt and pepper. Stir spinach into this and add green chiles, if desired. Pour into a greased 9-inch pie plate or quiche dish. Bake 30 minutes, or until set.

Cheddar Squash Bake

WENDY WISE CALVERT | EUSTACE, NEW ERA EC

2 eggs, separated
Salt, to taste
1 cup sour cream
1 tablespoon flour
6 cups thinly sliced, cooked squash
1½ cups shredded cheddar cheese
6–8 slices fried bacon, crumbled
1 tablespoon butter, melted

Preheat oven to 350 degrees. In a bowl, lightly beat egg yolks, then add salt, sour cream and flour; mix well. In a separate bowl, beat egg whites until stiff; fold into first mixture. Layer half the squash, egg mixture and cheese in a casserole dish; repeat layers and sprinkle the bacon and butter on top. Bake 25–30 minutes, or until golden brown. Serves 8–10.

Fresh Squash Fritters

BLANCA FORSHEE | BOERNE, BANDERA EC

2 cups finely chopped yellow squash
1 cup finely chopped onion
1 egg, beaten
1 teaspoon salt
1 teaspoon pepper
¾ teaspoon chopped fresh basil
½ cup flour

Mix yellow squash, onion, egg, salt, pepper and basil. Stir in the flour. Pour oil into a skillet to a depth of ½ inch. Heat over medium heat. Drop the squash mixture by tablespoonful into hot oil. Cook until browned, turning once. Drain on paper towels.

COOK'S NOTE: This is one of several recipes I developed in self-defense, when our garden overproduced squash.

Squash Dressing

DIANNE WENZEL | LINDEN, BOWIE-CASS EC

3 cups cooked, mashed yellow squash
1 large onion, chopped
1 package (6 ounces) Mexican cornbread mix
1 can (14.75 ounces) cream-style corn
2 tablespoons sugar
1 egg, beaten
1 teaspoon salt
½ teaspoon black pepper
¼ cup butter, melted

Preheat oven to 350 degrees. Mix all ingredients and pour into a 9-by-13-inch casserole dish. Bake 25–30 minutes, or until golden brown.

Indian Squash

MRS. PAT ADCOX | SNYDER, MIDWEST EC

3 ears corn
4 yellow squash, chopped
1 small onion, chopped
1 small bell pepper, chopped
2 tablespoons butter
Salt and pepper, to taste

Cut kernels from corn. Put in a skillet with other vegetables, butter, salt and pepper, and add a very small amount of water. Cover and steam until tender. Stir when about halfway done. If you like spicy food, add a small green chile.

COOK'S NOTE: An electric skillet is very good for preparing this dish.

Summer Squash

DORIS BURD | HENDERSON, RUSK COUNTY EC

2–2½ pounds yellow squash, cut up
6 tablespoons cream cheese
2 green onions, minced,
    or ¼ cup chopped white onion
¼ cup butter, melted
Salt and pepper, to taste
Buttered fresh breadcrumbs
¼ cup grated Parmesan cheese (optional)

Cook squash until tender, drain and mash. Stir in cream cheese, onions, butter, salt and pepper. Preheat oven to 350 degrees. Pour into a buttered 1-quart casserole dish. Top with buttered breadcrumbs and cheese, if desired. Bake 25 minutes.

Broiled Tomatoes

JEANETTA MCNEILL | HAPPY, SWISHER EC

3 tablespoons butter, melted
½ cup coarse cracker crumbs
2 tablespoons chopped green onion tops
⅛ teaspoon garlic salt
½ teaspoon salt
⅛ teaspoon pepper
4 medium ripe tomatoes

Preheat oven to 400 degrees. Mix butter, cracker crumbs, onion, garlic salt, salt and pepper. Cut tomatoes into quarters. Put crumb mix on tomatoes. Bake 7 minutes. Serve immediately.

COOK'S NOTE: I had an abundance of tomatoes and was looking for new ways to fix them. I found a recipe, but did not have all the ingredients. Since we live 33 miles from the nearest store, I had to change the recipe. So, this is an ORIGINAL RECIPE by me. Some relatives have it now, and everyone enjoys the partially cooked tomatoes and crunchy topping.

Scalloped Turnips

KITTY BAUCOM | SAN ANGELO, CONCHO VALLEY EC

1 pound boiled turnips, sliced and drained
1 teaspoon salt
⅛ teaspoon ground mace
½ cup breadcrumbs
2 tablespoons butter
1 can (10.75 ounces) cream of celery soup
1 cup evaporated milk

Preheat oven to 375 degrees. Grease a 1½-quart baking dish. Arrange a layer of turnips; sprinkle with salt, mace and breadcrumbs. Mix butter, celery soup and milk. Pour over layer of turnips. Repeat the layers until all ingredients are used. Bake 30 minutes.

Fried Zucchini Cakes

ELDA HUSE | WEST, HILL COUNTY EC

⅓ cup buttermilk baking mix
¼ cup grated Parmesan cheese
⅛ teaspoon salt
⅛ teaspoon pepper
2 large eggs, lightly beaten
2 cups coarsely grated zucchini (about 2 medium)
2 tablespoons butter

In a bowl, mix baking mix, cheese, salt and pepper. Stir in eggs until the mixture just becomes moist. Fold in zucchini. Melt the butter in a 10-inch skillet over moderate heat. Use 2 tablespoons batter for each zucchini cake. Fry zucchini cakes about 2–3 minutes on each side, or until brown. Makes 8–10 zucchini cakes.

COOK'S NOTE: Takes less than 10 minutes to prepare.

Zucchini and Tomatoes

CONNIE SANDEL | HUNTSVILLE, MID-SOUTH EC

½ cup chopped onion or chives
¼ cup olive or vegetable oil
1 cup chopped tomatoes
¼ teaspoon oregano
1 teaspoon parsley
Sweet basil
3–4 cups small zucchini, sliced in rounds
Grated Parmesan cheese, optional

Sauté onions or chives in oil; add tomatoes, oregano, parsley, basil and zucchini. Cook until tender. If desired, sprinkle Parmesan cheese over the top of the zucchini before serving.

COOK'S NOTE: Use fresh zucchini, tomatoes and herbs, if possible.

Vegetable Pizza

GARY MICHELS | GRANBURY, JOHNSON COUNTY EC

2 packages (8 ounces each) crescent rolls
1 cup mayonnaise
1 packet ranch dressing mix
16 ounces cream cheese
Fresh vegetables, cut into small pieces

Spread rolls flat on a large cookie sheet and bake 10 minutes at the temperature stated on the roll package. Mix together mayonnaise, dressing mix and cream cheese. Spread on crust. Arrange vegetables of your choice on top of cream cheese mixture. Cut into squares to serve.

Thai-Style Rice

PATTY JONES | CLUTE, NAVASOTA VALLEY EC

⅓ cup vegetable oil
3 cloves garlic, diced
Chicken breast, diced
1 medium onion, diced
2 cups cooked rice
1 teaspoon salt
1 teaspoon pepper
2 green peppers, diced
Soy sauce, optional
Cucumbers, green onions and tomatoes, for garnish

Add oil to skillet or wok and turn heat to high. Add garlic. Stir-fry until done. Add chicken and stir-fry until done. Stir-fry onion. Add rice, salt and pepper, stirring for 1 minute. Add green peppers and stir-fry for additional 2–3 minutes; add soy sauce, if desired. Garnish with sliced cucumbers, green onions and tomatoes.

Green Chile Rice

VENESHA SCHROEDER | LITTLEFIELD, LAMB COUNTY EC

2 cups grated Monterey jack cheese
8–12 ounces chopped green chiles
2 cups sour cream
2 eggs, beaten
4 cups cooked rice
1 cup grated cheddar cheese

Preheat oven to 350 degrees. Mix first 4 ingredients. Stir into rice. Pour into greased, 9-by-13-inch pan; top with cheddar cheese. Cover. Bake 35–40 minutes.

Spanish Rice

VANEITA NULL | WELLINGTON, GREENBELT EC

3 cups canned whole tomatoes
2 tablespoons vegetable oil
1 cup converted rice
1 large bell pepper, chopped
2 jalapeño peppers, chopped
1 large onion or 3 green onions, chopped
¾ cup water
1 teaspoon ground cumin
1 teaspoon black pepper
Dash crushed red pepper
1 tablespoon salt
3 teaspoons chili powder

Place tomatoes in a blender and blend until smooth; set aside. Heat oil in a 9-inch, nonstick skillet and cook rice until lightly browned. Add peppers and onion; sauté until translucent. Add tomatoes, water and seasonings to rice mixture. Stir well and cook over low heat 20–25 minutes, or until rice absorbs liquid. Stir often.

COOK'S NOTE: My son came up with this recipe when he could not find one he liked for Spanish rice. He knew what taste he preferred and kept experimenting until he came up with this. He and I just love it, and we prepare it often. It suits our taste for hot, spicy rice.

Nanny's Dressing

GERALDINE ELZEY | KEMP, KAUFMAN COUNTY EC

2 stalks celery, chopped
4 medium onions, chopped
½ cup butter
1 cooking apple, diced
4 slices toasted bread
1 teaspoon sage
3 eggs
1 9-inch pan prepared cornbread, crumbled
Garlic powder, to taste
Salt and pepper, to taste
3–4 cups chicken broth

Preheat oven to 350 degrees. In a skillet, cook celery and onions in butter until onions are clear. Add to a bowl with all other ingredients and mix well, adding enough chicken broth to make dressing moist but still hold its shape. Cook 1 hour. Serves 6.

Corn Pudding

EMILY EVANS ROBERSON | HICO, ERATH COUNTY EC

1 can (14.75 ounces) cream-style corn
1 cup grated cheddar cheese
½ cup cornmeal
⅓ cup vegetable oil
1 small can (4 ounces) chopped green chiles, not drained
1 teaspoon salt
¼ teaspoon garlic powder
⅛ teaspoon cayenne pepper
¼ cup chopped onion
2 eggs, well beaten

Preheat oven to 350 degrees. Mix thoroughly all ingredients except eggs. Blend in eggs. Pour into a 1-quart baking dish and cook 45 minutes.

COOK'S NOTE: Can be cooked and frozen. If frozen, thaw before heating.

MAIN DISHES

Bar-B-Q Chicken in the Oven

MRS. KENNETH CUDD | PERRYTON, NORTH PLAINS EC

1 whole chicken, cut into serving pieces
1 teaspoon salt
Pepper to taste
4 tablespoons water
3 tablespoons ketchup
3 tablespoons brown sugar
1 cup apple cider vinegar
1 teaspoon chili powder
1 teaspoon paprika
1 teaspoon mustard
2 tablespoons Worcestershire sauce
2 tablespoons lemon juice
2 tablespoons vegetable oil

Sprinkle chicken pieces with salt and pepper; set aside. In a saucepan, blend remaining ingredients; heat until dissolved. Preheat oven to 450 degrees. Line a large pan in heavy foil. Dip each piece of chicken in mixture and place on foil; pour remainder over and seal with more foil. Bake 15 minutes, then reduce heat to 350 degrees and bake 1 hour and 15 minutes.

Poppy Seed Chicken

CARLENE LONG | STANTON, CAP ROCK EC

2 pounds boneless, skinless chicken breasts,
    cooked and cut in large pieces
1 carton (8 ounces) sour cream
1 can (10.75 ounces) cream of chicken soup
1½ cups Ritz cracker crumbs (1 stack)
½ cup butter, melted
1 tablespoon poppy seeds

Preheat oven to 350 degrees. Place chicken in shallow casserole dish. Mix sour cream and soup; pour over chicken. Mix crumbs, butter and poppy seeds. Sprinkle over top. Bake 30 minutes.

Ruth's Chicken and Rice

DONA REED | FLOYDADA, LIGHTHOUSE EC

5 strips bacon
1 cup long-grain rice
Salt and pepper, to taste
1 whole chicken, cut into serving pieces
1 can (10.75 ounces) cream of chicken soup
1 can (10.75 ounces) cream of mushroom soup
Water
1 teaspoon chives
1 teaspoon oregano
1 teaspoon grated onion

Preheat oven to 250 degrees. Line a 9-by-13-inch baking dish with bacon strips. Cover with rice. Salt and pepper chicken and place on rice, skin side up. Mix soups with water (1 can each) and pour over chicken. Sprinkle chives, oregano and onion over top. Cover dish with foil, seal edges and bake 2½ hours. Do not open oven during baking time.

COOK'S NOTE: This recipe is a good dish to prepare when you have a busy day, as it does not have to be watched or checked until baking time is finished.

Chicken Enchilada Casserole

DIANNE MORGAN | HUGHES SPRINGS, BOWIE-CASS EC

½ cup chopped onion
Butter
3–4 chicken breasts, boiled, boned and chopped
1 can (10.75 ounces) cream of chicken soup
1 can (10.75 ounces) cream of mushroom soup
1 small can (4 ounces) chopped mild green chiles
1 carton (8 ounces) sour cream
Flour tortillas
Cheddar cheese, grated

Preheat oven to 350 degrees. Sauté onions in butter in a large skillet until clear. Add chicken, soups and chiles. Mix in sour cream. Grease casserole dish. Line bottom with tortillas, then spread half of chicken mixture over tortillas. Sprinkle with cheese. Repeat. Bake until cheese melts.

Chicken and Cheese Lasagna

M. JEAN HINES | SAN AUGUSTINE, DEEP EAST TEXAS EC

8 ounces lasagna noodles
1½ cups cottage cheese
3 cups diced cooked chicken
12 slices American cheese
½ cup grated Parmesan cheese
MUSHROOM SAUCE:
3 tablespoons butter
¾ cup chopped onion
¾ cup chopped green pepper
½ cup diced celery
1 can (10.75 ounces) cream of chicken soup
⅓ cup milk
1 can (12 ounces) sliced mushrooms, drained
¼ cup chopped pimientos
½ teaspoon basil

Cook noodles according to package directions. Rinse in cold water and drain again. Place half the noodles in a 9-by-13-inch casserole dish. Preheat oven to 350 degrees. Cover with half each of the Mushroom Sauce, cottage cheese, chicken, American cheese and Parmesan cheese. Repeat layers. For Mushroom Sauce, melt butter in a skillet and sauté onion, pepper and celery until tender. Stir in soup, milk, mushrooms, pimientos and basil and continue cooking slowly for 10 minutes. Bake for 45 minutes.

COOK'S NOTE: Can double recipe and freeze 1 casserole for future use.

Buttermilk Baked Chicken

MRS. STEPHEN LYON | NEW BADEN, NAVASOTA VALLEY EC

1 whole chicken, cut into serving pieces
1½ cups buttermilk, divided use
¾ cup flour
1½ teaspoons salt
¼ teaspoon pepper
¼ cup butter
1 can (10.75 ounces) cream of chicken soup

Preheat oven to 425 degrees. Dip chicken into ½ cup of buttermilk and roll in flour seasoned with salt and pepper. Melt butter in a 9-by-13-inch pan. Place chicken in pan, skin side down, and bake uncovered 30 minutes. Turn chicken and bake another 15 minutes. Blend remaining buttermilk and soup and pour around chicken. Bake 15 minutes more, or until drumstick is tender when pierced with a fork. Serves 6.

Party Chicken

TERRY MCWILLIAMS | ROBY, MIDWEST EC

6 boneless, skinless chicken breasts
Lemon pepper
1 can (10.75 ounces) cream of chicken soup
3 ounces cream cheese, softened
1 carton (8 ounces) sour cream

Preheat oven to 300 degrees. Lay chicken breasts in greased pan. Sprinkle with lemon pepper. Mix remaining ingredients and spread over chicken. Cover with foil and bake 2 hours. Uncover and bake 1 hour longer.

Stuffed Chicken Breasts

LYNDA MARSHALL | SLATON, SOUTH PLAINS EC

4–5 boneless, skinless chicken breasts
1 small can (4 ounces) chopped green chiles
1½ cups grated Cheddar cheese
Salt and pepper, to taste
½ cup butter, melted
2 cups crushed plain crackers

Pound chicken flat with a meat mallet. Preheat oven to 250 degrees. Cut each breast into large strips. Place small amount of chiles and cheese on each strip. Sprinkle salt and pepper, roll up and secure with a toothpick. Roll each breast in melted butter, then in crackers. Place in baking dish. Sprinkle with any remaining butter, chiles and cheese. Cover with foil and bake 2 hours.

Italian Chicken

VIRGINIA ZILLMANN | SAN ANTONIO, KARNES EC

1 2-pound chicken, cut into serving pieces
1 egg, beaten
Water
¾ cup dry breadcrumbs
2 tablespoons shortening
1 small can (8 ounces) tomato sauce
¼ cup chopped onion
½ teaspoon garlic
½ teaspoon basil
½ teaspoon oregano
½ cup mozzarella cheese

Dip chicken parts in egg mixed with 1 tablespoon water. Roll in bread crumbs. Brown chicken in shortening heated in a Dutch oven. Mix tomato sauce, water, onion, garlic, basil and oregano together and pour over browned chicken. Cover and simmer over low heat approximately 45 minutes. Sprinkle cheese on top before serving.

Chicken Fritters

LELA LOVE | GOLDTHWAITE, HAMILTON COUNTY EC

2 eggs, separated
½ cup minced celery
1 teaspoon grated onion
¼ cup flour
½ teaspoon salt
Dash of hot pepper sauce
2 cups chopped cooked chicken
Vegetable oil, for frying

Combine egg yolks, celery, onion, flour, salt and hot pepper sauce in a bowl; stir in chicken and mix well. Beat egg whites until stiff; fold into chicken mixture. Drop by the tablespoonful into heated oil. Brown on both sides. May be served with chicken gravy, creamed peas or rice. Serves 4.

Chicken Paprika

PHYLLIS A. HURLEY | RIO FRIO, BANDERA EC

¼ cup vegetable oil
2 medium onions, finely chopped
2–3 teaspoons paprika
1 whole chicken, cut into serving pieces
1 teaspoon salt
½ cup sour cream

Heat oil in 10- or 12-inch skillet over moderate heat; add and brown the onions. Add paprika and chicken; sprinkle with salt. Cover. Cook over very low heat 1 hour, or until tender, turning after 30 minutes. Pour sour cream over chicken; heat. Makes 4 servings.

Spicy Chicken Enchilada Casserole

MARY ATTLESEY | YANTIS, FARMERS EC

1 medium onion, chopped
2 tablespoons vegetable oil
1 can (14.5 ounces) whole tomatoes,
    cut up and drained
1 small can (8 ounces) tomato sauce
1 small can (4 ounces) chopped green chiles
1 packet enchilada sauce mix
¼ teaspoon garlic powder
½ teaspoon seasoned salt
3–4 cups shredded cooked chicken
12 corn tortillas
2 small cans (2.25 ounces each) sliced ripe olives
4 ounces Monterey jack cheese, grated

In a large Dutch oven, sauté onions in oil until tender. Add tomatoes, tomato sauce, green chiles, enchilada sauce mix, garlic powder, seasoned salt and chicken. Simmer, covered, 15–20 minutes. Preheat oven to 350 degrees. Place 4 corn tortillas on bottom of a greased 9-by-13-inch pan. Pour ⅓ of the chicken mixture over tortillas, spreading evenly. Add ⅓ of the olives and cheese; spread evenly. Repeat layers twice. Bake 30–40 minutes. Yields 6–8 servings.

Onion-Baked Chicken

CATHERINE FERGUSON | HENDERSON, RUSK COUNTY EC

1 cup biscuit mix
1 teaspoon salt
½ teaspoon pepper
¼ teaspoon paprika
1 whole chicken, cut into serving pieces
4 teaspoons butter
1 packet dry onion soup
2 cups hot water

Preheat oven to 325 degrees. Combine biscuit mix, salt, pepper and paprika. Mix thoroughly. Coat the chicken with the dry mixture and place in a 3-quart casserole dish. Dot with butter. Mix together dry onion soup and hot water. Pour over chicken. Cover the casserole dish and bake for 1½ hours.

Arroz Con Pollo (Rice With Chicken)

EDDIE HAM SPENCE | MULESHOE, BAILEY COUNTY EC

1 3-pound chicken, cut into serving pieces
Salt and pepper, to taste
1 cup vegetable oil
½ cup butter
1 cup rice
1 large garlic clove, minced
2 medium onions, chopped
3 cups chicken stock
¼ teaspoon pepper
¼ teaspoon ground cumin
¼ teaspoon ground oregano
2 tomatoes, peeled and chopped
1 small jar (2 ounces) pimientos, chopped

Sprinkle chicken with salt and pepper, and brown in oil in a large skillet; set aside chicken. Drain and discard oil, then melt butter in large skillet. Add rice and cook over very low heat, stirring until golden brown. Add remaining ingredients and mix gently. Preheat oven to 300 degrees. Pour mixture into baking dish and place chicken on top. Cover and bake 1 hour and 15 minutes. Serves 6–8.

E-Z Chicken

MRS. HILMAR MUELLER | LA VERNIA, GUADALUPE VALLEY EC

1 whole chicken
Salt and pepper, to taste
1 packet onion soup mix
1 packet ranch dressing mix

Preheat oven to 350 degrees. Place chicken in an oven-safe bag (such as Reynolds Oven Bags). Salt and pepper chicken. Pour mixes over chicken and close bag with a twist tie. Bake 1 hour and 15 minutes.

Almond Chicken

SUSAN POWELL | ATHENS, NEW ERA EC

Vegetable oil
2 pounds boneless, skinless chicken breast,
    cut into strips or cubes
1 can (8 ounces) bamboo shoots,
    drained and sliced in half
1 cup sliced celery
1 small can (4 ounces) mushroom pieces,
    or ¼ pound fresh mushrooms, sliced
¾ teaspoon MSG or salt
3 chicken bouillon cubes
3 cups water
6 teaspoons soy sauce
4½ tablespoons cornstarch
4½ tablespoons water
8 ounces snow or sugar snap peas (optional)
½ cup toasted, whole blanched almonds
Cooked rice

Heat oil in skillet. Add chicken and cook about 6 minutes. Add bamboo shoots, celery, mushroom pieces and MSG or salt. Stir fry 1 minute. Dissolve bouillon cubes in water and add to skillet along with soy sauce. Simmer, covered, over low heat for 3 minutes. Mix cornstarch with 4½ tablespoons water. Stir into pan. Bring to a boil and cook 1 minute. Add peas, if desired, and almonds. Heat thoroughly. Serve with rice.

Southern Fried Chicken

CLARA SLOUGH | COOPER, LAMAR COUNTY EC

1 2½-pound chicken, cut into serving pieces
Lemon juice
Salt and pepper, to taste
2 eggs
1 tablespoon milk
Flour
Butter or shortening
GRAVY:
3 tablespoons flour
1½ cups half-and-half
Salt and pepper, to taste

Put lemon juice, salt and pepper over chicken pieces. In a medium bowl, beat eggs and add milk. Put flour in a shallow dish. Dip chicken into egg mixture; roll in flour. Brown chicken in butter or shortening. Cover and cook over low heat until tender. For Gravy, remove chicken and add 3 tablespoons flour plus half-and-half to hot fat, stirring until thickened. Season with salt and pepper.

Imperial Chicken

EMILY EVANS ROBERSON | HICO, ERATH COUNTY EC

½ cup butter
4 chicken breasts
¼ cup flour seasoned with salt, pepper
    and garlic powder
1 pound mushrooms, quartered
1 tablespoon chopped onion
1 cup heavy whipping cream
¼ cup dry sherry
1½ teaspoons salt
½ teaspoon pepper

Melt butter in a large skillet. Dredge chicken in seasoned flour. Brown on all sides; remove from pan and reserve drippings. Over medium heat, in the same pan, sauté mushrooms and onion about 5 minutes. Meanwhile, in a small pan, combine cream and sherry and warm a little to prevent curdling. When warmed, add salt and pepper; pour into skillet with mushroom mixture. Return chicken to skillet, cover and simmer 20 minutes, or until fork tender.

Chicken Pie

RITA ADDICKS | WEIMAR, FAYETTE EC

PASTRY:

1½ cups flour

⅛ teaspoon salt

½ cup shortening

¼ cup milk or water

FILLING:

6 tablespoons butter

6 tablespoons flour

½ teaspoon salt

¼ teaspoon pepper

1¾ cups chicken broth

⅔ cup milk

2 cups chicken, cooked and diced

1 can mixed vegetables (2 cups)

For Pastry, combine flour and salt in mixing bowl; cut in shortening. Add milk or water as needed. Form into 2 balls: 1 with ⅔ dough; the other with the remaining ⅓. Roll out and place larger portion in casserole dish; set aside. For Filling, melt butter; add flour and seasonings. Cook over low heat, stirring constantly, until smooth (about 1 minute). Slowly add liquids, stirring often and cook until thickened. Add chicken and vegetables. Preheat oven to 425 degrees. Pour mixture into pastry-lined casserole dish. Top with remaining pastry. Pinch edges together; cut steam vents in top crust. Bake 35–40 minutes. Serves 6.

Granny's Chicken Spaghetti

EMILY EVANS ROBERSON | RICO, ERATH COUNTY EC

1 package (12 ounces) spaghetti

¼ cup chopped onion

¼ cup chopped green pepper

¼ cup chopped red bell pepper,
    or 1 small jar (2 ounces) pimientos

1 cup sliced mushrooms

Butter

Garlic powder

4–5 cups cubed cooked chicken (3 pounds)

12 ounces processed cheese, cubed
    (Velveeta preferred)

1 can (10.75 ounces) cream of mushroom soup

1 can (10.75 ounces) cream of chicken soup

1 can (14.5 ounces) chicken broth

Salt and pepper, to taste

Cook spaghetti according to package directions. In a skillet, sauté onion, peppers and mushrooms in a small amount of butter sprinkled with garlic powder. Combine spaghetti, vegetables, and remaining ingredients in a large pot. Heat 10 minutes over medium heat, or until desired thickness. Serve with tossed salad, Italian dressing and garlic bread.

COOK'S NOTE: I prefer to season the water for cooking the chicken with several celery leaves, lemon juice, salt, pepper, garlic powder and fajita seasoning.

Chicken and Dressing

MRS. WAYNE RUEDE | BANDERA, BANDERA EC

1 package (14 ounces) herb stuffing mix
3 cups cubed cooked chicken
½ cup butter
½ cup flour
½ teaspoon salt
Dash of pepper
4 cups chicken broth
6 eggs, slightly beaten
PIMIENTO AND MUSHROOM SAUCE:
1 can (10.75 ounces) cream of mushroom soup
1 carton (8 ounces) sour cream
¼ cup milk
¼ cup chopped pimientos

Prepare stuffing according to package instructions. Spread in a 9-by-13-inch pan. Top with a layer of chicken. Preheat oven to 325 degrees. In a large saucepan, melt butter. Blend in flour and seasonings. Whisk in broth. Cook and stir until mixture thickens. Remove from heat. Stir a small amount of the hot mixture into the bowl with the eggs. Return all to hot mixture; mix well. Pour over chicken. Bake 40–50 minutes. Cut into squares and serve with Pimiento and Mushroom Sauce: Combine all ingredients in saucepan and warm thoroughly. Serves 16.

Chicken and Dressing Casserole

BETTY BANKHEAD | CARTHAGE, RUSK COUNTY EC

4 chicken breasts, cooked and chopped
1 can (10.75 ounces) cream of chicken
    and mushroom soup
1 carton (8 ounces) sour cream
1 package (14 ounces) cornbread dressing mix
1 cup chicken broth

Preheat oven to 375 degrees. Spread chicken in bottom of a 9-by-13-inch casserole dish. Combine soup and sour cream and pour over chicken. Sprinkle dressing mix on top and pour chicken broth over dressing mix. Cover with foil. Bake 40–45 minutes.

Chicken Caruso

RITA SCHUETZE | KERRVILLE, BANDERA EC

4 boneless, skinless chicken breasts
Garlic salt and pepper, to taste
3 tablespoons butter
1 jar (15 ounces) spaghetti sauce
1 teaspoon Italian seasoning
2 cups sliced celery
3 cups hot cooked rice
Parmesan cheese

Cut chicken into thin strips. Season with garlic salt and pepper. In a large saucepan, sauté chicken 2 minutes in butter. Stir in sauce and Italian seasoning. Cover and simmer 10 minutes. Add celery and cook until tender-crisp. Serve over fluffy rice. Sprinkle with Parmesan cheese. Serves 6.

Chicken Cherokee

FRANK H. SLADE | HENDERSON, RUSK COUNTY EC

6–8 chicken thighs
Salt and pepper, to taste
2 tablespoons butter
½ clove garlic, minced
1 medium onion, chopped
½ cup water
2 teaspoons molasses
1 teaspoon Worcestershire sauce
1 teaspoon flour
Cooked rice

Sprinkle chicken thighs with salt and pepper. Brown them in butter with garlic over moderate heat in heavy skillet or Dutch oven. Remove chicken. Brown onion in same pan. Add water, molasses and Worcestershire sauce; blend. Cook 1 minute. Return chicken to pan, cover tightly, reduce heat to low and simmer 1 hour, basting often. About 10 minutes before chicken is done, sprinkle with flour, baste, re-cover and let thicken slowly. Serve chicken with rice, with the remaining juices poured on top. Serves 4–6.

Mexican Chicken and Rice

ETHEL KRAMER | GRAHAM, FORT BELKNAP EC

1 3-pound chicken
2 chicken bouillon cubes
1 cup converted rice (Uncle Ben's preferred)
2 cups water
1 onion, chopped
½ cup butter
½ teaspoon garlic powder
½ teaspoon ground cumin
1 teaspoon chili powder
1 small jar (2 ounces) pimientos
1 small can (4 ounces) green chiles
1 can (10.75 ounces) cream of chicken soup
½ cup chicken broth
1 carton (8 ounces) sour cream
8 ounces Monterey jack cheese, grated
8 ounces Cheddar cheese, grated

In a pot, stew chicken in water and bouillon cubes; cool, remove bones and chop meat into bite-size pieces. Cook rice in water just until tender. In a skillet, sauté onions in butter; then add garlic, cumin, chili powder, pimientos and green chiles. Set aside. In a saucepan, heat chicken soup, broth and sour cream; then add Monterey jack cheese. Stir until cheese melts and add onion mixture. Preheat oven to 350 degrees. Spray a 3-quart casserole dish with cooking spray. Put rice in bottom of dish, add chopped chicken and top with soup mixture. Bake about 20 minutes, until heated through. Add grated Cheddar cheese and return to oven for 5 minutes, until cheese melts. Serves 8.

COOK'S NOTE: This is my own recipe and my family does enjoy this.

Jalapeño Chicken

LAVONNE DROEMER | GIDDINGS, BLUEBONNET EC

6 boneless, skinless chicken breasts
2 tablespoons vegetable oil
2 cups sour cream
1 tablespoon flour
1 garlic clove, chopped
Salt and pepper, to taste
1 can (8 ounces) whole jalapeño peppers
¼ cup white wine (optional)
1 cup grated mozzarella cheese
1 large onion, sliced in rounds
4 tablespoons chopped green onion, including tops

Brown chicken in oil on both sides and arrange in a 9-by-13-inch baking dish. In a blender, combine sour cream, flour, garlic, salt, pepper, jalapeño peppers and wine, if desired. Blend until smooth to make sauce. Preheat oven to 350 degrees. Sprinkle cheese over chicken, top with sauce and onion rounds and sprinkle with green onions. Bake uncovered 1 hour, or until tender.

COOK'S NOTE: Guests always enjoy this one!

Chicken Taco Casserole

MRS. ED CONRADY | WINDTHORST, J-A-C EC

1 3-pound chicken
Corn chips
1 large can (28 ounces) enchilada sauce
1 can (10.75 ounces) cream of mushroom soup
1 large onion, chopped
½ teaspoon garlic salt
¼ teaspoon pepper
1 cup grated cheese
1 cup chicken broth

Cook chicken, debone and cut meat into small pieces. Preheat oven to 350 degrees. Grease baking dish and line with corn chips. Combine chicken, enchilada sauce, mushroom soup, onion, garlic salt and pepper, and spread over corn chips. Sprinkle with the grated cheese. Cover with additional corn chips and add the chicken broth. Bake for 30 minutes.

Chicken Flautas

GWEN ELLIOTT | HUNTSVILLE, MID-SOUTH EC

1 cup finely chopped cooked chicken or turkey
⅓ cup picante sauce
2 tablespoons green onion slices
¼ teaspoon ground cumin
Vegetable oil
16 corn tortillas
1 cup shredded Cheddar cheese

Combine chicken or turkey, picante sauce, onion and cumin; mix well. Preheat oven to 400 degrees. Heat about ½ inch oil in small skillet until hot but not smoking. Quickly fry each tortilla in oil to soften, about 2 seconds on each side. Drain on paper towel. Spoon 1 tablespoon chicken mixture and 1 tablespoon cheese down center of each tortilla. Roll tightly, secure with toothpick. Place seam side down on baking sheet. Bake 18–20 minutes, or until crisp. Serve with guacamole and picante sauce.

COOK'S NOTE: Makes 16 appetizers or serve with bowl of chili for a good dinner! Great way to use leftover turkey, too. We've made a meal with just these and a salad and ice cream for dessert.

Chicken Casserole

EVELYN REEVES | EDMONDSON, SWISHER COUNTY EC

1 package (8 ounces) wild rice
    (Uncle Ben's Original Recipe preferred)
Chicken broth
1 can (10.75 ounces) cream of celery soup
1 small jar (2 ounces) pimientos
½ cup mayonnaise
¼ cup chopped onion
2 cups diced cooked chicken
1 can (5 ounces) water chestnuts, sliced
Grated cheese
1 package (2 ounces) sliced almonds

Cook rice in chicken broth according to directions on box. Preheat oven to 350 degrees. Add soup, pimientos, mayonnaise, onions, chicken and water chestnuts. Mix together and pour into a casserole dish. Bake 30 minutes. Remove from oven and sprinkle with cheese and almonds. Return to oven long enough to melt cheese. Serve hot or cold.

COOK'S NOTE: Extra good! Everybody's favorite.

Chicken Enchiladas

KRISTI RICHARDSON | LUBBOCK, SOUTH PLAINS EC

18 corn tortillas, cut in halves
Chicken broth
1 whole chicken, cooked, boned and chopped
    (or 3 chicken breasts)
1 can (10.75 ounces) cream of chicken soup
1 can (10.75 ounces) cream of mushroom soup
1 can (12 ounces) evaporated milk
1 small can (4 ounces) chopped green chiles
1 onion, minced
Salt and pepper, to taste
Grated cheese

Preheat oven to 350 degrees. Spray a 9-by-13-inch casserole dish with cooking spray. Heat chicken broth in a shallow pan or skillet. Dip tortilla halves in hot chicken broth and line pan with them. In a bowl, mix chicken with soups, milk, green chiles, onion, salt and pepper. Cover tortilla layer with chicken mixture. Layer more tortillas, after dipping in broth, then chicken. Cover with grated cheese. Cover with foil and bake 30 minutes.

COOK'S NOTE: Sauté onion first, if you like. This recipe may be prepared ahead and is great after being frozen. Do not cook before freezing. From frozen, cook 1 hour at 350 degrees, or until bubbly.

Cheesy Chicken Tortilla Stack

CHRISTINE CHAMBERLAIN | WALLER, SAN BERNARD EC

½ cup vegetable oil
6 flour tortillas
1 carton (8 ounces) sour cream
½ teaspoon seasoned salt
½ teaspoon hot pepper sauce
2½ cups shredded cooked chicken breast
2½ cups shredded Monterey jack cheese
1¼ cups shredded longhorn cheese
½ cup minced green onions
1½ tablespoons butter
⅓ cup shredded lettuce
¼ cup chopped tomato

Heat oil to hot but not smoking in a 10-inch skillet. Fry tortillas, 1 at a time, in hot oil 3–5 seconds, or until they hold their shape and begin to crisp. Drain well on paper towels; set aside. Preheat oven to 400 degrees. Combine sour cream, seasoned salt and hot pepper sauce. Place 1 tortilla on a lightly greased baking sheet. Spread about 1 tablespoon sour cream mixture over tortilla. Sprinkle with ½ cup shredded chicken, ½ cup Monterey Jack cheese, ¼ cup longhorn cheese and 2 tablespoons green onions. Repeat all layers 4 times. Top with remaining tortilla. Brush top tortilla and sides of tortillas with melted butter. Cover with foil; bake 25 minutes. Immediately remove foil after baking; place tortilla stack on serving plate. Spread remaining sour cream mixture on top tortilla. Sprinkle with lettuce and tomato. Cut into wedges and serve immediately.

Quail Bake

PAULINE ELLIS | CORPUS CHRISTI, MEDINA EC

Butter
1 cup long-grain rice
1 cup warm water
1 packet onion soup mix
6–8 quail, cleaned and washed

Preheat oven to 350 degrees. Grease a roasting pan well with butter. Put rice in pan. Combine warm water and soup mix, stirring well. Pour over rice and mix well. Dot with small amounts of butter. Place quail, breasts down, in a circle on rice mixture. Cover and bake about 45 minutes, or until rice is done.

Quail or Dove, Texas-Style

JEFFREY K. ROST | LA GRANGE, FAYETTE EC

¾ onion, sliced
12 ribs celery with leaves, chopped
12 chile peppers (optional)
Salt, to taste
Lemon pepper, to taste
12 quails or doves
12 bacon strips
½ cup red wine or sherry
1 bottle Italian salad dressing

Combine onion, celery, chiles, salt and lemon pepper. Stuff cavities of quails or doves with this mixture. Wrap bacon around each bird and secure with toothpicks. Mix wine with dressing, reserving ½ cup marinade. Marinate birds in bulk of wine mixture for 6 hours. Broil in oven or on outside grill. Baste with reserved marinade while cooking. Bake 45 minutes, or until brown.

COOK'S NOTE: I have always been a game hunter and enjoy eating game very much. My dad and grandad were bird hunters and I, like them, hunt quail and dove along with other types of game. My profession as a taxidermist puts me in touch with other game hunters on a daily basis.

Smoked Dove Breast

RITA SCHUETZE | KERRVILLE, BANDERA EC

Dove breasts
Garlic salt, to taste
1 slice raw bacon
1 slice jalapeño pepper

Clean, wash and drain each dove breast. Sprinkle with garlic salt. Place 1 slice jalapeño pepper in the middle of each breast. Wrap with bacon and secure the bacon with a toothpick. Cook on the grill 10–15 minutes, or until done.

Venison Roast

MYRTLE N. SHEEHAN | POWDERLY, LAMAR COUNTY EC

1 venison roast
Bacon slices
1 small can (8 ounces) tomato sauce
1 medium onion, chopped
Salt and pepper, to taste
2 small garlic cloves, chopped
2 tablespoons vinegar
2 tablespoons sugar
2 tablespoons Worcestershire sauce
1 bay leaf
1 teaspoon sage
3–4 drops liquid smoke flavoring
2 tablespoons flour or cornstarch
½ cup water
1 cup beef bouillon (optional)

Preheat oven to 300 degrees. Put roast on heavy-duty foil in a baking dish, using enough foil to be able to fold and seal it over the roast. Cover venison roast with bacon slices. Mix remaining ingredients together—except flour, water and beef bouillon, if using—and pour over roast. Fold and seal foil. Bake 3 hours. Remove bay leaf. Process juices from baking dish in blender, pour into saucepan and bring to a boil. Mix flour or cornstarch in water. Mix well. Add to boiling sauce. Add beef bouillon, if desired, and boil until slightly thickened.

Venison Sausage

NANCY WHITWORTH | ROBY, MIDWEST EC

3 pounds ground venison
1 pound ground smoked ham
8 slices bacon, ground
1 tablespoon ground sage
1 teaspoon ground thyme
1 teaspoon salt
1 teaspoon pepper
¼ teaspoon ground red pepper
Vegetable oil, to cook

Combine first 8 ingredients and mix well. To cook, shape about 1 pound of sausage into 6 patties. Cook in small amount of oil until brown. Serve with gravy and hot biscuits for supper. Will make about 4½ pounds.

Venison Meatloaf

JANIE WALLACE | SEGUIN, GUADALUPE VALLEY EC

2 pounds ground venison
2 pounds bulk pork sausage
2 onions, chopped
1½ cups cracker crumbs
½ cup evaporated milk
3 eggs
1 cup barbecue sauce
1 teaspoon salt
½ teaspoon pepper
1 small can (8 ounces) tomato sauce, divided use

Combine meat, onions and cracker crumbs. Mix well. Add milk, eggs, barbecue sauce, salt, pepper and half the can of tomato sauce. Mix well. Let stand 15 minutes. Preheat oven to 350 degrees. Place in greased baking pan or loaf pan. Bake 30 minutes. Top with remaining tomato sauce and bake for 1 hour longer, or until done.

Venison Burgers

MRS. A.J. SPERIER | ORE CITY, UPSHUR-RURAL EC

1 pound ground venison
1 tablespoon chili sauce
1 stalk celery, finely chopped
1 onion, chopped
1 carrot, ground

Mix ingredients together, form into thick patties and fry until brown in heavy skillet. Cover pan and cook slowly until done.

Pot-Roasted Rabbit

MRS. REINHOLD ALTWEIN | MARION, GUADALUPE VALLEY EC

2½–3 pound rabbit, cleaned
    and cut into serving pieces
¼ pound salt pork
¼ cup flour
1 teaspoon salt
¼ teaspoon pepper
¼ cup butter
½ cup hot water
½ cup sliced onion
1 bay leaf

Make deep cuts into fleshy parts of meat. Cut salt pork into strips and stick into the slits. Dust lightly with flour seasoned with salt and pepper. Melt butter in Dutch oven and brown rabbit slowly on all sides. Add water, onion and bay leaf. Cover and cook 1½–2 hours until tender. Serve at once. Makes 4 servings.

Dad's Day Off Bar-B-Que

EDNA M. BERGER | PORT O'CONNOR, VICTORIA COUNTY EC

3 tablespoons liquid smoke flavoring
3 teaspoons garlic salt
2 teaspoons onion salt
2 teaspoons celery salt
1 3- to 5-pound brisket
Pepper
3 tablespoons Worcestershire sauce

Mix liquid smoke and garlic, onion and celery salts into a paste; paint meat with it. Wrap tightly in heavy foil and seal well. Refrigerate overnight. Next morning, preheat oven to 225 degrees, then rub on pepper and Worcestershire sauce. Put back into foil and place in shallow roasting pan. Bake 6–10 hours.

Chuckwagon Casserole

MRS. RILEY VAN MATRE | JOHNSON CITY, PEDERNALES EC

2 cups cubed cooked beef
Flour
Vegetable oil
1 can (14.75 ounces) whole kernel corn, drained
1 can (10.75 ounces) tomato soup
1 cup shredded Cheddar cheese
1 tablespoon finely chopped onion
1 teaspoon chili powder
1 can (10 count) biscuits or your own
2 tablespoons butter, melted
¼ cup cornmeal

Toss beef cubes in a little flour to coat, then brown them in oil in a skillet. Preheat oven to 400 degrees. Mix next 5 ingredients together in a bowl; stir in browned beef. Place this in a 2½-quart casserole dish. Bake 10 minutes. Dip biscuits in melted butter, then in cornmeal. Arrange on top of casserole. Bake 20–25 minutes longer, or until biscuits are brown.

COOK'S NOTE: This is absolutely delicious!

Sweet and Sour Meatballs

MR. AND MRS. CLAUDE AYOTTE | FORT WORTH, WISE EC

1 pound ground beef
½ onion, finely chopped
1 egg
Salt and pepper, to taste
¼ teaspoon garlic powder or garlic salt
¼–½ cup fine breadcrumbs
1 tablespoon vegetable oil
1 can (14 ounces) whole cranberry sauce
1 small can (8 ounces) pineapple chunks, with juice
Barbecue sauce

Mix beef, onion, egg, salt, pepper and garlic powder or salt well, then work in breadcrumbs until thick enough to form into balls. Form small meatballs, about ¾–1 inch in diameter. Fry in oil in a deep skillet. Drain off fat and add cranberry sauce, pineapple and barbecue sauce to pan. Simmer for about 1½ hours.

COOK'S NOTE: This recipe is good when served over steamed rice. The sauce may also be used with chicken, ribs or any of your favorite meats. I mostly use this recipe for Christmas gatherings as a buffet food, keeping it warm in a slow cooker. Most every time we go to a gathering, I am asked to bring this dish.

Texas-Size Meatballs

GLADYS CLARK | BAGWELL, LAMAR COUNTY EC

1 pound ground beef
1 cup oats
1 egg
1 teaspoon salt
1 onion, chopped
2 cups whole milk
1 can (10.75 ounces) cream of chicken soup
2 tablespoons flour
Milk

Mix ground beef, oats, egg and salt together and form into large meatballs. Put onion in skillet and add meatballs. Fry slowly, turning once. When slightly brown, add milk and cream of chicken soup. Cook slowly for a few minutes. Mix flour with small amount of milk. Add to meatballs and stir until thick as gravy.

Rolled Steak

DOROTHY BUCKNER | LOCKHART, DEWITT COUNTY EC

½ cup sliced fresh mushrooms
½ cup plus 2 tablespoons butter, divided use
1½–2 cups breadcrumbs
6 stuffed green olives, sliced
1 egg
1 clove garlic, chopped
⅓ cup chopped onion
¼ cup pimientos
1 round steak
Salt and pepper, to taste

Sauté mushrooms in 2 tablespoons butter and set aside. In a bowl, combine breadcrumbs, olives, egg, remaining butter (melted), garlic, onion and pimientos. Preheat oven to 350 degrees. Trim fat from edge of steak and sprinkle with salt and pepper. Lay steak flat and cover with mixture. Roll steak jellyroll style; secure with skewers or toothpicks. Place roll in sprayed pan and cover with mushrooms. Roast 45–55 minutes.

Pepper Steak

MRS. C.A. CONNER | ANTELOPE, J-A-C EC

1 pound sirloin or round steak
2 tablespoons shortening
¼ cup soy sauce
1½ cups water
2 medium onions, cut into strips
2 bell peppers, cut into strips
2 tablespoons cornstarch
Fluffy rice

Cut steak into small cubes. Brown in shortening about 5 minutes or until tender. Add soy sauce and water. Simmer 10 minutes. Add onions. Simmer for 5 minutes. Add bell peppers. Cook until tender. Thicken with cornstarch and serve over rice or in a rice ring.

Tejas Frijo-Ole Fajitas

SUSAN POWELL | ATHENS, NEW ERA EC

2 cans (12 ounces each) beer, chilled
1 cup barbecue sauce
2 teaspoons Worcestershire sauce
2 heaping tablespoons chili powder
½ heaping teaspoon black pepper
15–20 drops hot pepper sauce
2 teaspoons oregano
2 teaspoons garlic salt
3 pounds beef skirt steak with fat well trimmed
FAJITA FIXINGS:
Flour tortillas
Shredded Cheddar cheese
Shredded lettuce
Chopped tomatoes
Picante sauce
Chopped onions
Guacamole
Sour cream

To make marinade, mix first 8 ingredients together until seasonings are dissolved. Place meat in marinade for at least 24 hours; I usually leave it for 3 days. Barbecue meat quickly and slice thinly across grain. Serve prepared meat with Fajita Fixings.

Chalupa Loaf

MRS. J.R. MEANS | TEMPLE, MCLENNAN COUNTY EC

1–1½ pounds ground beef
1 teaspoon salt
2 tablespoons chili powder
⅓ cup chopped green bell pepper
⅓ cup chopped onion
1 cup evaporated milk
1 cup tomato sauce
10 corn tortillas
½ pound grated cheese

Brown meat with salt, chili powder, green pepper and onion. Simmer until onion is done and drain fat. Add milk and tomato sauce. Preheat oven to 300 degrees. In a casserole dish, cut tortillas into strips and alternate layers of tortillas, meat mixture and cheese. Bake 40 minutes.

Beef Sour Cream Enchiladas

MOLLIE L. GARDNER | HAMILTON, HAMILTON COUNTY EC

1 pound lean ground beef
½ cup chopped onion
½ teaspoon salt
8 corn tortillas
½ cup vegetable oil
½ cup canned or bottled taco sauce
1 cup shredded Monterey jack cheese
¼ cup butter
6 tablespoons flour
2 teaspoons instant chicken bouillon granules
2 cups water
1 cup sour cream
¼ cup chopped green chiles
Red chili sauce, optional

In a skillet, cook beef and onions until meat is brown; drain fat. Add salt. Heat oil in a small skillet. Dip tortillas in hot oil to soften and drain on paper towels. Spoon equal portions of the meat mixture onto tortillas. Top each with 1 tablespoon each of taco sauce and cheese. Roll up; place seam-side down in a lightly greased 6-by-10-inch baking dish. Preheat oven to 400 degrees. In medium saucepan, melt butter; add flour and bouillon granules, stirring until smooth. Gradually add water. Cook, stirring often, until thick. Remove from heat and stir in sour cream and chiles. Pour mixture over rolled tortillas. Top with remaining cheese. Bake 15 minutes. Serves 4.

COOK'S NOTE: These are truly delicious! A little red chili sauce can be mixed with the taco sauce for a spicier and hotter flavor.

Beef Stroganoff

BETH PENDERGRASS | LEVELLAND, LAMB COUNTY EC

2 cups sliced mushrooms
1 large onion, chopped
¼ cup butter, divided use
2 pounds round steak, cut into ¼-inch slices
Flour
1 teaspoon salt
2 cups beef broth
1 carton (8 ounces) sour cream
Cooked egg noodles

Sauté mushrooms and onion in 2 tablespoons butter. Remove from pan. Melt remaining butter and brown strips of steak coated with flour. Add salt and broth and cook until tender. Add mushrooms, onion and sour cream. Serve over egg noodles.

Jo's Barbecue Beef Ribs

KATHRYN J. ROBERTS | ARCHER CITY, J-A-C EC

5 pounds pork or beef short ribs
BARBECUE SAUCE:
2 cups chopped onion
6 cloves garlic, minced
1 cup strong black coffee
1 cup Worcestershire sauce
1 cup ketchup
½ cup cider vinegar
½ cup brown sugar
¼ cup minced fresh or frozen hot peppers
3 tablespoons chili powder
2 teaspoons salt

Pierce meat with large fork. Place ribs in large plastic bag; pour in Barbecue Sauce and close bag. To make Barbecue Sauce, combine all ingredients in a saucepan and simmer 25 minutes. Purée in blender or food processor. Marinate in refrigerator at least 8 hours, turning once. Cook over hot coals for 10 minutes, then brush with marinade and cook 5 minutes more.

COOK'S NOTE: You can also bake these, covered, 1½ hours at 350 degrees.

Lone Star Sauerbraten (Best in the West)

KATIE LESCHNITZER | NOCONA HILLS, COOKE COUNTY EC

1 4- to 5-pound beef roast (top or bottom)
1 tablespoon salt
Pepper, to taste
2 bottles (12 ounces each) beer (Lone Star preferred)
1 cup vinegar
1–2 cups water
1 onion, sliced
3 bay leaves
10 whole black peppercorns
2 tablespoons sugar
4 whole cloves
¼ teaspoon allspice
Flour
3 ounces slab bacon
6 gingersnaps, crushed
½ cup raisins

Rub beef with salt and pepper. Place in large glass bowl. In a saucepan, heat beer, vinegar, water, onion, bay leaves, peppercorns, sugar, cloves and allspice, but do not boil. Pour heated mixture over beef to partially cover. Cool, then cover with plastic wrap securely and place in refrigerator. Turn beef once or twice each day for 7 days. When ready to cook, drain beef, reserving marinade, and pat dry. Dredge lightly in flour. Using an iron pot (Dutch oven), cut up bacon and fry until soft. Remove. Add beef and sear quickly on all sides. Lower heat to very low; add beer and vinegar mixture, including onion and bacon. Simmer 3 hours, or until very tender. By this time, liquid should be cooked down. Remove beef; keep warm. Add crushed gingersnaps to thicken gravy. Add raisins and a little water, if necessary. Slice beef with electric knife or sharp knife, as the meat will be soft. Serve beef and sauce with red cabbage and your favorite dumplings.

Beef Roast With Gravy

MRS. P.E. GARDNER | HAMILTON, HAMILTON COUNTY EC

1 4-pound roast
1 tablespoon salt
1 tablespoon Worcestershire sauce
1 medium onion, chopped
1 teaspoon sugar
¼ cup ketchup
Flour

Cut roast into serving-size pieces and place in a cold pressure cooker. Add the other ingredients. Cover with cold water and seal lid. Cook 45 minutes at 10 pounds pressure. Allow pressure to reduce normally. When pressure is all out, remove lid and place meat in a casserole dish. Preheat oven to 350 degrees. Make gravy with a little of the beef broth from cooker. Cover meat with gravy and bake 10 minutes, or until brown on top.

Bavarian Steak Rolls

MRS. T.F. CLARDY | LEVELLAND, LYNTEGAR EC

1 1-pound steak
Prepared mustard
Salt and pepper
½ cup chopped dill pickles
½ cup chopped onion
1 small can (4 ounces) mushrooms, chopped or minced
Flour
Butter or shortening

Pound or tenderize steak. Spread lightly with prepared mustard and sprinkle on salt and pepper. Mix pickles, onion and mushrooms and spread on steak. Roll up as tightly as possible and tie at each end and wherever needed with twine. Roll in flour and brown quickly on all sides in small amount of butter or shortening in skillet. Place in pan with tight cover. Add just enough hot water to cover. Lower heat and simmer until tender.

Bazziola

MRS. J.T. HODGES JR. | FLOYDADA, LIGHTHOUSE EC

1 pound ground beef
2 tablespoons butter
1 large onion, chopped
1 green pepper, chopped
1 package spaghetti
1 can (15 ounces) sweet young peas
1 can (10.75 ounces) cream of mushroom soup
1 can (10.75 ounces) tomato soup
1 small can (4 ounces) mushrooms, chopped
1 jar stuffed olives
Worcestershire sauce
Garlic salt
Salt and pepper

In a skillet, brown meat in butter with onion and pepper. In pot, cook spaghetti, drain and return to pot; add browned meat, peas, soups, mushrooms and olives to pot. Season with Worcestershire sauce, garlic salt, salt and pepper, to taste. Preheat oven to 350 degrees. Pour spaghetti mixture into a casserole dish. Cover and bake 45 minutes.

Five-Layer Dinner

WINNIE RAMEY | HENDERSON, RUSK COUNTY EC

1½ pounds ground beef
1 large bell pepper, chopped
1 large onion, chopped
5 potatoes, peeled and sliced into rounds
Salt and pepper, to taste
1 large can (28 ounces) whole tomatoes, chopped

Preheat oven to 350 degrees. Arrange in layers in casserole dish in order listed. Pour tomatoes over top, cover and bake about 1½ hours or until meat and potatoes are done. Makes 6–8 servings.

Enchilada Burgers

DONNA J. TYREE | BULLARD, CHEROKEE COUNTY EC

1 pound ground beef, cooked and drained
½ cup chopped onion
½ cup sour cream
1½ tablespoons chopped parsley
Salt and pepper, to taste
1½ cups shredded Cheddar cheese

Combine browned meat with remaining ingredients. Serve on toasted hamburger buns.

Green Enchilada Casserole

JACINTA CRANFORD | ABILENE, TAYLOR EC

1 small onion, chopped
1 pound ground beef
1 can (10 ounces) enchilada sauce
1 small can (4 ounces) chopped green chiles
1 can (10.75 ounces) cream of chicken soup
10 corn tortillas
1 or more cups grated Cheddar cheese

In a large skillet, cook onion and meat until brown, stirring with fork to crumble meat. Add enchilada sauce, chiles and soup; mix well. Cook 5–10 minutes, or until heated. Preheat oven to 350 degrees. Place a layer of tortillas in the bottom of a lightly greased 2½-quart casserole dish. Cover with some of the meat-soup mixture; sprinkle with cheese. Then repeat layers, ending with cheese. Bake 20 minutes, or until hot.

Taco Twists

MRS. J.B. SMITH | PILOT POINT, COOKE COUNTY EC

1 pound ground beef
1 can (15 ounces) chili beans
2 tablespoons onion flakes, or
    1 tablespoon onion powder
1 teaspoon garlic salt
2 teaspoons chili powder
¼ cup cornmeal
1 can (10 count) flaky biscuits
¾ cup grated Cheddar cheese
½ cup crushed corn chips

In large skillet, brown beef; then drain. Mash beans; add onion flakes and seasonings; mix well. Preheat oven to 350 degrees. Sprinkle cornmeal on dough board, then place 2 rows of 5 biscuits together, pressing to form an 8-by-16-inch rectangle. Spread meat mixture over dough. Roll up like jellyroll. Cut into 10 slices and place in greased 9-by-13-inch baking dish. Sprinkle with cheese and corn chips. Bake 35–40 minutes.

Cowboy Casserole

MRS. AUDIE MASTERSON | DAWSON, NAVARRO COUNTY EC

2 strips bacon, cut into small pieces
1 medium onion, chopped
1 pound ground beef
2 cans (15 ounces each) pork and beans
½ cup molasses
½ cup ketchup
1 tablespoon Worcestershire sauce
1 teaspoon salt
½ teaspoon dry mustard

Preheat oven to 375 degrees. Cook bacon in frying pan with onion. Add beef and cook until meat is no longer pink. Add other ingredients. Spoon into casserole dish and bake 30 minutes.

Mama's Day Off Casserole

BERTHA GISH | NEDERLAND, JASPER-NEWTON EC

1 pound lean ground chuck
1 can (10.75 ounces) cream of chicken soup
1 bag (32 ounces) frozen tater tots

Preheat oven to 375 degrees. Flatten beef into the bottom of a 1½-quart casserole dish. Pour soup over beef. Arrange tater tots on top. Bake uncovered 45–55 minutes, or until the meat is done the way you like it and top is browned.

    COOK'S NOTE: Cooking time may vary depending on size and type of casserole used.

Beefy Mexican Lasagna

SAMMIE MONIS | SEYMOUR, B-K EC

1 pound ground beef
1 can (14.5 ounces) diced tomatoes
1 packet taco seasoning
1 can (6 ounces) French-fried onions, divided use
2 eggs, slightly beaten
1½ cups cottage cheese
1½ cups shredded Cheddar cheese, divided use
12 6-inch corn tortillas
1 small onion, chopped
1 tomato, chopped
Shredded lettuce

In a large skillet, brown beef and drain. Add canned tomatoes and taco seasoning. Simmer uncovered 5 minutes. Stir in ½ can French-fried onions. In a separate bowl, combine eggs, cottage cheese and 1 cup Cheddar cheese. Preheat oven to 350 degrees. Place 3 tortillas on bottom of 8-by-12-inch baking dish. Overlap 6 tortillas around sides of dish. Spoon meat mixture into dish. Top with 3 more tortillas, then with cheese mixture. Bake covered 45 minutes. Sprinkle with onion and remaining cheese and bake 5 minutes more. To serve, arrange lettuce and tomatoes around edges. Serves 6–8.

Texas Rice and Beans

RAYMOND L. HARTMAN | ELGIN, BLUEBONNET EC

1 small onion, diced
1 small green pepper, diced
2 teaspoons bacon drippings
1 pound ground beef
1 large can (28 ounces) diced tomatoes
½ teaspoon hot pepper sauce
Salt and pepper
1 can (15 ounces) red beans
Cooked white rice

Sauté onion and green peppers in bacon drippings. Add meat and stir until well browned. Add tomatoes, hot pepper sauce, and salt and pepper to taste. Simmer over low heat about 30 minutes or until meat is done. Add beans with juice and heat through. Serve over heaps of white rice.

Main Dish at JC Bar

RUTH CARNES | VICTORIA, DEWITT COUNTY EC

3 tablespoons butter
1 bell pepper, chopped
10 green onions, chopped
1 pound ground meat
1 garlic clove, minced
1 can (29 ounces) hominy, drained
1 can (15 ounces) no-bean chili
1 can (10.75 ounces) cream of mushroom soup
12 ounces processed cheese, sliced or cubed
    (Velveeta preferred)
½ cup crushed corn chips

Melt butter in a large skillet. Add pepper and onions. Sauté until crisp-tender. Add meat and cook until it's no longer pink. Stir in garlic, hominy, chili and soup. Preheat oven to 350 degrees. Put mixture in a 9-by-13-inch baking dish. Cover with cheese and top with chips. Bake about 45 minutes, until bubbly and light brown. Serves 12.

COOK'S NOTE: Can be made ahead of time. Also can freeze, but hold off on the cheese and chips until time to bake.

Pasta de Scuitta (Mock Ravioli)

MARTHA MILLER | TATUM, RUSK COUNTY EC

8 ounces shell pasta
Salt, to taste
1 package (10 ounces) frozen spinach,
    cooked and drained
1 cup chopped green pepper
1 cup chopped celery
1 large onion, chopped
3 cloves garlic, chopped
1 pound ground beef
1 small can (8 ounces) tomato sauce
1 small jar (15 ounces) pasta sauce with mushrooms
1 cup grated cheese
1 tablespoon olive oil
1 tablespoon chili powder
½ teaspoon ground cumin

Cook pasta in boiling, lightly salted water until tender. Place a layer of pasta in baking dish. Next, layer spinach, then top with remaining pasta. In a large skillet, sauté pepper, celery, onion and garlic 5 minutes. Add ground beef and cook until no longer pink. Pour in tomato sauce, heat through, and pour over pasta in dish. While that is standing, about ½ hour, preheat oven to 350 degrees and make a second sauce using pasta sauce, grated cheese, olive oil, chili powder and ground cumin. Pour over other mixture. Bake 25 minutes, or until heated.

Coke Steak

RICKIE WARREN | MULESHOE, BAILEY COUNTY EC

Flour
Salt and pepper, to taste
1 pound tenderized round steak
½ cup chopped onion
2 tablespoons vegetable oil
6 tablespoons ketchup
1 can Coke

Flour, salt and pepper steak. Brown steak with onion on both sides in a skillet using vegetable oil. Add ketchup and cover steak with Coke. Bring to boil and then simmer until sauce is thick and steak is tender.

Italian Stuffed Banana Peppers

BETTY MCGOWEN | CLYDE, TAYLOR EC

1 pound ground beef
1 medium onion, finely chopped
1 bunch green onions, finely chopped
4 cloves garlic, finely chopped
4 tablespoons chopped parsley
1 cup Italian breadcrumbs
1 egg, beaten
16–18 banana peppers, seeded and halved
1 cup jarred pasta sauce
Salt and pepper, to taste
4 tablespoons grated Parmesan cheese

In a skillet, sauté ground beef until no longer pink. Add onions, garlic and parsley. Cook for 2 minutes. Remove from heat and add breadcrumbs and egg. If too dry, add small amount of water. Preheat oven to 350 degrees. Fill peppers with mixture and place in greased casserole dish. Pour sauce over peppers and sprinkle with salt, pepper and cheese. Bake 25 minutes. Makes 8 servings.

Black-Eyed Pea Cornbread

LANY LAHAIE | HENDERSON, RUSK COUNTY EC

1 pound ground beef
1 cup canned black-eyed peas, drained
1 cup chopped onion
¾ cup cream-style corn
1 cup cornmeal
½ cup flour
1 cup buttermilk
¼ cup vegetable oil
2 eggs
1 teaspoon salt
½ teaspoon baking soda
2 chopped jalapeño peppers
1 cup grated Cheddar cheese

Preheat oven to 350 degrees. Brown meat, drain and break into small pieces. Mix all ingredients, adding cheese last. Cook in well-greased 9-by-13-inch pan 45 minutes, or until done. Makes a large batch.

Salisbury Steaks

GLADYS GRIMES | NORMANGEE, NAVASOTA VALLEY EC

1 can (10.75 ounces) cream of chicken soup
1 can (10.75 ounces) cream of mushroom soup
1 tablespoon prepared mustard
2 teaspoons Worcestershire sauce
1 teaspoon horseradish
½ cup water
1½ pounds ground beef
1 egg
¼ cup dry bread crumbs
1 packet onion soup mix
2 teaspoons parsley (optional)

Mix together soups, mustard, Worcestershire sauce, horseradish and water and set aside. In a separate bowl, combine remaining ingredients, adding ¼ cup of soup mixture. Shape beef mixture into oval patties and brown on both sides in oiled skillet. Drain off excess grease. Add 2 tablespoons water to the soup mixture, stir well, then pour over patties in skillet and cook over low heat 30 minutes, or put all in a covered casserole dish and bake about 40 minutes at 350 degrees. Spoon soup mixture over patties occasionally while cooking.

Tangy Make-Ahead Lasagna

SANDRA MAYO | SPUR, DICKENS EC

3 ounces cream cheese, softened
1 cup sour cream
½ medium onion, minced,
    or ½ tablespoon onion powder
1 clove garlic, minced, or ⅛ teaspoon garlic powder
1 pound ground beef
1 small can (8 ounces) tomato sauce
1½ teaspoons salt, divided use
Pepper
1 package lasagna noodles
1 cup grated mozzarella, Monterey jack
    or Swiss cheese

Beat cream cheese, then gradually add sour cream. Stir in onion and garlic; set aside. In a skillet, brown ground beef, stirring until it is no longer pink. Stir in tomato sauce, 1 teaspoon salt and pepper to taste; set aside. Cook lasagna noodles according to package directions. Rinse noodles with cold water and drain. Preheat oven to 350 degrees. Spray a deep 2-quart baking dish with nonstick cooking spray. Spread a thin layer of meat sauce on the bottom of the dish. Then layer half of the noodles, half of sour cream mixture and half of meat sauce. Repeat layers in same order. Sprinkle with cheese. Bake immediately, or cover tightly with plastic wrap and refrigerate overnight. (The flavors blend better if it is refrigerated overnight.) Bake about 30 minutes. Let stand 10 minutes to set layers. Serves 6.

Swedish Meatballs

PAULA STEGEMOELLER | SAGERTON, STAMFORD EC

½ cup breadcrumbs
¼ cup milk
1 pound lean ground beef
¼ cup finely chopped onion
1 teaspoon salt
⅛ teaspoon nutmeg
⅛ teaspoon pepper
1 jar (12 ounces) grape jelly
1 bottle (12 ounces) chili sauce

In a small bowl, soak breadcrumbs in milk for 5 minutes. Preheat oven to 350 degrees. In a larger bowl, mix beef, soaked breadcrumbs, onion, salt, nutmeg and pepper. Form into 1½-inch balls on cookie sheet. Bake until brown, 20–30 minutes. Meanwhile, in a saucepan, heat the jelly and chili sauce slowly. Drain meatballs and place in casserole dish; pour sauce over them. Return to oven until bubbly.

COOK'S NOTE: The chili sauce comes in a jar and is found by the ketchup in the store. Great for parties! My dad, Wilton Payne (Jim), was the manager at Lyntegar EC in Tahoka, Lynn County, for more than 40 years. I have the first cookbook and love it.

Mexican Pizza

MRS. T.F. HENSON | DUBLIN, ERATH COUNTY EC

Large flour tortilla
Melted butter
Grated longhorn Cheddar cheese
Chopped green onion
Chopped tomato
Diced green chiles
Chorizo sausage, cooked

Warm tortilla under broiler. Using a pastry brush, spread tortilla lightly with butter. Sprinkle generously with cheese, green onion, tomatoes, green chiles and cooked chorizo. Place under broiler until cheese melts.

Texas Beef Skillet

KAY CREECH | GUSTINE, COMANCHE COUNTY EC

1 pound ground beef
¾ cup chopped onion
1 can (14.5 ounces) diced tomatoes
1 can (15 ounces) ranch-style beans
½ cup quick-cooking rice
3 tablespoons chopped green pepper
1½ teaspoons chili powder
½ teaspoon garlic salt
½ cup water
½ teaspoon salt
¾ cup shredded American cheese
Crushed corn chips

In a skillet, cook ground beef and onion until meat is done and onion is tender. Drain off fat. Stir in tomatoes, beans, rice, green pepper, chili powder, garlic salt, water and salt. Bring to boil. Reduce heat and simmer 15–20 minutes, stirring as needed. Sprinkle cheese on top. Cover and heat 2–3 minutes until cheese melts. Sprinkle crushed chips around the edge.

COOK'S NOTE: This recipe may easily be doubled for a large crowd. You may also use many substitutions and still have a very good dish: tomato sauce or juice for tomatoes, leftover pinto beans for canned beans, leftover plain rice or Spanish rice for quick-cooking rice, any kind of cheese that you have on hand, or leftover chili for the ground beef. Also, you may use crushed tortilla chips or cornbread topping instead of corn chips. Place in oven on low heat to hold over for a time. May easily be prepared ahead of time and reheated in a casserole dish. This recipe is hard to mess up, even for the most inexperienced cook.

Great Steak

ROSIE ROSS | TAYLOR, BARTLETT EC

2 teaspoons minced fresh garlic
2 teaspoons coarsely ground black pepper
2 teaspoons dry mustard
2 teaspoons paprika
2 teaspoons chili powder
1 teaspoon dried thyme leaves, crumbled
½ teaspoon salt
½ teaspoon crushed red pepper
1 tablespoon olive oil
2 boneless steaks (1-inch-thick, 12 ounces each), fat trimmed
Fresh thyme sprigs, for garnish, optional

Make the dry rub: In a small bowl, mix garlic, black pepper, mustard, paprika, chili powder, thyme, salt and red pepper until well blended. Brush the oil on both sides of the steaks and place each steak on a large sheet of plastic wrap. Rub the spice mixture on both sides of steaks. Wrap tightly and refrigerate at least 1 hour or up to 24 hours. When ready to cook, unwrap the steaks. Heat a gas grill to high, prepare a hot charcoal fire until the coals form white ash, or heat a broiler. Grill or broil the steaks 4–6 inches above the heat source, 5–7 minutes on each side for rare, 7–9 minutes for medium, or 9–11 minutes for well done. Remove the steaks to serving plates and let stand a few minutes after grilling to give juices a chance to settle. Garnish with thyme sprigs, if desired.

Mexican Ranch Casserole

SHEILA SOCIA | JACKSONVILLE, CHEROKEE COUNTY EC

2 pounds ground beef
Salt and pepper, to taste
2 cans (10.75 ounces each) cream of mushroom soup
1 can (10 ounces) diced tomatoes and green chiles
1 can (15 ounces) ranch-style beans, drained
10 corn tortillas
1 pound processed cheese, grated
  (Velveeta preferred)

Brown beef with salt and pepper and drain. Add soup, tomatoes and beans. Preheat oven to 400 degrees. In an oblong dish, layer half the corn tortillas, top with some of the cheese, then pour half of the above mixture over this. Top with cheese and repeat the above. Bake about 30 minutes.

COOK'S NOTE: I make this dish for a lot of church socials, and it is always a success with most everyone.

Green Chile Casserole

SHIRLEY HADSELL | MARFA, RIO GRANDE EC

12 corn tortillas
Vegetable oil
1 can (15.5 ounces) hominy, drained
2½ cups grated cheese, divided use
1 onion, chopped, divided use
2 small cans (4 ounces each) chopped green chiles,
  divided use
1 pound ground beef, browned
2 cups green chile salsa

Preheat oven to 350 degrees. Heat oil in a skillet and quickly fry tortillas in it. Cover bottom of 9-by-13-inch casserole dish with half of tortillas. Layer all of hominy, 1 cup cheese, half the onion, and half the chopped green chiles over tortillas. Cover with remaining tortillas, ground beef, 1 cup cheese, remaining onion and green chiles. Pour salsa over top and sprinkle with cheese. Bake 30 minutes.

Individual Pizza

BARBARA BEDNARZ | SLATON, SOUTH PLAINS EC

2 cans (10 count each) biscuits
1 small can (8 ounces) tomato sauce
1 teaspoon chili powder
½ teaspoon oregano
½ teaspoon pepper
¼ teaspoon garlic salt
¼ teaspoon dry mustard
1 pound ground beef or sausage, cooked
¼ cup chopped onion
Cheese, grated or sliced
Other toppings: olives, bell peppers, etc.

Preheat oven to 400 degrees. Separate and roll out biscuits on floured board. Mix tomato sauce with other spices and spread over biscuits. Top with meat, onion, cheese and other toppings. Bake 15 minutes.

COOK'S NOTE: You can use also use refrigerated pizza crust. Bake as directed. This is one way the kids can make pizza like they want to.

Pizzaburgers

CINDY HELLESVIG | LIBERTY HILL, PEDERNALES EC

1 pound ground beef
1 can (12 ounces) canned meat (Spam preferred)
2 cups pasta sauce
½ cup chopped fresh parsley
1 tablespoon dried oregano
1 teaspoon dried sage
⅓ teaspoon salt
⅔ pound cheese, grated
9 hamburger buns

In a skillet, brown beef and drain. Preheat oven to 400 degrees. Smash canned meat with a fork; add to beef, along with sauce, seasonings and cheese. Put all 18 hamburger bun halves on a jellyroll pan and spoon meat mixture evenly among buns. Bake 10–12 minutes. Serve open-face.

Spinach Meatballs With Tomato Sauce

MARG AMES | BAY CITY, JACKSON EC

1 package (10 ounces) frozen chopped spinach

1 medium onion, finely chopped

1 clove garlic, minced or mashed

1½ pounds lean ground beef

3 tablespoons fine dry breadcrumbs

3 tablespoons grated Parmesan cheese, plus more
    for serving

1 egg, slightly beaten

1 teaspoon salt

¼ teaspoon pepper

2 tablespoons butter

2 tablespoons flour

2 cans (15 ounces each) tomato sauce

1 cup water

Grated Parmesan cheese

Defrost spinach and drain by pressing through a wire strainer; chop finely. Preheat oven to 500 degrees. Combine spinach with onion, garlic, beef, breadcrumbs, cheese, egg, salt and pepper; mix until well blended. Form into balls about the size of a golf ball and arrange in a single layer in a shallow-rimmed baking pan. Bake 7–9 minutes or until well browned. Meanwhile, melt butter in a large frying pan over medium heat, or in an electric skillet. Stir in flour and cook until bubbly. Gradually stir in tomato sauce and water, cooking slowly, stirring until thickened. Add the meatballs and some of their juices and cook uncovered until meatballs are heated through. Serve over pasta. Serves 4–6. Serve with additional grated Parmesan cheese.

COOK'S NOTE: This is a good way to "sneak" spinach into a meal for people who avoid eating it.

Bar-B-Qued Meatballs

PEGGY BAIN | LUBBOCK, SOUTH PLAINS EC

1½ pounds ground beef

½ cup milk

2 teaspoons pepper

2 tablespoons vegetable oil

1 cup ketchup

¼ cup Worcestershire sauce

½ onion, chopped

1 teaspoon sugar

2 tablespoons vinegar

1 tablespoon water

Mix beef, milk and pepper thoroughly. Shape into medium meatballs. In a skillet, heat oil and brown meatballs all over in oil. Combine remaining ingredients in a bowl. Pour over meatballs in skillet and cover. Cook about 10 minutes, turning meatballs occasionally.

COOK'S NOTE: This is an old recipe. My children grew up enjoying it. It is very tasty!

Old Settlers Beans

MARIE FLOURNOY | BAGWELL, LAMAR COUNTY EC

1 pound ground beef

1 onion, chopped

1 can (15 ounces) pork and beans

1 can (15 ounces) pinto beans

1 can (15 ounces) ranch-style beans

⅓ cup barbecue sauce

⅓ cup ketchup

⅓ cup brown sugar

1 tablespoon mustard

1 teaspoon salt

1 teaspoon pepper

1 teaspoon garlic salt

¼ teaspoon chili powder

Brown beef and onion in large pot. Add all other ingredients and simmer 25 minutes.

Texhoma Beans

CLARA SLOUGH | COOPER, LAMAR COUNTY EC

1 pound dried pinto beans
1 pound ground beef
1 large onion, chopped
1 teaspoon garlic powder
1 large can (28 ounces) diced tomatoes
2 tablespoons taco sauce
2 teaspoons salt
½ teaspoon ground cumin
½ teaspoon oregano

Cook beans until tender; drain and set aside. Sauté ground beef with onion and garlic powder. Add rest of ingredients and heat through. Then add beans and simmer until thick.

Beef Pot Pie

MONIQUE SWALLOW | ROBSTOWN, NUECES EC

1 pound ground beef
1 onion, chopped
Garlic salt
1½ cups diced potatoes
1½ cups diced carrots
1 cup corn or peas
1 can (10.75 ounces) cream of celery soup
1 can (10.75 ounces) cream of mushroom soup
¾ cup milk
1 package refrigerated pie crusts
1 cup grated Cheddar cheese

Brown meat, onion and garlic in a skillet; drain. Stir in all other ingredients, except pie crust and cheese. Preheat oven to 350 degrees. Place 1 pie crust into a deep dish pie pan. Pour in meat mixture. Sprinkle with cheese. Place other pie crust on top; pinch the edges. Put holes on top of crust with fork. Bake 45 minutes.

Spanish Rice Meatloaf

GEORGIA LOWE | TEXARKANA, BOWIE-CASS EC

1 pound ground beef
1 can (15 ounces) Spanish rice
1 small onion, chopped
Salt and pepper, to taste
Tomato sauce (optional)

Preheat oven to 350 degrees. Mix all ingredients together and mold. Place in baking dish and cook 45 minutes to 1 hour. If desired, top with tomato sauce or other topping.

Mexican Mini Meatloaves

MRS. JOHN D. HANES | QUEEN CITY, BOWIE-CASS EC

1½ pounds ground beef
1 cup medium picante sauce, divided use
½ cup crushed tortilla chips or corn chips
1 medium onion, chopped
1 egg
1½ teaspoons ground cumin
1 teaspoon salt
½ cup shredded sharp Cheddar
    or Monterey jack cheese

Preheat oven to 350 degrees. Combine ground beef, ¾ cup of picante sauce, chips, onion, egg, cumin and salt. Shape to form 6–8 loaves. Place in 9-by-13-inch baking dish. Bake about 35 minutes, or to desired doneness. Spoon remaining picante sauce over meatloaves; sprinkle with cheese while hot. Cover with foil until serving time. Serve with more picante sauce, if desired.

COOK'S NOTE: Busy cooks with an eye on the clock will appreciate the convenience of these individual servings, which bake far faster than a standard meatloaf.

Spaghetti Meatloaf

MRS. O.M. SANDERS | VALLEY MILLS, MCLENNAN EC

1 pound ground beef
½ cup chopped onion
1 egg, slightly beaten
1 teaspoon seasoned salt
1 large jar (16 ounces) pasta sauce with cheese

Preheat oven to 350 degrees. Lightly grease an 8-inch square baking pan. Toss together all ingredients until combined. Turn into prepared pan and press down with back of spoon. Bake uncovered for 1 hour. Let stand a few minutes before cutting into squares. Serves 6.

Gourmet Meatloaf

GLORIA DULIN | TULIA, SWISHER EC

1 tablespoon butter
1 cup sliced fresh mushrooms
¼ cup chopped onion
1 cup sour cream
1 pound ground beef
1 cup old-fashioned rolled oats
1 egg, beaten
¼ cup tomato juice
1 teaspoon Worcestershire sauce
1 teaspoon salt
1 teaspoon ground black pepper

To make filling, melt butter in a small frying pan. Sauté mushrooms and onion 5 minutes, stirring. Remove from heat and stir in sour cream; set aside. Preheat oven to 300 degrees. In a large bowl, combine all remaining ingredients; mix well. In lightly greased loaf pan, place half of meatloaf mixture. Lengthwise, down the center, make an indentation. Spoon sour cream mixture into the indentation. Spoon remaining meatloaf mixture over all of the filling. Press top and bottom meat layers together around the edges. Bake 45 minutes. Let stand 5 minutes before slicing. Makes 4 servings.

Favorite Meatloaf

MRS. CALVIN ADAMEK | MART, NAVASOTA VALLEY EC

2 pounds ground meat
1 cup bread crumbs
½ cup sour cream
2 eggs
1 onion, chopped
2 teaspoons salt
1 can (4 ounces) mushroom pieces, drained
1 cup ketchup, divided use

Preheat oven to 350 degrees. Mix all the ingredients, except ketchup. Then add ½ cup ketchup. Pat meat mixture into loaf pan. Bake 50 minutes. To serve, pour off fat from pan and spoon remaining ketchup over top of meatloaf.

Delicious Meatloaf

MRS. L. KARCHER | LA GRANGE, FAYETTE EC

1 pound ground beef
½ cup evaporated milk
⅓ cup old-fashioned rolled oats
¼ cup finely chopped onion
1½ teaspoons salt, divided use
⅛ teaspoon pepper
1 cup tomato sauce
2 tablespoons brown sugar
1 tablespoon vinegar
1 teaspoon Worcestershire sauce
¼ teaspoon dry mustard
½ teaspoon chili powder

In a bowl, mix together the ground beef, evaporated milk, oats, chopped onions, 1 teaspoon salt and pepper. In a saucepan, cook the tomato sauce, brown sugar, vinegar, Worcestershire sauce, dry mustard, chili powder and ½ teaspoon salt 5 minutes. Preheat oven to 350 degrees. Stir half of the tomato mixture into the beef mixture and place in a loaf pan. Pour rest of sauce over the top and bake 50 minutes.

Individual Meatloaves With Barbecue Sauce

GLADYS MADDOX | MULESHOE, BAILEY COUNTY EC

1½ pounds ground beef
2 tablespoons minced onion
1½ tablespoons chopped green pepper
1⅓ cups cubed stale bread or croutons
½ teaspoon salt
1 egg
3 tablespoons ketchup
2½ teaspoons horseradish
½ teaspoon dry mustard
½ cup milk
1 cup barbecue sauce

Preheat oven to 350 degrees. In a bowl, mix together all ingredients except barbecue sauce; blend well. Shape into 6 small loaves; place in greased baking dish. Bake 1 hour. Serve with warmed barbecue sauce.

Cornbread Meatloaf

MRS. HOMER SWINSON | STANTON, CAP ROCK EC

1½ pounds ground meat
½ cup chopped onion
¼ cup chopped green pepper
1 can (14.5 ounces) diced tomatoes
3 tablespoons Worcestershire sauce
1 tablespoon onion salt
2 tablespoons chili powder
Salt and pepper to taste
1 package (6.5 ounces) cornbread mix
¾ cup milk
1 egg

In a heavy skillet, brown ground meat with onion and green pepper. Drain fat, reserving 3 tablespoons; add tomatoes, Worcestershire sauce, onion salt, chili powder, and salt and pepper, to taste. Preheat oven to 400 degrees. Pour mixture into an ungreased 8-by-12-inch baking dish. Top with following: To cornbread mix, add ¾ cup of milk and 1 egg. Mix well. Bake until cornbread is brown, but taking caution not to bake until meat is dry.

Meal-in-One Meatloaf

MRS. O.C. INGRAM | PILOT POINT, COOKE COUNTY EC

1 pound ground beef
1 small onion, chopped
2 medium potatoes, peeled and diced
2 carrots, peeled and diced
½ cup diced celery
1 can (16 ounces) green beans, chopped
1 can (10.75 ounces) tomato soup
1 teaspoon salt
½ teaspoon black pepper

Preheat oven to 350 degrees. In a skillet, brown meat and onion, then add other ingredients and mix. Place in casserole dish and bake for 1 hour. Yields 4–6 servings.

Hoboes' Supper

MRS. EMMETT D. KING | TIPTON, SOUTHWEST RURAL EC

Ground beef
Onion, sliced ⅓ inch thick
Potatoes, sliced
Salt and pepper

Make hamburger patties to desired size; salt and pepper each side. Salt and pepper onion and potato slices, too. Preheat oven to 325 degrees. Lay out as many 1-foot square pieces of foil as you have patties. Grease foil or spray with nonstick cooking spray. Lay a few onion slices and a few potato slices on each piece of foil. Lay a hamburger patty on top. Enclose tightly in the foil and bake at least 1½ hours.

COOK'S NOTE: Slices of carrots can be added too. Do not open foil until ready to eat.

Dorito Casserole

MRS. H.E. BLAND | HASKELL, STAMFORD EC

1 pound ground beef
1 small onion, chopped
1 can (10.75 ounces) cream of mushroom soup
1 large can (12 ounces) evaporated milk
1 small can (4 ounces) chopped green chiles
5 ounces flavored tortilla chips (Doritos preferred)
8 slices American cheese

Brown meat and onions in skillet until meat is cooked. Add mushroom soup, milk and chiles; mix well. Add chips and mix together. Lay slices of cheese on top. Cover and heat until cheese melts. Makes 5 large servings.

Shepherd's Pie

MRS. OSCAR REED | IREDELL, ERATH COUNTY EC

4 cups mashed potatoes
3 cups ground meat
½ cup breadcrumbs
½ cup milk or beef stock
¼ cup chopped onion
½ cup diced cooked carrots
1 egg, beaten
1 teaspoon salt

Preheat oven to 350 degrees. Line baking dish with half the potatoes. Mix all other ingredients together and put on top of potatoes. Cover with remaining potatoes and bake until brown.

Skillet Meal

MRS. BILL DARBY | VALLEY MILLS, MCLENNAN EC

¾ pound ground meat
⅔ cup quick-cooking rice
1 medium onion, chopped
Salt and pepper
3 cups boiling water
2 cups packed shredded cabbage

Use skillet with lid to fry meat about 5 minutes. Pour off all but 2–3 tablespoons of fat; add rice, onion, and salt and pepper, to taste. Cook 5 minutes stirring well, add boiling water and cabbage. Cook at high heat for 5 minutes. Reduce heat to medium for 15 minutes or longer, stir and keep covered until served.

Texas Goulash

MONIQUE SWALLOW | ROBSTOWN, NUECES EC

1 pound ground beef
1 onion, chopped
1 small bell pepper, chopped
3 stalks celery, chopped
1 clove garlic, minced
Salt and pepper
½ teaspoon Italian seasonings
Dash chili powder
1 can (14.5 ounces) stewed tomatoes
2 cans (14.5 ounces each) tomato sauce
2 cans water
1 can (10 ounces) diced tomatoes with green chiles
1 can (14.5 ounces) whole new potatoes
1 can (14.75 ounces) kernel corn (or frozen, if desired)
2 cups Texas-shaped pasta or macaroni

Brown meat, onion, bell pepper, celery and garlic; salt and pepper to taste. Drain meat. Add all other ingredients and simmer for 40 minutes, until pasta is done.

German Goulash

MRS. EDWIN MOELLER | ROWENA, COLEMAN COUNTY EC

½ pound beef stew meat, cubed
2 cups diced potatoes
1 cup diced carrots
1 cup shredded cabbage
3 tablespoons bacon drippings
1 cup sweet peas
Salt and pepper

Put meat in saucepan, cover with water and boil until almost done. Add potatoes, carrots and cabbage and boil until tender before adding bacon drippings and peas. Salt and pepper to taste.

Seven-Layer Casserole

KATHRYN THOMPSON | GIDDINGS, BLUEBONNET EC

1 cup uncooked rice
1 cup corn kernels
Salt and pepper
2 small cans (8 ounces each) tomato sauce,
    divided use
Water
½ cup chopped onion
½ cup chopped green pepper
1 pound ground beef
4 slices bacon

Preheat oven to 350 degrees. Place rice and corn in layers in a greased 2-quart casserole dish. Sprinkle with salt and pepper. Pour 1 can tomato sauce and ½ can water over layers. In a bowl, mix together onion, green pepper and uncooked beef; add salt and pepper to taste. Add the second can of tomato sauce and ¼ can of water. Cover meat with 4 strips of bacon, halved. Cover and bake 1 hour. Uncover and bake 30 minutes more.

Petti's Spaghetti Pie

PETTI MONIQUE SWALLOW | ROBSTOWN, NUECES EC

6 ounces spaghetti
2 tablespoons butter
⅓ cup Parmesan cheese
2 eggs, well beaten
1 cup cottage cheese
1 pound lean ground beef
1 onion, chopped
1 green pepper, chopped
1 can (14.5 ounces) diced tomatoes
1 small can (6 ounces) tomato paste
1 teaspoon sugar
1 teaspoon oregano
½ teaspoon garlic salt
½ cup shredded mozzarella cheese

Cook spaghetti and drain; stir in butter. Stir in Parmesan cheese and eggs. Form spaghetti into 10-inch, buttered pie plate. Spread cottage cheese over spaghetti. In skillet, cook meat, onion and pepper until done. Drain fat. Stir in undrained tomatoes, tomato paste, sugar, oregano and garlic salt; heat. Preheat oven to 350 degrees. Turn mixture into spaghetti crust. Bake uncovered 20 minutes. Sprinkle with mozzarella cheese and bake 5 minutes longer, or until cheese melts.

Persian Cabbage Dolma

MARY NELL FERDOWSIJAH | HENDERSON, RUSK COUNTY EC

1 large head cabbage
½ cup split peas
1 pound ground lamb or beef
1 cup chopped onions
½ cup chopped fresh parsley
½ teaspoon cinnamon
2 teaspoons salt, divided use
½ teaspoon freshly ground black pepper, divided use
1½ cups canned beef broth
¼ cup sugar
½ cup lemon juice

Wash cabbage, leaving whole. Cover with water, bring to a boil and cook over low heat 15 minutes. Drain and carefully remove 24 leaves; set aside. Cook the peas in boiling water 30 minutes, or until tender; drain. Mix together peas, meat, onions, parsley, cinnamon, 1 teaspoon salt and ¼ teaspoon pepper. Put a heaping tablespoon of the mixture on each cabbage leaf. Fold in the opposite ends; then roll up into sausage shapes. If any meat is left, use a few more cabbage leaves. Line the bottom of a deep skillet with cooked cabbage leaves. Arrange the rolls on them, in layers, placing more leaves between the layers. Mix broth with remaining 1 teaspoon salt and ¼ teaspoon pepper, and pour over all; lay over a final layer of cabbage leaves, if any remain. Cover and cook over low heat 30 minutes. Mix sugar into lemon juice and pour over all. Cook 30 minutes more; taste for seasoning. Serves 6–8.

COOK'S NOTE: Instead of the split peas, you can substitute uncooked instant rice.

Cabbage Roll

ELNA BIGGS | CUERO, DE WITT EC

1 head cabbage, divided use
2 pounds ground meat
1 small can (8 ounces) tomato sauce
½ cup instant or cooked rice
¼ cup chopped onion
½ cup cracker crumbs
Salt and pepper
Bacon drippings
CHEESE SAUCE:
2 tablespoons butter
⅓ cup flour
1 cup milk
⅓ cup grated cheese

Place 10 cabbage leaves in boiling, salted water for 2–3 minutes. Cool. Preheat oven to 350 degrees. Mix meat, tomato sauce, rice, onion and cracker crumbs in a bowl. Mix and season with salt and pepper, to taste. Put meat mixture in cabbage leaves and roll up. Pin with toothpicks. Bake in covered dish 40 minutes. Shred and boil the rest of the cabbage head. Season with bacon drippings, salt and pepper, to taste. Place cooked rolls on top of drained cooked cabbage. Top with Cheese Sauce: Melt butter in a saucepan, stir in flour until smooth. Continue stirring over medium heat while pouring in milk slowly. Stir in cheese until melted. Cook until thickened.

Oven-Fried Liver With Herbed Onion Rings

JEANETTE JACOBS | CAMERON, BELFALLS EC

1 cup crushed cornflakes
½ teaspoon salt
¼ teaspoon pepper
2 pounds calf, veal or lamb liver, sliced
½ cup butter, melted
1 package (16 ounces) frozen breaded onion rings
¼ teaspoon marjoram
4 strips bacon, diced

Preheat oven to 425 degrees. Mix cornflake crumbs, salt and pepper. Dip liver in melted butter, then in seasoned crumbs. Arrange liver slices and frozen onion rings in a single layer on a baking sheet lined with foil. Sprinkle onion rings with marjoram and liver slices with diced bacon. Bake 10–15 minutes, or until onions are crisp and liver slices are browned. Makes 6 servings.

COOK'S NOTE: My family won't eat liver any other way.

Calabacita (Squash Casserole)

BLANCA FORSHEE | BOERNE, BANDERA EC

1 pound pork, cut into small cubes
Shortening
½ cup chopped onion
2 cups chopped fresh or canned tomatoes
1 cup whole kernel corn
1 Mexican squash or zucchini
1 teaspoon ground cumin
½ teaspoon garlic powder
Salt and pepper, to taste

Brown the meat in shortening; add onion and sauté. Add tomatoes, corn, squash and seasonings. Stir all ingredients a few minutes. Cover and simmer on low heat until squash is tender, about 30 minutes.

COOK'S NOTE: This is my grandmother's (Mauricia Sifuentes) recipe. All her recipes were verbally given to me.

Pork Chops in Orange Sauce

MRS. CHARLES SCHROEDER | LITTLEFIELD, LAMB COUNTY EC

4 pork chops, 1-inch thick
Salt and pepper
Paprika
2 tablespoons vegetable oil
⅓ cup water
½ cup sugar
½ teaspoon cornstarch
½ teaspoon cinnamon
1 tablespoon plus 1 teaspoon grated orange zest
1 cup orange juice
6 whole cloves
Hot cooked rice

Sprinkle pork chops with salt, pepper and paprika. Heat oil in skillet. Over medium heat, brown pork chops on both sides. Add water to skillet. Cover, reduce heat and simmer 40–45 minutes, or until pork chops are tender, turning once. Combine sugar, cornstarch and cinnamon in a medium saucepan; stir in orange zest, orange juice and cloves. Cook over medium heat, stirring constantly, until mixture is thickened and bubbly. Remove cloves. Serve pork chops over rice and spoon the sauce over chops, as desired.

COOK'S NOTE: This dish is great for bridge luncheons or Christmas Eve. I have never found this old recipe in a cookbook. This was given to me in the 1960s, but when we moved it was lost, then I found it now that we've moved again.

Chalupa
(Pork Roast With Pinto Beans)

SUSAN BOHNENBERGER | SEGUIN, GUADALUPE VALLEY EC

1½ pounds dried pinto beans
12 cups water
1½ cups chopped onions
1 5- to 6-pound pork loin roast
⅓ cup chili powder
2 tablespoons minced and seeded
   canned jalapeño peppers
1½ teaspoons ground cumin
2–3 cups chicken broth
1 tablespoon salt
ACCOMPANIMENTS:
1 large head lettuce, shredded
1 pint sour cream
3 bunches green onions, chopped
6 tomatoes, chopped
Picante sauce
32 flour tortillas

Wash beans; discard any stones or shriveled beans. Combine water and beans in large Dutch oven. Cover and bring to a boil. Preheat oven to 325 degrees. Add remaining ingredients, except chicken broth and salt, to beans. Cover and bake 4 hours. Remove from oven. Place pork on cutting board; remove bones and excess fat. Shred meat into bite-sized pieces; return to Dutch oven. Add 2 cups chicken broth and salt. Return to oven and bake uncovered 30 minutes. Can be made ahead to this point. Cool, cover and refrigerate up to 48 hours. To reheat, remove fat and bake, covered, 1 hour at 325 degrees, or until heated through. Or simmer covered over low heat, stirring occasionally. Chalupa should have a thick, stew-like consistency. If necessary, add additional chicken broth. Serve with Accompaniments, allowing guests to make their own combinations, using a flour tortilla as the base. Makes about 32 chalupas.

   COOK'S NOTE: This is a delicious recipe for a large number of people. We serve it at parties, along with guacamole, tortilla chips and margaritas. It freezes well.

Scalloped Potatoes
With Pork Chops

MONIQUE SWALLOW | ROBSTOWN, NUECES EC

6 pork chops
6 tablespoons vegetable oil
5 cups sliced potatoes, divided use
6 slices American cheese
Salt and pepper
½ cup chopped onion
2 cans (10.75 ounces each) cream of celery soup
2½ cups milk

Brown pork chops on one side in hot oil. Remove chops as they brown; reserve drippings. Place half of potatoes in greased 9-by-13-inch baking dish. Top with cheese slices and then remaining potatoes. Place pork chops, browned side up, on potatoes. Sprinkle with salt and pepper. Preheat oven to 350 degrees. Sauté onions in drippings until tender, but do not brown. Spoon over pork chops. Heat soup with milk and pour over chops. Bake 1 hour, covered. Remove cover and bake 30 minutes more.

Apple Baked Pork Chops

MAGGIE BEZNER | CELINA, GRAYSON-COLLIN EC

4 pork chops
Salt and pepper
2 apples
2 teaspoons butter
4 teaspoons brown sugar

Preheat oven to 350 degrees. Trim all visible fat from pork chops. Place pork chops in baking dish. Salt and pepper each. Cut apples in half and remove cores. Place each half-apple on a pork chop. Spread butter on each apple and sprinkle each with 1 teaspoon brown sugar plus a little salt and pepper. Bake 45 minutes to 1 hour.

Favorite Pork Chop Casserole

NANCY WHITWORTH | ROBY, MIDWEST EC

6 pork chops
1 cup cooked rice
2 small onions, sliced
2 large tomatoes, sliced
1 green pepper, cut into rings
Salt and pepper
2 cans (14 ounces each) beef broth
¼ teaspoon thyme
¼ teaspoon marjoram

Brown pork chops. Preheat oven to 350 degrees. Place chops on top of rice on bottom of deep casserole dish. Add pork chop drippings. Place a thick slice of onion, tomato and green pepper rings on each chop. Salt and pepper to taste. Pour in broth, thyme and marjoram. Cover and bake 1 hour, or until chops are tender.

Pork Chop Dinner

HEDWIG A. DEHART | HALLETTSVILLE, GUADALUPE VALLEY EC

6 pork chops
½ teaspoon salt
¼ teaspoon pepper
2 pounds sauerkraut
1 onion, chopped
½ teaspoon caraway seed
1 bay leaf
2 cans kidney beans
¾ can beer (9 ounces)

Brown pork chops seasoned with salt and pepper; set aside. Preheat oven to 350 degrees. Using a large casserole dish, layer the following: squeezed-out sauerkraut, chopped onion, caraway seed and broken bay leaf. Add beans and pork chops on top. Pour beer over all and bake 45 minutes.

COOK'S NOTE: This dish is very good for a winter evening supper with cornbread sticks or muffins.

Creole Pork Chops

ALTA MOORE | MULESHOE, BAILEY COUNTY EC

Salt and pepper
4 thick pork chops
1 onion, sliced into rings
1 bell pepper, sliced into rings
1 can (10.75 ounces) tomato soup
1 can (10.75 ounces) cream of mushroom soup
Water

Salt and pepper pork chops. Place in hot skillet and sear on both sides. Place onion and bell pepper rings on top of chops. Pour soups mixed with 1 cup water over this. Simmer 1½ hours.

Cheesy Bacon Spaghetti

MELINDA WOODS | CLEBURNE, JOHNSON COUNTY EC

6 slices bacon
¼ cup diced green onions
6 ounces spaghetti
½ cup grated Parmesan cheese
1 teaspoon salt
¼ teaspoon pepper

In a medium skillet, cook bacon until browned. Remove from skillet and crumble. Drain all but 1 tablespoon of bacon drippings. Sauté onion in drippings until tender. Combine with crumbled bacon. Prepare spaghetti according to package directions; drain. Toss spaghetti with bacon and onion mixture. Add Parmesan cheese, salt and pepper. Toss well. Serves 4.

Hot Sausage Jambalaya

HARRIET HUFF | CARTHAGE, RUSK COUNTY EC

2 packages hot link sausage, or 1 hot and 1 mild
3 onions, chopped
2 cups chopped celery
1 large bell pepper, chopped
Vegetable oil
1 box (6 ounces) wild rice (Uncle Ben's preferred)
1 box Rice-A-Roni, chicken flavor
1 can (10 ounces) diced tomatoes and green chiles
   (Rotel preferred)
1 can (10.75 ounces) cream of onion soup
2 cans (10.75 ounces each) cream of chicken soup

Cut sausage into bite-size pieces and cook. Sauté onions, celery and bell pepper in oil. Cook wild rice and Rice-A-Roni according to package directions. Preheat oven to 350 degrees. In a bowl, mix tomatoes and chiles, onion soup and chicken soup. Add sausage, onion mixture and rices to soup mixture, and pour all into a casserole dish. Bake until hot throughout.

New Year's Black-Eyed Peas With Sausage

MELANIE PEVEY | LUBBOCK, SOUTH PLAINS EC

3 cans (15 ounces each) black-eyed peas
1 pound sausage, sliced
2 tablespoons vegetable oil
1 large onion, chopped
1 small can (4 ounces) chopped green chiles
1 can (15 ounces) whole tomatoes
Salt and pepper, to taste

Place black-eyed peas in large stew pan to simmer. Fry sausage in oil until well browned. Drain all but 2 tablespoons drippings from skillet. Sauté onion in remaining oil. Add onions with oil and remaining ingredients, including sausage, to black-eyed peas. Simmer for 30 minutes over low heat.

Brazos Quiche

LEE BAILEY | GRANBURY, JOHNSON COUNTY EC

1 9-inch pie crust
½ pound bulk pork sausage
1 cup grated cheese, your choice
4 eggs
1½ cups heavy whipping cream
2 tablespoons butter, melted
1 tablespoon flour
½ cup chopped mushrooms
2 tablespoons chopped onion
Salt, to taste
Ground red pepper, to taste
Pinch of nutmeg

Place pie crust in deep dish pie pan or quiche pan. Cook sausage; drain and place over pie crust. Sprinkle grated cheese over sausage. Preheat oven to 375 degrees. Combine remaining ingredients. Whip with wire whisk and pour into pan. Bake 40 minutes, or until puffy and golden brown.

Sausage and Egg Casserole

FLORINE GRIFFIN | GONZALES, GUADALUPE VALLEY EC

1 pound ground sausage
6 slices bread, cubed
1 cup grated sharp cheese
4–6 eggs
2 cups milk
1 teaspoon seasoned salt (Lawry's preferred)
1 teaspoon salt
½ teaspoon dry mustard
Chopped chives

Fry sausage and set aside. Put breadcrumbs in a 2½-quart buttered casserole dish, then cheese. Mix remaining ingredients and beat well. Pour over bread and cheese. Refrigerate overnight, then bake 45 minutes at 350 degrees.

Meat and Vegetable Puffs

BETTY MCGOWEN | CLYDE, TAYLOR EC

½ cup flour
1 teaspoon baking powder
1 teaspoon salt
3 tablespoons milk
2 eggs
1 cup diced cooked ham
1 cup mashed potatoes
1 tablespoon chopped parsley
Vegetable oil

Mix all ingredients together. Drop from spoon into hot oil and cook until puffed and golden brown.

COOK'S NOTE: May add bits of leftover vegetables.

Cheese Enchiladas

DOLORES WILLIS | JASPER, JASPER-NEWTON EC

12 flour tortillas
1 onion, chopped
12 ounces Monterey jack cheese, grated
1 teaspoon melted butter
¼ cup flour
1 can chicken broth
1 carton (8 ounces) sour cream
Cheddar cheese, grated

Preheat oven to 350 degrees. Fill tortillas with onion and Monterey jack cheese. Roll up and place in baking dish. Mix butter, flour, chicken broth and sour cream together. Pour over enchiladas. Sprinkle with cheese. Bake 20 minutes.

Chiles Rellenos

KATHY GIBSON | LOMETA, HAMILTON COUNTY EC

8 canned whole green chiles
8 ounces Monterey jack cheese
¼ cup plus 3 tablespoons flour, divided use
½ onion, minced
1 clove garlic, minced
1 tablespoon vegetable oil, plus more for frying
1 can (14.5 ounces) diced tomatoes
1 cup chicken broth
½ teaspoon chili powder
½ teaspoon dried oregano leaves
Salt and pepper
3 eggs, separated
1 tablespoon water

Drain, rinse and gently remove seeds and membranes from chiles. Cut cheese into strips. Place strips inside chiles. Coat outside of stuffed chiles using ¼ cup flour. Set aside. To make the sauce, sauté onion and garlic in 1 tablespoon oil in a skillet until golden brown. Add tomatoes, broth, chili powder, oregano, salt and pepper to taste. Simmer for 10 minutes. Meanwhile, in a bowl, beat egg whites until they form soft peaks. In a separate bowl, beat egg yolks until creamy with 1 tablespoon water, 3 tablespoons flour and salt to taste. Fold into whites. Heat 1 inch of oil in a frying pan. Dip stuffed chiles into fluffy egg batter. Ease into hot oil. Fry 3–4 minutes, or until a deep golden brown on each side. Drain on paper towels. Serve with heated sauce. Makes 4 servings.

Granny's Baked Eggs

EILEEN SINKS | CHARLOTTE, KARNES EC

⅓ cup mayonnaise
½ cup milk
1 cup grated cheese
½ teaspoon Worcestershire sauce
Salt, pepper and paprika, to taste
8 eggs

Heat mayonnaise, milk, cheese, Worcestershire sauce and seasonings; stir until smooth. Preheat oven to 400 degrees. Break eggs carefully into a buttered baking dish. Pour sauce over eggs. Set baking dish in pan of water and bake about 30 minutes, or until well done.

COOK'S NOTE: Good to eat at supper with hot biscuits and bacon.

Breakfast Trash

BESSIE GOODEN | SEADRIFT, VICTORIA COUNTY EC

1 pound bulk sausage
4–5 medium potatoes, peeled and diced
1 large onion, chopped
1 medium bell pepper, chopped
Salt and pepper
½ pound processed cheese, cubed, or
    grated Cheddar cheese
5 eggs, beaten
Sliced jalapeños and jalapeño juice (optional)
Flour tortillas
Picante sauce

Cook sausage in large skillet until it starts to get done. Add potatoes, onion and pepper. Add salt and pepper to taste. Cook until potatoes are done. Add cheese, stir, then add beaten eggs. You can add a couple of jalapeño slices and jalapeño juice. Warm flour tortillas, and serve with picante sauce and peppers.

COOK'S NOTE: Can be made ahead. Also good for camping.

Ham and Cheese Quiche

FRANCES L. GARDNER | HAMILTON, HAMILTON COUNTY EC

12 slices bacon
2 onions, sliced
2 cups coarsely chopped ham
2 cups grated Cheddar cheese
2 cups grated Swiss cheese
1 tablespoon flour
2 deep dish pie crusts, baked
6 eggs, beaten
2 cups half-and-half, heated
1 teaspoon salt
½ teaspoon coarsely ground black pepper
½ teaspoon dry mustard
⅛ teaspoon cayenne
½ teaspoon nutmeg
Paprika
Parsley flakes

In a skillet, fry bacon until crisp, remove bacon, pat dry with paper towel and crumble into small pieces. Sauté onion in bacon drippings until soft; set aside. Sauté ham in drippings for approximately 5 minutes. In a bowl, combine cheeses and toss with flour. Sprinkle bacon, then onion, over bottom of pie crusts. Layer half of the ham and half of the cheeses. Add the remaining ham. Top with the cheese. Beat the eggs with the warm half-and-half, salt, pepper, dry mustard, cayenne and nutmeg. Pour egg mixture over the filled pie crusts; let stand 10 minutes. Preheat oven to 350 degrees. Sprinkle quiches lightly with nutmeg, paprika and parsley. Bake 30–40 minutes, or until custard is set.

COOK'S NOTE: These freeze well. To freeze, bake quiches only 20 minutes, then cool, wrap with foil and freeze. To reheat, preheat oven to 350 degrees and bake 25 minutes from frozen, or until heated throughout.

Cheesy Ham and Broccoli Bake

MRS. PAUL A. JONES | NOCONA HILLS, COOKE COUNTY EC

1 package (10 ounces) frozen chopped broccoli
1 can (10.75 ounces) Cheddar cheese soup
½ cup sour cream
1 can chunked ham, chicken or turkey,
　　flaked with fork
1 cup cooked rice
½ cup buttered breadcrumbs

Preheat oven to 350 degrees. Cook broccoli until barely tender; drain well. In a large bowl, stir soup and sour cream together. Add broccoli, meat and rice. Spoon into 1½-quart casserole dish. Sprinkle with breadcrumbs. Bake 30–35 minutes.

Baked Deviled Egg Casserole

MRS. JEAN BODINE | KAUFMAN, KAUFMAN COUNTY EC

6 hard-boiled eggs
2 teaspoons prepared mustard
¼ teaspoon salt
3 tablespoons plus ¾ cup sour cream, divided use
2 tablespoons butter
½ cup chopped green pepper
⅓ cup chopped onion
¼ cup chopped pimiento
1 can (10.75 ounces) cream of mushroom soup
½ cup grated cheese

Halve eggs lengthwise; remove yolks. Mash yolks, mustard and salt together with 3 tablespoons sour cream. Fill egg whites with yolk mixture. Melt butter in large skillet. Sauté pepper and onion until tender. Remove from heat; stir in pimiento, soup and remaining ¾ cup sour cream. Preheat oven to 350 degrees. Place ½ of soup mixture in 1½-quart shallow baking dish. Arrange eggs, cut side up, in single layer on top. Pour on remaining soup mixture. Sprinkle with cheese. Bake 20 minutes, or until heated through.

COOK'S NOTE: This may be made in advance and refrigerated until ready to bake. Just bake a few minutes longer.

Korny Dogs

WINNIE L. FELPS | LEANDER, PEDERNALES EC

1 egg
½ cup milk
½ cup flour
½ cup cornmeal
½ teaspoon baking powder
½ teaspoon salt
1 package wieners
Vegetable oil for frying

Mix first 6 ingredients to make a batter. Dip wieners in batter and fry in hot oil.

Roasted Leg of Lamb

MRS. FORD GREENHAW | LORENZO, SOUTH PLAINS EC

1 4- to 5-pound leg of lamb
Salt and pepper
1 can or jar purple plums (about 15 ounces)
2 tablespoons lemon juice
1 tablespoon soy sauce
1 teaspoon Worcestershire sauce
½ teaspoon dried basil, crumbled
½ clove garlic, crushed

Preheat oven to 325 degrees. Place leg of lamb in shallow roasting pan, fat side up, and season all over with salt and pepper. Bake 2½–3 hours, or until meat thermometer reads 175–180 degrees. Meanwhile drain purple plums, reserving ¼ cup of syrup. Pit plums and force through a sieve. Combine with reserved syrup and remaining ingredients to create sauce. Baste lamb with plum sauce 4 times during last hour of roasting. Simmer remaining sauce 5 minutes. To serve, pass sauce with meat.

Mexican Lamb Chops

HAZEL KING | ALTO, CHEROKEE COUNTY EC

4 shoulder lamb chops, 1-inch thick
Flour, seasoned with salt and pepper
3 tablespoons butter
1 small can (8 ounces) pineapple slices, drained
¾ cup orange juice
¼ cup lemon juice
⅔ cup dry white wine
½ cup raisins
2 tablespoons light brown sugar
¼ teaspoon cinnamon
¼ teaspoon ground nutmeg
2 medium green-tipped bananas, cut into chunks
½ cup slivered toasted almonds
Hot cooked rice

Dredge lamb chops in seasoned flour. Cook in butter in a skillet until brown on both sides. Preheat oven to 350 degrees. Place in a shallow baking dish and top each chop with 1 pineapple slice. Combine juices, wine, raisins, sugar and spices and pour over chops. Bake 40 minutes, or until chops are tender. Add bananas and almonds; then bake 5 minutes longer. Serve with rice. Makes 4 servings.

Scalloped Oysters

GINGER TEST | NOVICE, COLEMAN COUNTY EC

1 pint fresh oysters, or 2 cans oysters
2 cups coarsely crushed saltine cracker crumbs
½ cup butter, melted
2 cups sliced fresh mushrooms
¾ cup half-and-half
¼ teaspoon Worcestershire sauce
Black pepper, coarsely ground, to taste

Preheat oven to 350 degrees. Drain oysters, reserving ¼ cup liquid. In a bowl, combine crumbs and melted butter. Set aside ½ cup buttered crumbs. Combine remaining crumbs with other ingredients and oysters. Turn into a buttered 8-inch round baking dish. Top with reserved crumbs. Bake 30–40 minutes.

COOK'S NOTE: We always have these at Thanksgiving and Christmas with turkey and dressing.

Fishermen's Macaroni Casserole

KATHY GIBSON | LOMETA, HAMILTON COUNTY EC

1½ cups macaroni or shell pasta
Salt
1 can (14.75 ounces) salmon
Milk
3 tablespoons butter
3 tablespoons flour
1 teaspoon seasoned salt
1 teaspoon instant minced onion
2 teaspoons black pepper
½ teaspoon dry mustard
1¼ cups grated Cheddar cheese, divided use
1 tablespoon Worcestershire sauce
1 tablespoon lemon juice
½ cup sour cream
1 cup frozen peas, thawed
2 tablespoons minced parsley
6 crackers, crushed

Cook macaroni in boiling salted water for 10 minutes, or until tender. Drain and set aside. Drain salmon liquid into 1-pint measuring cup. Add enough milk to make 2 cups; set aside. Flake salmon into a small bowl; set aside. Melt butter in heavy saucepan. Stir in flour, seasoned salt, instant onion, black pepper and dry mustard. Remove from heat. Stir in milk mixture. Cool slightly, stirring until thickened. Add 1 cup of the cheese. Stir until melted and blended. Fold in macaroni, salmon, Worcestershire sauce, lemon juice, sour cream, peas and parsley. Preheat oven to 375 degrees. Turn into greased shallow 1½-quart baking dish. Mix remaining ¼ cup cheese with cracker crumbs and sprinkle on top. Bake 30–35 minutes, or until bubbly and golden brown. Makes 4 servings.

Stuffed Crab

HARRIETT E. HUDSON | BAY CITY, JACKSON EC

1 large onion
5 ribs celery
4 slices bacon
6 slices lightly toasted bread
2 eggs
Salt and black pepper, to taste
½ teaspoon cayenne
1 teaspoon curry powder

Grind onion, celery and bacon in food chopper, then scrape into a bowl. Soak the slices of bread in water and squeeze dry. Mix with onion mixture and add crab meat. Then add eggs, salt and black pepper, cayenne and curry powder; mix well. Put in casserole dish. Bake 1 hour at 400 degrees, starting with a cold oven.

COOK'S NOTE: If you used fresh crab, you can stuff the cleaned crab shells and bake in them.

Baked Trout or Bass

JEAN WHITWORTH | ROBY, MIDWEST EC

1 14- to 16-inch trout or bass
3–4 fresh onions, sliced
Butter
Garlic salt
Salt
Black pepper
1½ ounces red wine
1 lemon

Preheat oven to 450 degrees. Place fish over onion on heavy foil that has been sprayed with vegetable spray. Add a pat of butter inside and out of fish. Sprinkle well with garlic salt, salt and pepper to taste. Add wine. Squeeze lemon over fish, then drop rind into package of foil. Place package into a roasting pan and bake 30 minutes.

COOK'S NOTE: You can also bake this outside over hot coals. Double-wrap in foil and turn over after 15 minutes.

New Orleans Catfish

RUBY FLENTGE | ROSEBUD, BELFALLS EC

2 pounds catfish
½ teaspoon salt
½ teaspoon pepper
2 cups cooked rice
2 tablespoons grated onion
½ teaspoon curry powder
6 thin lemon slices
¼ cup butter
Chopped parsley

Preheat oven to 350 degrees. Cut fish into serving pieces and place in a well-greased 9-by-13-inch baking dish. Sprinkle fish with salt and pepper. In a bowl, combine rice, onion and curry powder. Spread over fish. Top with lemon slices and dot with butter; cover. Bake 25–30 minutes, or until fish flakes easily when tested with a fork. Remove cover the last few minutes of cooking to allow for slight browning. Sprinkle with parsley.

Country-Fried Catfish

LAVERNE CABLA | TEMPLE, BELFALLS EC

1 cup prepared mustard
6 cups milk
5 pounds catfish fillets
4 cups flour
4 cups cornmeal
Salt and pepper
Vegetable oil, for frying

In a bowl, mix mustard and milk together. In another bowl, mix flour with cornmeal and salt and pepper to taste. Dip fish in milk mixture, then roll in flour mixture. Deep fry until golden brown. Feeds 8–10.

Bass Casserole

MRS. PAUL KOLWYCK | PORT NECHES, JASPER-NEWTON EC

2 medium bass
2½ tablespoons vegetable oil
½ cup chopped onions
½ cup chopped green peppers
Salt
½ teaspoon dry mustard
1 teaspoon Worcestershire sauce
½ teaspoon cayenne
1 teaspoon seasoned salt
1 cup water
1 egg
½ cup milk
2½ cups breadcrumbs, divided use
Butter

Skin and fillet bass. Cook in skillet with oil long enough to remove fish from bones; flake fish. Sauté onions and peppers; add fish to skillet with onions and peppers, and add salt, mustard, Worcestershire sauce, cayenne, seasoned salt and water. Cook until fish cooks down. Preheat oven to 350 degrees. Beat egg in milk and add to fish mixture; stir in 2 cups breadcrumbs. Taste for salt; add more, if needed. Place in buttered casserole dish. Sprinkle remaining breadcrumbs on top. Pat with butter. Cook until top browns and butter melts, about 35 minutes.

Scampi a la Marinara

MARY ALICE YELVERTON | BOERNE, BANDERA EC

5 tablespoons olive oil
2 cloves garlic, minced
1 can (28 ounces) Italian tomatoes (such as San Marzano)
2 tablespoons snipped fresh parsley
½ teaspoon dried basil
2½ teaspoons salt
¼ teaspoon pepper
1 teaspoon dried oregano
⅔ cup canned tomato paste
½ teaspoon garlic salt
2 pounds cooked, peeled and deveined shrimp
Grated cheese
1 package spaghettini or vermicelli, prepared according to package directions

Cook garlic in oil in large skillet. Add tomatoes, parsley, basil, salt and pepper; simmer uncovered 30 minutes. Stir in oregano and tomato paste; cook uncovered 15 minutes. Stir in garlic salt and shrimp. Heat through and serve topped with grated cheese over pasta.

Shrimp Hurry Curry

MRS. BENNIE ELDRED | MONTGOMERY, MID-SOUTH EC

1½ pounds raw, peeled, deveined shrimp (fresh or frozen)
2 teaspoons butter
1 can (10.75 ounces) cream of shrimp soup
1 can (10.75 ounces) cream of mushroom soup
¾ cup sour cream
1½ teaspoons curry powder
2 tablespoons chopped parsley

Melt butter in a 10-inch skillet. Add shrimp and cook over low heat 3–5 minutes, stirring frequently. Add the soups and stir until blended. Stir in cream, curry powder and parsley. Serve over rice or toast points.

Shrimp Quiche

BILLIE ROLLINS | CORPUS CHRISTI, BANDERA EC

1 cup sliced fresh mushrooms
4 green onions, chopped
¼ cup butter
4 eggs, well beaten
1½ cups light cream
1 teaspoon salt
⅛ teaspoon dry mustard
⅛ teaspoon nutmeg
1 cup shredded mozzarella cheese
¾ pound shrimp, boiled and chopped
1 9-inch pie shell

Preheat oven to 400 degrees. In a small saucepan, cook mushrooms and green onions in butter until tender. In a large bowl, whisk together eggs, cream, salt, mustard, nutmeg and cheese. Fold in shrimp, mushrooms and green onions. Pour mixture into pie shell. Bake 15 minutes, then reduce heat to 300 degrees and continue to bake for 30 minutes, or until knife comes out clean when inserted in center. Let stand 5 minutes before serving. Makes 6 servings.

Tuna Spinach au Gratin

MRS. QUENTIN W. GILL | HAPPY, SWISHER EC

1 slice bread, torn into bite-size pieces
¼ teaspoon salt
Dash of pepper
1 tablespoon lemon juice
1 can (5 ounces) tuna, drained
2 tablespoon grated Parmesan cheese, plus more
    for top
1 package (10 ounces) frozen chopped spinach,
    cooked and drained
½ cup salad dressing (Miracle Whip preferred)

Preheat oven to 350 degrees. Stir all ingredients together. Put in a pie pan. Sprinkle with additional Parmesan cheese. Bake 20 minutes. Serves 4.

COOK'S NOTE: Sounds awful, looks terrible, but tastes delicious.

Tuna Patties

ROSIE ROSS | TAYLOR, BARTLETT EC

2 cans (5 ounces each) tuna in water, well drained
1 egg
½ cup breadcrumbs
¼ cup chopped onion
Salt and pepper
Cooking oil

Mix tuna, egg, breadcrumbs and onion. Shape into ½-inch thick patties. Sprinkle both sides of patties with salt and pepper. Heat oil in pan over medium heat and fry patties until golden brown.

Tuna Casserole

MRS. QUENTIN W. GILL | HAPPY, SWISHER EC

7 ounces canned tuna
1 clove garlic, pressed
2 cups sliced mushrooms
½ onion, chopped
2 tablespoons butter
½ cup breadcrumbs
1 chicken bouillon cube, crushed
½ cup warm water
1 tablespoon dried parsley leaves
¼ teaspoon thyme
2 tablespoons Parmesan cheese

Drain tuna and flake into a bowl; set aside. In a skillet, sauté garlic, mushrooms and onion in butter. Stir in breadcrumbs, bouillon cube, water, parsley and thyme. Fold in tuna. Preheat broiler. Put in individual au gratin dishes. Sprinkle with Parmesan cheese. Broil until tops brown.

DESSERTS

Apple Brown Betty Cake

DON CRANE | KIRBYVILLE, JASPER-NEWTON EC

½ cup butter, softened
¾ cup plus 2 tablespoons sugar
1 egg
1 cup flour
½ teaspoon baking soda
1 teaspoon cinnamon
½ cup chopped pecans
2 cups sliced apples

Preheat oven to 375 degrees. In a large bowl, cream butter, sugar and egg together. In a separate bowl, mix flour, soda and cinnamon together. Add flour mixture, a little at a time, to butter mixture, stirring to combine. Mix in pecans and apples. Pour into a 9-by-9-inch baking pan and bake for 35 minutes, or until done. Cake will be moist.

Fresh Apple Cake

JOANN SKIDMORE | SULPHUR BLUFF, FARMERS EC

1¼ cups vegetable oil
2 cups sugar
3 eggs
2 teaspoons vanilla extract
3 cups flour
1 teaspoon baking soda
½ teaspoon salt
1¼ teaspoons cinnamon
1 cup chopped pecans
3 cups diced apples, preferably Rome
GLAZE:
¼ cup butter
½ cup brown sugar
¼ cup half-and-half or milk

Preheat oven to 350 degrees. In a large bowl, mix first 4 ingredients. In a separate bowl, combine flour, soda, salt and cinnamon, then add to sugar mixture. Fold in pecans and apples. Pour into greased, floured Bundt pan. Bake 1 hour. Test for doneness. For Glaze, mix all ingredients in saucepan and boil 1–3 minutes. Pour over hot cake.

Applesauce Cake

WANDA ROBINSON | MULESHOE, BAILEY COUNTY EC

1 cup shortening
2 cups sugar
2 eggs
2 teaspoons baking soda
2 cups applesauce
3½ cups flour
2 teaspoons cinnamon
1 teaspoon ground cloves
Pinch of salt
2 teaspoons vanilla extract
2 cups mixed nuts, raisins and dates

Preheat oven to 350 degrees. In a large bowl, cream shortening and sugar; stir in eggs. In a separate bowl, mix soda with applesauce, then add to sugar mixture. Add flour, spices and vanilla. Beat 1 minute. Fold in nuts and fruit. Turn into greased and floured Bundt pan. Bake 40 minutes.

Apricot Nectar Cake

VIOLET VOGES | NEW BRAUNFELS, PEDERNALES EC

1 package yellow cake mix
¾ cup vegetable oil
1 small can (5½ ounces) apricot nectar
4 eggs, separated
2 teaspoons lemon extract
TOPPING:
Juice and rind of 1 lemon
1½ cups powdered sugar

Preheat oven to 350 degrees. In a large bowl, beat egg whites until stiff. In a mixing bowl, put cake mix, oil, nectar, egg yolks and lemon extract. Beat on low speed 5 minutes. Fold in stiffly beaten egg whites. Pour into greased Bundt pan. Bake 40–45 minutes. Remove from oven and allow to rest 5 minutes. For Topping, combine grated rind and juice with sugar and stir until smooth. If icing is too thin, add a bit more sugar. Spread over top and sides of warm cake.

Banana Cake With Sour Cream

PHYLLIS A. HURLEY | RIO FRIO, BANDERA EC

2½ cups flour
2 teaspoons baking powder
1 teaspoon baking soda
1¼ teaspoons salt
½ cup butter, softened
1½ cups sugar
3 eggs, beaten
1 teaspoon vanilla extract
1 cup sour cream
1 cup mashed ripe bananas
½ cup chopped nuts (pecans or walnuts)
BUTTER CREAM FROSTING:
¾ cup butter, divided use
3 tablespoons flour
¾ cup milk
¾ cup sugar
⅓ teaspoon vanilla extract

Preheat oven to 350 degrees. In a large bowl, sift flour, baking powder, soda and salt together. In a separate bowl, cream butter, sugar and eggs; add vanilla. Add sour cream, bananas and nuts, alternating with dry ingredients. Bake in 2 well-greased and floured 9-inch round cake pans. Bake 30–45 minutes, or until cake tests done. For Butter Cream Frosting, melt ¼ cup butter in a saucepan. Slowly, add flour and milk over low heat. Cook to a pudding consistency and chill thoroughly in refrigerator. In a bowl, cream remaining ½ cup butter and gradually add sugar. Beat until sugar seems to dissolve. Add pudding mixture gradually, beating until fluffy. Add vanilla and continue to beat until light, about 1 minute. Frost cool cake.

Banana Frosting

MRS. GARY PICKRELL | SUDAN, LAMB EC

1 box (16 ounces) powdered sugar
½ cup butter, softened
1 ripe banana, mashed
1 tablespoon heavy whipping cream
1 teaspoon vanilla extract
½ cup pecans

Mix in order given and spread on cake.

Blackberry Wine Cake

FRAN ANDERSON | SAN MARCOS, PEDERNALES EC

1 box white cake mix
1 small box (3 ounces) blackberry Jell-O
½ cup vegetable oil
1 cup blackberry wine
4 eggs
½ cup chopped nuts
GLAZE:
1 cup powdered sugar
½ cup blackberry wine
½ cup butter

Preheat oven to 325 degrees. In a mixing bowl, combine all ingredients, except nuts, and beat 2 minutes. Heavily grease Bundt pan. Sprinkle nuts in bottom. Gently pour batter over nuts. Bake 50 minutes. For Glaze, mix sugar and wine in saucepan; bring to a boil. Add butter as you remove from heat and mix well. Remove cake from pan and pour Glaze gently over cake while warm.

COOK'S NOTE: This cake is better if made a day or two before serving.

Banana Nut Cake

MRS. IVA STARK | NEWPORT, J-A-C EC

1½ cups sugar
½ cup shortening
2 eggs
2 cups flour
2 teaspoons baking soda
Dash salt
6 tablespoons buttermilk
3 mashed bananas
1 cup pecans
1 tablespoon vanilla extract

Preheat oven to 375 degrees. In a large bowl, cream sugar and shortening. Add eggs 1 at a time, beating after each. In a separate bowl, sift flour, soda and salt. Add dry ingredients alternately with buttermilk to creamed mixture. Add mashed bananas, nuts and vanilla and mix. Pour into 2 greased 9-inch cake pans. Bake 30 minutes.

Carrot Cake

LOUISE WILSON | BONHAM, FANNIN COUNTY EC

1½ cups vegetable oil
2 cups sugar
4 eggs
2 cups flour
1 teaspoon baking powder
1 teaspoon baking soda
1 teaspoon cinnamon
½ teaspoon salt
1½ cups carrots, grated
ICING:
1½ cups butter, softened
8 ounces cream cheese
1 box (16 ounces) powdered sugar
1 cup nuts

Preheat oven to 350 degrees. In a large bowl, combine oil and sugar. Add the eggs, 1 at a time. In a separate bowl, mix together the flour, baking powder, soda, cinnamon and salt. Add dry ingredients to wet ingredients; beat, then fold in the carrots. Bake 35 minutes. For Icing, combine all ingredients and mix well. Ice cool cake.

14-Karat Cake

PERLA WILSON | JAYTON, DICKENS EC

2 cups flour
2 teaspoons baking powder
1½ teaspoons baking soda
1½ teaspoons salt
2 teaspoons cinnamon
2 cups sugar
1½ cups vegetable oil
4 eggs
2 cups grated carrots
1 small can (8 ounces) crushed pineapple, drained
½ cup nuts
7 tablespoons sweetened flaked coconut
FROSTING:
½ cup butter, softened
8 ounces cream cheese
1 teaspoon vanilla extract
1 box (16 ounces) powdered sugar

Preheat oven to 350 degrees. In a large bowl, sift together dry ingredients. Add oil and eggs; mix well. Add remaining 4 ingredients. Bake in 3 9-inch cake pans 35–40 minutes. For Frosting, in a mixing bowl, beat butter, cream cheese and vanilla until smooth. Add powdered sugar. Spread on cooled cake.

Buttermilk Cake

MYRTLE REYNOLDS | GRAFORD, ERATH COUNTY EC

2 cups sugar
1 cup shortening
4 eggs
1 cup buttermilk
½ teaspoon baking soda
3 cups flour
1 teaspoon vanilla extract

Preheat oven to 350 degrees. In a large bowl, cream together sugar and shortening. Add the eggs and remaining ingredients. Put in greased and floured 10-inch Bundt pan. Bake 1 hour.

Cherry Cake

EULA WEST | GAINESVILLE, COOKE COUNTY EC

1 box Duncan Hines Strawberry Supreme cake mix
3 eggs
1 teaspoon lemon extract
1 can (21 ounces) cherry pie filling
ICING:
1 cup sour cream
1½ cups sugar
1 medium container (12 ounces) whipped topping
Sweetened flaked coconut

Preheat oven to 350 degrees. In a large bowl, combine cake mix, eggs and lemon extract; mix well. Stir in pie filling. Bake in 3 9-inch cake pans 30–35 minutes. For Icing, mix first 3 ingredients. Ice the 3-layer cake, filling between layers and covering top and sides. Sprinkle the top with coconut and lightly press more onto the sides. Let sit in refrigerator 3 days.

COOK'S NOTE: This is a delicious cake or dessert: full of calories, but great for special occasions.

Cherry Surprise Cake

MRS. LEON SCHILLING | BOVINA, DEAF SMITH COUNTY EC

1 cup vegetable oil
1½ cups sugar, divided use
4 eggs
1 teaspoon vanilla extract
2 cups flour
1 teaspoon baking powder
1 teaspoon cinnamon
1 can (15 ounces) cherries

Preheat oven to 325 degrees. In a mixing bowl, mix oil and 1 cup sugar thoroughly. Add eggs and beat until fluffy. Add vanilla. In a separate bowl, sift flour and baking powder. Add to wet ingredients and beat. In another bowl, mix remaining ½ cup sugar with cinnamon for topping. Grease a 9-by-13-inch pan and pour half the batter across bottom. Sprinkle half of topping over batter. Pour cherries over topping. Pour rest of batter over cherries and sprinkle rest of topping. Bake 50 minutes.

Cherry Dump Cake

BONNIE DIXON | ALVARADO, JOHNSON COUNTY EC

1 can cherry pie filling
1 cup pecans
1 large can (20 ounces) crushed pineapple, drained
1 cup sweetened flaked coconut
1 box yellow cake mix
1 cup butter, melted

Preheat oven to 350 degrees. In a bowl, mix first 4 ingredients together. Put in greased 9-by-13-inch pan. Sprinkle dry cake mix over this. Pour melted butter over cake mix. Bake 1 hour. Serve plain, or with whipped topping or ice cream.

Joyce's Cake

EDYTHE HAND | ELM MOTT, HILL COUNTY EC

2 cups sugar
½ cup shortening
3 teaspoons cocoa powder
2 eggs
½ cup buttermilk
2 cups flour
1 teaspoon baking soda
½ teaspoon salt
1 teaspoon vanilla extract
1 cup coffee
ICING:
6 tablespoons butter, melted
¼ cup sweetened flaked coconut
1 cup packed brown sugar
1 cup chopped pecans
1 small can (5 ounces) evaporated milk

Preheat oven to 350 degrees. In a large bowl, combine sugar, shortening, cocoa and eggs; beat well. Add buttermilk, flour, soda, salt and vanilla; beat well again. Bring coffee to a boil and add to mixture; mix well. Pour into a 9-by-13-inch pan and bake 40–45 minutes or until done. Make Icing while cake is baking: Mix all Icing ingredients together and blend well. Take cake out of oven and spread Icing on top of hot cake. Put under broiler and cook only a few seconds. When Icing starts to bubble, remove cake from oven.

COOK'S NOTE: This cake is great any time of year and is named after a friend who gave me the recipe.

Almond Joy Cake

MRS. RAYMOND HOOD | MURCHISON, NEW ERA EC

1 box chocolate cake mix
1½ cups evaporated milk, divided use
2½ cups sugar, divided use
24 large marshmallows
1 large package (14 ounces) sweetened flaked
    coconut
½ cup butter
1 small package (6 ounces) chocolate chips
1 cup chopped almonds or pecans

Bake cake in 9-by-13-inch pan, according to package directions. In a large saucepan, combine 1 cup milk and 1 cup sugar. Add marshmallows; heat and stir until marshmallows are melted. Remove from heat and add coconut. Pour hot marshmallow mixture over warm, prepared cake. Bring remaining ½ cup milk, 1½ cups sugar and butter to a boil. Stir in chocolate chips until melted, then add nuts. Pour on cake when cool.

Black Forest Dump Cake

MRS. WALDO LUEDEKER | NEW ULM, SAN BERNARD EC

1 small can (8 ounces) crushed pineapple
1 can (21 ounces) cherry pie filling
1 box devil's food cake mix
1 cup chopped pecans
½ cup butter
Whipped topping

Preheat oven to 350 degrees. Drain pineapple; reserve liquid. Spread pineapple in lightly greased 9-by-13-inch pan. Add pie filling and spread gently. Sprinkle dry cake mix over pie filling; top with pecans. In a small saucepan, combine butter and reserved pineapple liquid; melt butter over low heat and stir to combine. Drizzle over mixture in pan. Bake 35–40 minutes. When cool, cut into squares and serve with whipped topping.

Black Bottom Cupcakes

FRANCES WHITSEL | DIME BOX, BLUEBONNET EC

8 ounces cream cheese
1 egg
⅓ cup sugar
⅛ teaspoon salt
½ teaspoon vanilla extract
1 cup chocolate chips
1½ cups flour
1 cup sugar
¼ cup cocoa powder
½ teaspoon salt
1 teaspoon baking soda
1 cup water
⅓ cup vegetable oil
1 tablespoon vinegar
1 teaspoon vanilla extract
Chopped pecans (optional)

Preheat oven to 350 degrees. In a mixing bowl, beat first 5 ingredients together until fluffy. Add chocolate chips and set aside. For chocolate batter, use a separate bowl to mix together remaining ingredients except pecans with a mixer until smooth. Put 2 tablespoons of the chocolate batter into paper cupcake liners in muffin pans. Add 2 teaspoons of the cream cheese batter on top of the chocolate batter. Add pecans on top, if desired. Bake 25–30 minutes, or until done. May sprinkle sugar on top after they are baked. Makes 24 cupcakes.

Chocolate Chip Cupcakes

JUNE FREEMAN | MT. PLEASANT, BOWIE-CASS EC

½ cup butter, softened
6 tablespoons sugar
6 tablespoons brown sugar
½ teaspoon vanilla extract
1 egg
1 cup plus 2 tablespoons flour
½ teaspoon baking soda
½ teaspoon salt
TOPPING:
½ cup packed brown sugar
1 egg
⅛ teaspoon salt
1 package (6 ounces) chocolate chips
½ cup chopped nuts
½ teaspoon vanilla extract

Preheat oven to 375 degrees. In a large bowl, combine all ingredients and beat until creamy. Spoon a tablespoon of mixture into 2½-inch cupcake liners and bake 10–12 minutes. Remove from oven. Prepare the Topping while cupcakes are baking: In a mixing bowl, combine first 3 ingredients and beat until very thick. Add remaining ingredients. Put 1 tablespoon of topping over each baked cupcake. Return to oven and bake another 15 minutes. Cupcakes rise in center, but when you remove from oven the first time, the centers fall and make an indentation for the topping. Yields approximately 18.

COOK'S NOTE: These are very pretty and make great party, tea and shower desserts if baked in mini-cupcake pans.

Chocolate Italian Cream Cake

MRS. MILBURN CARROLL | CROWELL, SOUTHWEST RURAL EA

5 eggs, separated
½ cup butter, softened
½ cup shortening
2 cups sugar
2 cups flour
1 teaspoon baking soda
¼ cup cocoa powder
1 cup buttermilk
1 teaspoon vanilla extract
1 cup coconut
1 cup chopped pecans
FROSTING:
8 ounces cream cheese
½ cup butter, softened
1 teaspoon vanilla extract
1 box (16 ounces) powdered sugar
¼ cup cocoa powder
1 cup chopped pecans

Preheat oven to 325 degrees. Stiffly beat egg whites and set aside. In a mixing bowl, cream butter, shortening and sugar. Add egg yolks, 1 at a time, beating after each. In a separate bowl, sift together flour, soda and cocoa. Alternate adding dry ingredients and buttermilk to butter mixture a little at a time, beginning and ending with dry ingredients. Stir in vanilla, coconut and pecans. Fold in stiffly beaten egg whites. Bake in 3 greased and floured layer cake pans 25–30 minutes. Let cool before frosting. For Frosting, cream together cream cheese and butter in a mixing bowl. Add vanilla. In a separate bowl, sift together powdered sugar and cocoa. Beat into butter mixture a little at a time. Add pecans. Frost between layers and tops and sides of cake.

COOK'S NOTE: This cake won first place in chocolate cake contest at the 1983 Texas State Fair in Dallas.

Double Hershey Cake

JANIVIE LYKINS | HAMILTON, HAMILTON COUNTY EC

1 cup butter, softened
2 cups sugar
4 eggs
6 packages (1.55 ounces each) Hershey's milk
    chocolate bars, melted in double boiler
1 small can (5.5 ounces) Hershey's chocolate syrup
¼ teaspoon baking soda
1 cup buttermilk
2½ cups flour
2 teaspoons vanilla extract
1 cup chopped nuts

Preheat oven to 325 degrees. In a mixing bowl, cream butter with sugar. Add eggs, 1 at a time, beating well after each. Add melted chocolate and syrup. In a separate bowl, dissolve baking soda in buttermilk. Add to butter mixture alternately with flour. Add vanilla and chopped nuts; blend well. Bake in greased and floured Bundt pan 1½ hours. Serve without icing.

COOK'S NOTE: This is a truly outstanding chocolate cake. The recipe is very old, and the original called for eight 5-cent Hershey bars. I acquired this recipe in Waco about 1954.

German's Sweet Chocolate Cake

MARY WESTBROOK | ITASCA, HILL COUNTY EC

1 cup butter, softened
2 cups sugar
5 eggs
1 bar (4 ounces) German's sweet chocolate, melted
1 teaspoon vanilla extract
1 cup buttermilk, divided use
2½ cups sifted cake flour
1 teaspoon baking soda

Preheat oven to 350 degrees. In a large bowl, cream butter and add sugar gradually until light and fluffy. Beat in eggs, melted chocolate and vanilla. Add ⅔ cup buttermilk and flour, a small amount at a time. Dissolve soda in remaining ⅓ cup buttermilk and add to mixture. Bake in 10-inch Bundt pan 1 hour or until done.

Pudding Cake

AURLEEN KASPAR | LA GRANGE, FAYETTE EC

1 cup flour
½ cup butter, softened
1 cup chopped pecans
1 cup powdered sugar
8 ounces cream cheese
1 small container (8 ounces) whipped topping,
    divided use
1 large box (5.9 ounces) instant chocolate
    pudding mix
1 small box (3.4 ounces) instant chocolate
    pudding mix
3 cups milk
Chopped nuts (optional)

Preheat oven to 350 degrees. In a bowl, mix together first 3 ingredients thoroughly and press into greased 9-by-13 inch pan. Bake 20 minutes; cool. In a mixing bowl, combine powdered sugar and cream cheese. Add 1 cup whipped topping. Beat until smooth and spread over crust. In a separate bowl, mix together the packages of pudding mix with the milk. Beat until smooth and pour over cream cheese layer. Spread the rest of the whipped topping over this layer and top with chopped nuts, if desired. Refrigerate until ready to eat.

COOK'S NOTE: This recipe is liked by young and old at our house. Can be made the day before, so it saves time, also. The dish always gets licked clean!

Turtle Cake

DEEN MCDONALD | RAINBOW, LYNTEGAR EC

1 box German chocolate cake mix
½ cup vegetable oil
1½ cups water
2 eggs
7 tablespoons sweetened condensed milk
1 large bag caramels, unwrapped
¾ cup butter
½ cup evaporated milk
1 cup chocolate chips
1 cup chopped nuts
FROSTING:
¼ cup butter
2 tablespoons cocoa powder
½ can sweetened condensed milk (7 ounces)
Powdered sugar
1 cup chopped nuts

Preheat oven to 350 degrees. In a large bowl, combine first 5 ingredients and mix well. Pour half of batter in a 9-by-13- inch pan that has been greased and floured. Bake 20–25 minutes. Melt caramels and butter together; add evaporated milk; mix well. Punch holes in warm cake. Pour caramel mixture over baked cake. Sprinkle with chocolate chips and nuts. Pour the other half of cake batter over the top of caramel mixture and bake 25–35 minutes longer. For Frosting, melt butter in a saucepan and add cocoa. Stir in milk, powdered sugar and nuts (using enough powdered sugar to make Frosting an easy-to-spread consistency). Spread on warm cake.

Mississippi Fudge Cake

RUTH COOMER | NEWARK, TRI-COUNTY EC

2 cups butter
⅓ cup cocoa powder
1½ cups flour
¼ teaspoon salt
4 eggs
2 cups sugar
1 teaspoon vanilla extract
1 cup chopped nuts
1 package (16 ounces) miniature marshmallows
ICING:
1 box (16 ounces) powdered sugar
⅓ cup cocoa powder
½ cup butter, melted
6 tablespoons milk
1 teaspoon vanilla extract

Preheat oven to 350 degrees. In a large saucepan, melt butter and cocoa together. In a large bowl, sift flour and salt together. Pour butter mixture into flour and mix. In a separate bowl, beat eggs and sugar together; mix into flour mixture. Fold in vanilla and nuts. Bake in 9-by-13-inch pan 40–45 minutes. Remove from oven and cover with marshmallows while hot. For Icing, sift sugar and cocoa into a bowl; add butter, milk and vanilla, and mix well. Spread on cooled cake.

D'lish Cupcakes

MRS. EARL BUENGER | CUERO, DE WITT COUNTY EC

1 cup butter
4 ounces semisweet chocolate
1¾ cups sugar
1 cup flour
1 teaspoon vanilla extract
4 large eggs
1 cup pecans

Preheat oven to 325 degrees. In a saucepan, melt butter and chocolate together and cool. Put sugar, flour, vanilla and eggs in a bowl; do not beat. Add pecans and chocolate mixture. Stir all until well mixed. Fill cupcake liners half full. Bake 25 minutes.

Chocolate Cake

MRS. MILBURN CARROLL | CROWELL, SOUTHWEST RURAL EA

1 cup butter
½ cup water
3 tablespoons cocoa powder
2 cups flour
2 cups sugar
½ teaspoon salt
2 eggs
1 teaspoon baking soda
1 cup buttermilk
1 teaspoon vanilla extract
ICING:
½ cup butter
3 tablespoons cocoa powder
6 tablespoons milk
1 box (16 ounces) powdered sugar
½ cup pecans, chopped
1 teaspoon vanilla extract

Preheat oven to 350 degrees. In a saucepan, bring to boil butter, water and cocoa. In a large bowl, mix flour, sugar and salt. Pour melted mixture over flour mixture and mix well. Add eggs, soda, buttermilk and vanilla. Bake in greased 9-by-13-inch pan until done. The last 5 minutes while cake is cooking, begin Icing: In a large saucepan, bring to boil butter, cocoa and milk. Mix in sugar, pecans and vanilla. Ice cake while hot.

Frosty Delight Cake

MRS. J.W. DAY JR. | FLOYDADA, LIGHTHOUSE EC

2 cups brown sugar (not packed)
½ cup butter
3 eggs
2 squares semisweet chocolate, melted
1½ teaspoons vanilla extract
1 teaspoon red food coloring
2 cups flour, sifted
2 teaspoons baking powder
½ teaspoon salt
1 cup Dr Pepper
1 cup chopped nuts
ICING:
2 egg whites
½ cup sugar
½ cup brown sugar
1 tablespoon dark corn syrup
½ teaspoon cream of tartar
½ cup Dr Pepper
Chopped nuts (optional)

Preheat oven to 350 degrees. Grease and flour 2 cake pans. In a large bowl, cream together sugar, butter and eggs. Add chocolate, vanilla and food coloring. Add flour, baking powder and salt alternately with Dr Pepper. Add nuts and bake for 30 minutes. For Icing, beat egg whites in a mixing bowl until stiff. In a saucepan, cook rest of ingredients, except nuts, until soft-ball stage. Drizzle slowly into egg whites while beating. Ice cake and sprinkle nuts on top, if desired.

Marshmallow Fudge Cake

MRS. BILLY J. SIMMONS | HONEY GROVE, FANNIN COUNTY EC

2 cups sugar
1 cup butter
4 eggs
1½ cups flour
¼ teaspoon salt
1 cup chopped nuts
2 teaspoons vanilla extract
6 tablespoons cocoa powder
1 package (16 ounces) miniature marshmallows
ICING:
4 tablespoons evaporated milk
½ cup butter
4 tablespoons cocoa powder
1 box (16 ounces) powdered sugar
1 teaspoon vanilla extract

Preheat oven to 350 degrees. Put sugar in a large bowl. Melt butter, pour into sugar and cream together. Add eggs, then stir in flour, salt, nuts, vanilla and cocoa. Bake in loaf pan for 30–35 minutes at 350 degrees. When done, remove from oven and cover top of hot cake with marshmallows. For Icing, heat milk and melt butter in a large saucepan; add cocoa, sugar and vanilla. Mix well and pour over warm cake.

Date Cake

MRS. PAUL KOLWYCK | PORT NECHES, JASPER-NEWTON EC

2 cups boiling water
1 cup chopped dates
2 teaspoons baking soda
½ cup butter, softened
2½ cups sugar
2 eggs
3 cups flour
1 teaspoon vanilla extract
1 cup chopped pecans

Preheat oven to 350 degrees. In a heatproof bowl, pour boiling water over dates and stir in soda. Let cool. In a large bowl, cream butter and sugar; add eggs and mix. Add all other ingredients, including undrained dates. Bake 1 hour.

Coconut Supreme Cake

BONNIE FIELDS | BLOOMING GROVE, NAVARRO COUNTY EC

1 box white cake mix
1 small box (3.4 ounces) vanilla instant pudding mix
¼ cup vegetable oil
4 egg whites
1 cup water
FROSTING:
1 large container (16 ounces) whipped topping
1 small box (3.4 ounces) vanilla instant pudding mix
1 small can (8 ounces) crushed pineapple, drained
Sliced banana
Sweetened flaked coconut

Preheat oven to 350 degrees. In a large bowl, combine all ingredients and beat well. Pour into 3 oiled and floured 9-inch cake pans. Bake 25 minutes or until done. Cool completely before frosting. For Frosting, beat whipped topping and pudding mix together in a bowl. Frost each layer, then spread on drained pineapple, sliced banana and coconut. On top of cake, just spread Frosting and sprinkle with coconut. Chill and serve.

Sunshine Cake

LINNETTE HABERMANN | SEGUIN, GUADALUPE VALLEY EC

1 box Duncan Hines Butter Recipe Golden cake mix
4 eggs
½ cup vegetable oil
1 can (11 ounces) mandarin oranges, with juice
ICING:
2½ large cans (20 ounces each) unsweetened, crushed pineapple, undrained
1 small box (3.4 ounces) instant vanilla pudding mix
1 small container (8 ounces) whipped topping

Preheat oven to 350 degrees. Put all ingredients together in a large bowl and mix together. Pour into 9-by-13-inch pan. Bake 35 minutes. Let cool before icing. For Icing, in a bowl, mix all ingredients together. Cake can be split or just frosted on top and sides.

Velvet Almond Fudge Cake

JOANN SALTER | ROCKDALE, BARTLETT EC

1½ cups slivered almonds, chopped, divided use
1 cup sour cream
4 eggs
1 small box (3.4 ounces) chocolate instant
     pudding mix
1 box chocolate cake mix
½ cup water
¼ cup vegetable oil
½ teaspoon vanilla extract
½ teaspoon almond extract
1 large package (12 ounces) chocolate chips

Preheat oven to 350 degrees. Toast almonds 3–5 minutes in oven. Sprinkle ½ cup almonds on bottom of well-greased 10-inch Bundt pan. In mixing bowl, combine sour cream, eggs, pudding mix, cake mix, water, oil and extracts. Blend, then beat at medium speed 4 minutes. Stir in chocolate chips and reserved almonds. Pour batter into pan. Bake 70 minutes, or until cake pulls away from pan. Cool in pan 15 minutes. Remove and finish cooling on rack.

Chocolate-Chip Date Nut Cake

JAN FLYNN | SCHERTZ, GUADALUPE VALLEY EC

1 cup dates
1 cup boiling water
1 cup sugar
2 cups flour
1 cup Miracle Whip
2 teaspoons baking soda
Pinch of salt
½ cup brown sugar
½ cup chopped nuts
1 small package (6 ounces) chocolate chips

Preheat oven to 350 degrees. In a heatproof bowl, combine dates and boiling water; let stand until cool. In a large bowl, stir together sugar, flour, Miracle Whip, soda and salt. Add date mixture and mix. Put in greased 9-by-13-inch cake pan. Top with mixture of brown sugar, nuts and chocolate chips. Bake 40–50 minutes. Serve with ice cream or whipped cream.

Deluxe Sour Cream Coconut Cake

GLADYS IVINS | CORSICANA, NAVARRO COUNTY EC

2 cups sugar
1 cup butter, softened
5 eggs
1 cup coconut milk or regular milk
2 teaspoons vanilla extract
1 teaspoon coconut flavoring
3½ teaspoons baking powder
⅛ teaspoon salt
2¾ cups sifted flour
FILLING:
2 cups powdered sugar
1 small container (8 ounces) whipped topping
2 cups sour cream
1 teaspoon vanilla extract
3 cups freshly grated coconut

Preheat oven to 350 degrees. In large bowl, cream sugar and butter, beat in eggs, then alternate wet and dry ingredients, mixing well. Bake 25–30 minutes in 3 8-inch round cake pans. Cool completely, then split each cake to form 6 thin layers. For Filling, combine all ingredients, adding coconut last. Spread between the split layers and on top (not on sides). Seal in airtight container and refrigerate for 3 days before serving. Makes a 6-layer, 8-inch cake.

COOK'S NOTE: This is a deluxe cake that takes a little more effort, but it is excellent for special occasions. This cake is beautiful in looks, too. It won me a place in the State Fair of Texas Cake Bake-Off in 1987, and it isn't found in every cookbook.

Piña Colada Cake

FLORENCE BAKER | GONZALES, GUADALUPE VALLEY EC

1 box white cake mix
3 eggs
½ cup water
⅓ cup white rum
¼ cup vegetable oil
1 cup sweetened flaked coconut
FROSTING:
1 small can (8 ounces) crushed pineapple
1 small box (3.4 ounces) vanilla instant pudding mix
⅓ cup white rum
1 small container (8 ounces) whipped topping,
    thawed
1 cup sweetened flaked coconut

Preheat oven to 350 degrees. In a bowl, blend all cake ingredients except coconut. Beat 4 minutes with electric mixer at medium speed. Fold in coconut. Pour into 2 greased and floured 9-inch layer cake pans. Bake 25–30 minutes, or until cake springs back when lightly pressed. Cool 15 minutes in pans. Remove and cool on racks. For Frosting, combine pineapple, pudding mix and rum in bowl. Beat until blended. Fold in whipped topping. Fill and frost cake layers. Sprinkle with coconut and chill. Refrigerate leftovers.

Italian Cream Cake

IDA EDWARDS | NEW HOME, LYNTEGAR EC

5 eggs, separated
2 cups sugar
½ cup butter, softened
½ cup shortening
2 cups flour
1 teaspoon baking soda
1 cup buttermilk
1 cup sweetened flaked coconut
1 cup chopped pecans
1 teaspoon vanilla extract
FROSTING:
16 ounces cream cheese, softened
½ cup butter, softened
2 cups sifted powdered sugar
1 teaspoon vanilla extract
1 cup chopped pecans

Preheat oven to 350 degrees. In a mixing bowl, beat egg whites until stiff; set aside. In large bowl, cream sugar, butter and shortening. Add egg yolks 1 at a time; beat well. Sift together flour and soda, add to butter mixture alternating with buttermilk. Add coconut, pecans and vanilla. Gently fold in beaten egg whites. Bake in 3 9-inch pans 25 minutes. For Frosting, cream together the cream cheese and butter. Mix in the vanilla, then gradually stir in the powdered sugar. Frost cake and then sprinkle pecans over top.

Sock It To Me Sour Cream Cake

ELDA RUSE | WEST, HILL COUNTY EC

½ cup sugar
¾ cup vegetable oil
4 eggs
1 box Duncan Hines Butter Recipe Golden cake mix
1 cup sour cream
2 tablespoons brown sugar
2 teaspoons cinnamon
½ cup chopped pecans
GLAZE:
1 cup powdered sugar
2 tablespoons butter, melted
3 tablespoons milk

Preheat oven to 325 degrees. In a bowl, mix first 5 ingredients together and pour half into Bundt pan. In a separate bowl, mix brown sugar, cinnamon and chopped pecans. Pour pecan mixture on top of cake mixture. Add last half of cake batter to Bundt pan. Bake 1 hour. For Glaze, combine all ingredients in a bowl and mix until smooth. Pour Glaze over warm cake.

Kahlua Cake

MRS. L.T. HARGROVE | BOWIE, WISE EC

1 box yellow cake mix
1 carton (8 ounces) sour cream
4 eggs
1 small box (3.4 ounces) instant vanilla pudding mix
¾ cup vegetable oil
1 teaspoon vanilla extract
1 cup brown sugar
½ cup chopped pecans
⅓ cup Kahlua coffee liqueur

Preheat oven to 350 degrees. Mix first 6 ingredients with mixer. Divide into halves. To first half, mix brown sugar, pecans and Kahlua. Grease and flour Bundt pan. Put half of plain mixture in pan. Add half of the Kahlua mixture. Add the rest of the plain mixture and top with Kahlua mixture. Cut through with knife. Bake 1 hour.

Milky Way Cake

BETTY SMITH | SLATON, SOUTH PLAINS EC

8 Milky Way candy bars (1.84 ounces each)
1 cup butter, softened, divided use
2 cups sugar
4 eggs
2¼ cups flour
½ teaspoon baking soda
1¼ cups buttermilk
ICING:
2½ cups sugar
1 cup evaporated milk
1 small package (6 ounces) chocolate chips
1 cup marshmallow cream
½ cup butter

Preheat oven to 325 degrees. In a saucepan, melt candy and ½ cup butter; set aside. In a large bowl, cream sugar and ½ cup butter; add eggs. Add flour and soda, alternating with the buttermilk. Add melted candy mixture. Bake in Bundt pan 1 hour and 10 minutes. For Icing, cook sugar and milk to soft-ball stage in a saucepan. Add chocolate chips, marshmallow cream and butter. Stir until melted. Pour over cooled cake.

Peach Cake

CLAUDIA HEYWOOD | AZLE, TRI-COUNTY EC

3 eggs, beaten
1¾ cups sugar
1 cup vegetable oil
2 cups flour
1 teaspoon salt
1 teaspoon baking soda
1 teaspoon cinnamon
2 cups chopped peaches
½ cup chopped nuts

Preheat oven to 350 degrees. In a large bowl, mix eggs, sugar and oil thoroughly by hand. In a separate bowl, mix dry ingredients together and add to sugar mixture. Fold in peaches and nuts. Pour into greased and floured Bundt pan. Bake 1 hour, or until cake tests done. Can use canned or frozen peaches or pears.

Fig Cake

MRS. REESIE L. EDDINS | SAN AUGUSTINE, DEEP EAST TEXAS EC

4 egg whites
1½ cups sugar
¾ cup butter, softened
1 cup milk
3 cups plus 2 tablespoons flour, divided use
½ teaspoon salt
4 teaspoons baking powder
1 teaspoon lemon extract
1 tablespoon molasses
1 teaspoon cinnamon
1½ cups chopped fresh figs

Preheat oven to 375 degrees. In a mixing bowl, beat egg whites until stiff; set aside. In a large bowl, cream sugar and butter. Add milk. In a separate bowl, sift 3 cups flour, then measure by lightly spooning into measuring cup and leveling with a butter knife. Resift measured flour with salt and baking powder. Add half of flour mixture to butter mixture. Fold in stiffly beaten egg whites, and the remainder of flour mixture, plus lemon extract. Separate batter evenly into two bowls. Dredge figs in 2 tablespoons flour, and add to half the batter along with molasses and cinnamon. Fill a greased and floured Bundt pan, alternating spoonfuls of light and dark mixtures. Bake 55 minutes.

Blackberry Jam Cake

FRANCES HRABAL | SULPHUR SPRINGS, FANNERS EC

1 cup butter, softened
1½ cups dark brown sugar
3 cups flour
½ teaspoon salt
1 teaspoon baking soda
½ teaspoon nutmeg
1 teaspoon cinnamon
1 teaspoon allspice
1 cup buttermilk
3 eggs, slightly beaten
1 cup seedless blackberry jam
1 cup chopped pecans

Preheat oven to 350 degrees. In a large bowl, cream butter and sugar. In a separate bowl, sift together the dry ingredients, then add to butter mixture alternately with buttermilk. Add eggs and blend well. Fold in jam and nuts. Pour in 2 greased and floured cake pans. Bake 25–30 minutes.

COOK'S NOTE: You can make a powdered sugar icing by using a little jam to flavor sugar and make the mixture spreadable.

Punch Bowl Cake

FAYE ANN NELSON | SHALLOWATER, SOUTH PLAINS EC

1 box yellow cake mix (plus ingredients on box)
2 large boxes (5.9 ounces each) vanilla instant
   pudding mix (plus ingredients on packages)
2 cans (21 ounces each) cherry pie filling
2 large cans (20 ounces each) crushed pineapple,
   drained
2 bananas, sliced and sprinkled with Fruit Fresh
   to keep from turning dark
1 cup pecan pieces
1 large container (16 ounces) whipped topping
1 can (7 ounces) sweetened flaked coconut

Bake cake according to package directions; set aside. Make two batches of pudding according to package directions; set aside. After cake cools, crumble up finely. Layer ingredients in large glass bowl. Start with crumbled cake, add 1 can cherry pie filling, 1 can pineapple, 1 sliced banana, 1 batch of pudding, a layer of pecans, a layer of whipped topping and coconut. Make a second layer. Cover with plastic wrap and chill overnight. Yields 24 servings.

COOK'S NOTE: Make this in a large punch bowl or a bowl on a stand so the layers will show up. It makes a nice Christmas cake if you substitute pistachio instant pudding for the vanilla, which makes the layers red and green.

Brown-Sugar Oatmeal Cake

MARY WALKER | HUGHES SPRINGS, BOWIE-CASS EC

1½ cups hot water
1 cup quick-cooking oats
1 cup packed brown sugar
1 cup plus 4 teaspoons sugar
½ cup vegetable oil
2 eggs
1 teaspoon baking soda
1 teaspoon cinnamon
½ cup chopped pecans
2 cups flour
GLAZE:
½ cup butter
½ cup nuts
1 cup brown sugar
½ cup evaporated milk
1½ cups sweetened flaked coconut

Preheat oven to 350 degrees. In a heatproof bowl, mix the water and oats together; let cool. In a large bowl, mix the remaining ingredients together. Add the cooled oatmeal mixture last; mix well. Bake in a 9-by-13-inch pan that has been greased and floured. While still hot, cover with Glaze and bake 5 more minutes. For Glaze, cook butter, nuts, sugar and milk in a saucepan over medium heat until thick, about 15 minutes. Remove from heat and stir in the coconut.

Peanut Butter Cake

JEANNIE OWENS | COVINGTON, HILL COUNTY EC

½ cup peanut butter
⅓ cup butter, softened
1½ cups sugar
2 eggs, beaten
1 teaspoon vanilla extract
2 cups sifted flour
3 teaspoons baking powder
1 teaspoon salt
½ teaspoon cinnamon
1 cup milk

Preheat oven to 350 degrees. In a large bowl, cream peanut butter, butter and sugar. Add eggs and stir in vanilla. Add dry ingredients, alternating with milk. Pour into greased 9-by-13-inch pan. Bake 45 minutes. Cool and frost with a fudge frosting, if desired.

Pecan Cake

MRS. JIM HOWLE | ROSEBUD, BELFALLS EC

½ cup butter, softened
1 cup sugar
2 eggs
1 teaspoon vanilla extract
2 cups sifted flour
½ teaspoon baking soda
½ teaspoon baking powder
½ teaspoon salt
1 cup sour cream
1 cup finely chopped pecans
Powdered sugar

Preheat oven to 350 degrees. In a mixing bowl, cream butter until fluffy. Gradually beat in sugar. Add eggs, 1 at a time, beating well after each addition. Stir in vanilla. Sift together dry ingredients into a bowl. In thirds, blend flour mixture and sour cream into sugar mixture, mixing just until smooth. Fold in pecans. Turn batter into greased and floured 9-inch Bundt pan, or fancy cake pan. Bake 1 hour, or until done. Before serving, sprinkle lightly with powdered sugar.

Orange Date Cake

MARGOT FOSTER | HUBBARD, NAVASOTA VALLEY EC

1 cup butter, softened
2 cups sugar
4 eggs
1 teaspoon baking soda
1½ cups buttermilk
4 cups flour
2 teaspoons grated orange zest
1 cup chopped dates
1 cup chopped pecans
TOPPING:
1 cup orange juice
1½ cups sugar
1 teaspoon grated orange zest

Preheat oven to 350 degrees. In a large bowl, cream butter and sugar until fluffy. Add eggs 1 at a time, beating after each. In a separate bowl, combine soda and buttermilk; add alternately with flour to butter mixture. Fold in orange zest, dates and pecans. Bake in greased Bundt pan 1 hour. When cool, remove from pan and pour Topping over. For Topping, combine ingredients in saucepan. Simmer (do not boil), stirring until sugar is dissolved. Poke holes in top of cake with a toothpick. Pour Topping slowly over cake.

COOK'S NOTE: Cake improves with age.

Maple-Pecan Chiffon Cake

BILLIE L. HOLCOMB | ROBY, MIDWEST EC

2¼ cups sifted cake flour
¾ cup sugar
3 teaspoons baking powder
1 teaspoon salt
¾ cup packed brown sugar, free of lumps
½ cup vegetable oil
¾ cup cold water
5 egg yolks
2 teaspoons maple flavoring
1 cup (8–10) egg whites
½ teaspoon cream of tartar
1 cup finely chopped pecans
BROWN BUTTER ICING:
¼ cup butter
2 cups sifted powdered sugar
2 tablespoons heavy whipping cream
1 teaspoon vegetable oil
1½ teaspoons vanilla extract

Preheat oven to 325 degrees. Sift together flour, sugar, baking powder and salt in mixing bowl. Mix in the brown sugar. Make a well in the dry ingredients and add, in order, oil, water, egg yolks and maple flavoring. Beat on medium speed for 1 minute. In a large mixing bowl, beat the egg whites and cream of tartar. Beat 3–5 minutes on high speed. Egg whites are stiff enough when a rubber spatula drawn through leaves a clean path. Pour egg yolk mixture gradually over beaten egg whites, gently folding with rubber spatula just until blended. Sprinkle pecans over top of batter and gently fold in. Pour immediately into ungreased 10-inch Bundt pan with 4-inch-high sides. Bake 55 minutes, then increase oven temperature to 350 degrees and bake 10–15 minutes more. Immediately turn pan upside down with the hole over a glass bottle. Let hang free of table until cold. (Or cool upside down on a rack.) Slide a knife in between the pan and the cake to remove; ice cooled cake. For Icing, let butter brown over low heat in a saucepan, then blend in sugar, cream, oil and vanilla. Stir vigorously until of consistency to spread. If too thick, stir in a little hot water.

Chocolate-Frosted Texas Pecan Torte

MRS. WEDA REYNOLDS | ARLINGTON, WISE EC

⅓ cup cake flour
½ teaspoon baking powder
¼ teaspoon salt
1½ cups finely ground pecans
3 eggs, separated
¾ cup sugar, divided use
½ teaspoon vanilla extract
BUTTER CREAM FROSTING:
½ cup butter, softened
4 cups sifted powdered sugar
4 squares unsweetened chocolate,
    melted and slightly cooled
¼ teaspoon salt
1 cup heavy whipping cream, whipped

Preheat oven to 325 degrees. In a small bowl, mix together flour, baking powder and salt. Sift twice, then mix in nuts. In a mixing bowl, beat egg whites until foamy. Gradually add 6 tablespoons of the sugar. Beat until stiff, but not dry; set aside. In a large bowl, beat egg yolks with the remaining sugar until thick and lemon-colored. Add vanilla. Fold in flour mixture. Fold in egg whites. Pour into 3 well-greased, lightly floured 9-inch round cake pans. Bake 35 minutes. Remove from pans and cool on racks. Frost cooled cake. For Butter Cream Frosting, cream butter in mixing bowl, adding half the sugar gradually; beat well after each addition. Add chocolate, and beat thoroughly. Add remaining sugar and salt. Beat until smooth and creamy. To frost torte, place first layer on a serving plate and frost. (It helps to put a dollop of frosting under the first layer to "glue" it to the plate.) Add second layer and repeat frosting. Add top layer and frost top and sides generously. Top with whipped cream and chill. If desired, decorate with rosette piping of icing when ready to serve.

COOK'S TIP: I like to "age" it for a day or more before serving.

Sour Cream Cake

MRS. DOR JOHNSON | RICHLAND SPRINGS, MCCULLOCH EC

¾ cup butter, softened

2 cups sugar

3 eggs

1 teaspoon vanilla extract

2 cups flour

1 teaspoon baking powder

¼ teaspoon salt

1 carton (8 ounces) sour cream

STREUSEL:

2 tablespoons brown sugar

½ teaspoon cinnamon

½ cup pecans, chopped

Preheat oven to 350 degrees. In a mixing bowl, cream butter and sugar. Add eggs, 1 at a time, mixing after each. Add vanilla. In a separate bowl, mix flour, baking powder and salt together and add alternately with sour cream. Make Streusel by mixing all ingredients together. Pour half of batter into greased Bundt pan and sprinkle on half of Streusel. Pour in remaining batter and sprinkle with remainder of Streusel. Bake 1 hour.

Fresh Pear Cake

THUSNELDA HUESKE | BRENHAM, BLUEBONNET EC

4 cups peeled and thinly sliced fresh, soft pears

2 cups sugar

1 cup chopped pecans

3 cups flour

½ teaspoon cinnamon

½ teaspoon salt

2 teaspoons baking soda

1 cup vegetable oil

1 teaspoon vanilla extract

2 eggs, well beaten, room temperature

In a large bowl, mix pears with sugar and nuts and let stand 1 hour. Stir often. Mixture makes its own juice. Preheat oven to 350 degrees. Add dry ingredients to pear mixture. Add oil, vanilla and eggs. Mix by hand. Pour batter into greased and floured 9-by-13-inch pan. Bake about 1½ hours.

Hummingbird Cake

MRS. RICHARD H. GERMAINE | UVALDE, MEDINA EC

3 cups flour

2 cups sugar

1 teaspoon baking soda

1 teaspoon salt

1 teaspoon cinnamon

3 eggs, beaten

1 cup vegetable oil

1½ teaspoons vanilla extract

1 small can (8 ounces) crushed pineapple, undrained

1 cup chopped pecans

2 cups mashed bananas

CREAM CHEESE FROSTING:

8 ounces cream cheese, softened

½ cup butter, softened

1 teaspoon vanilla extract

1 box (16 ounces) powdered sugar, sifted

½ cup chopped pecans or 1½ cups sweetened flaked coconut

Preheat oven to 350 degrees. Combine flour, sugar, baking soda, salt and cinnamon in a large mixing bowl. Add eggs and oil. Stir until dry ingredients are moistened. Do not beat. Mix in vanilla, crushed pineapple, pecans and bananas. Spoon batter into 3 greased and floured 9-inch round cake pans. Bake 25–30 minutes or until a wooden toothpick inserted in center comes out clean. Cool in pans 10 minutes. Remove from pans and cool completely before frosting. For Cream Cheese Frosting, combine cream cheese and butter in a mixing bowl and beat until smooth. Add vanilla and powdered sugar. Beat until light and fluffy. Makes enough frosting for 1 3-layer cake. Spread frosting on all layers and sprinkle pecans on top, or completely cover with coconut for snowball effect.

COOK'S NOTE: This cake makes a great bake-sale item. You may bake it in 12-inch Bundt pan. Spoon batter into Bundt pan, following same instructions as above, but bake 50–60 minutes. Add 1 tablespoon milk to Frosting for Bundt cake, if you want a drip effect.

Tropical Chiffon Cake

MRS. JACK COOK | SHALLOWATER, SOUTH PLAINS EC

2½ cups cake flour
1½ cups sugar
3 teaspoons baking powder
1 teaspoon salt
½ cup vegetable oil
5 egg yolks
¾ cup cold water
3 tablespoons grated orange zest
1 cup (8–10) egg whites
½ teaspoon cream of tartar
PINEAPPLE-COCONUT ICING:
3 egg whites
2¼ cups sugar
¼ teaspoon salt
½ teaspoon cream of tartar
½ cup pineapple syrup
½ cup crushed pineapple, drained
½ cup sweetened flaked coconut

Preheat oven to 350 degrees. Into a large bowl, sift together cake flour (spooned lightly to measure), sugar, baking powder and salt. Make a well and add oil, unbeaten egg yolks, cold water and orange zest. Mix until smooth. In a separate bowl, beat egg whites and cream of tartar into very stiff peaks (stiffer than for meringue). Pour egg yolk mixture gradually over egg whites, gently folding just until blended. Pour quickly into ungreased Bundt pan. Bake 55 minutes, then increase to 350 degrees and bake 10–15 minutes more, or until top springs back when lightly touched. Turn pan upside down, placing opening of Bundt over glass bottle to cool. When cool, loosen from sides of pan with spatula. Turn pan over and hit edge sharply to loosen. Using toothpicks in side as marks, split cake into 3 layers. Ice with Pineapple-Coconut Icing: Combine all ingredients, except pineapple and coconut, in top of double boiler over boiling water. Beat with rotary beater 7 minutes, or until icing peaks. Remove from heat; beat until cool. Reserve 1½ cups of Icing for top. Spread remaining Icing between layers and on sides. Add drained pineapple to the reserved Icing; spread on top of cake. Toast coconut under broiler. Sprinkle sides of cake with toasted coconut.

COOK'S NOTE: This is a pretty cake for parties.

Better Than Sex Cake

FRANCES BAXTER | CAMERON, BELFALLS EC

1 box yellow cake mix with pudding
    (plus ingredients on box)
1 large can (20 ounces) crushed pineapple, undrained
1 cup sugar
1 small box (3.4 ounces) vanilla instant pudding mix
    (plus ingredients on package)
1 small container (8 ounces) whipped topping
Sweetened flaked coconut
Chopped pecans

Bake cake mix in 9-by-13-inch pan as directed on box. Boil pineapple and sugar together for 5 minutes. Cool and spread over cooled cake. Prepare pudding according to package directions and spread over pineapple mixture. Spread whipped topping over this. Sprinkle with coconut and pecans.

COOK'S TIP: Freezes well. Serves a bunch. It is!!

German Crumb Cake

MRS. BILL DARBY | VALLEY MILLS, MCLENNAN EC

1 cup butter, softened
1 cup sugar
1 cup brown sugar
2 cups flour
1 teaspoon cinnamon
½ cup chopped nuts
1 teaspoon baking soda
1 cup buttermilk
2 eggs
½ teaspoon salt

Preheat oven to 350 degrees. In a large bowl, mix butter, sugars, flour and cinnamon into a crumb mixture. Into a separate bowl, remove ½ cup crumbs mixture; add nuts and set aside. Add other ingredients to first crumb mixture and spread in 9-by-13-inch pan. Spread crumb and nut mixture over top of batter and bake cake until brown and springs back.

Mexican Wedding Cake

BARBARA RASCO | ROBY, MIDWEST EC

2 cups sugar
2 cups flour
1 teaspoon baking soda
1 teaspoon vanilla extract
1 large can (20 ounces) crushed pineapple, undrained
½ cup chopped pecans
ICING:
½ cup butter, melted
8 ounces cream cheese
¾ cup sugar
1 teaspoon vanilla extract
½ cup chopped pecans

Preheat oven to 350 degrees. In a large bowl, mix all ingredients together and bake in a greased and floured 9-by-13-inch pan. Bake 30 minutes. For Icing, beat first 4 ingredients in a mixing bowl until stiff and fluffy. Fold in pecans and spread on warm cake.

Poppy Seed Cake

BELINDA ANDERSON | KARNACK, PANOLA-HARRISON EC

1 box yellow cake mix
4 eggs
¾ cup cream sherry
¾ cup vegetable oil
¼ cup poppy seeds
1 small box (3.4 ounces) butterscotch pudding mix
GLAZE:
¼ cup cream sherry
1 cup powdered sugar

Preheat oven to 350 degrees. In a large bowl, mix all cake ingredients and pour into Bundt pan. Bake about 1 hour. Remove from oven, and while in pan, poke holes in cake with ice pick; pour Glaze over hot cake. For Glaze, mix sherry and powdered sugar.

Mother's Potato Cake

SHIRLEY BROCKWAY | KAUFMAN, KAUFMAN COUNTY EC

1 cup cooked, mashed potatoes
1 cup butter, softened
½ cup whole milk
4 eggs
2 cups sugar
2¼ cups flour
½ teaspoon salt
2 teaspoons baking powder
1 teaspoon vanilla extract
ICING:
1 heaping tablespoon flour
1 cup sugar
Juice of 1 orange
Juice of 1 lemon
Grated zest of 1 lemon
½ cup boiling water
1 small bag (7 ounces) sweetened flaked coconut
1 cup pecans

Preheat oven to 350 degrees. In a large bowl, mix potatoes, butter, milk and eggs. In a separate bowl, mix sugar, flour, salt and baking powder; stir into potato mixture. Add vanilla. Bake 35 minutes in 4 round cake pans. For Icing, mix flour and sugar in a saucepan, then add juices, zest and water and cook until thick. Remove from heat and stir in coconut and pecans.

COOK'S NOTE: Double icing recipe, if you like lots of icing. This is a Christmas tradition cake.

Banana Pound Cake

JOLENE FONDY | SLATON, COMANCHE COUNTY EC

1½ cups shortening
2½ cups sugar
4 eggs
6 bananas
1 teaspoon vanilla extract
3 cups sifted flour
2 teaspoons baking soda
Pinch of salt

Preheat oven to 300 degrees. In a large bowl, cream shortening and sugar. Add eggs 1 at a time, mixing after each. Mash bananas and add; mix well. Add vanilla, flour, soda and salt. Bake 1½ hours in a greased and floured large Bundt pan, or 1 hour in 4 loaf pans.

Best-Ever Pound Cake

BERNIECE HULLUM | BURNET, PEDERNALES EC

3 cups sugar
1½ cups shortening
1 cup whole milk
6 eggs
1 teaspoon lemon extract
1 teaspoon vanilla extract
3½ cups flour
½ teaspoon salt

In a mixing bowl, cream sugar, shortening and milk; beat well. (The more it is beaten, the better.) Add eggs 1 at a time, mixing after each. Blend in extracts. Add sifted flour and salt, a small amount at a time; mix well. Pour in greased and floured Bundt pan. Start in a cold oven and bake at 350 degrees for 1½ hours.

COOK'S NOTE: This cake has the best texture of any pound cake I have ever eaten. The beating of this cake is the secret.

Chocolate Intrigue Pound Cake

EDNA ZOCH | HARROLD, SOUTHWEST RURAL EA

3 cups sifted flour
2 teaspoons baking powder
½ teaspoon salt
1 cup shortening
2 teaspoons butter flavoring
2 cups sugar
3 eggs
1 cup milk
1½ teaspoons vanilla extract
¾ cup chocolate syrup
¼ teaspoon baking soda

Preheat oven to 350 degrees. Sift together flour, baking powder and salt into a bowl; set aside. In a mixing bowl, cream together shortening, butter flavoring, sugar and eggs (added 1 at a time). Beat well after each addition. Combine milk and vanilla; alternately add to creamed mixture along with dry ingredients. Blend well after each addition. Turn two-thirds of the batter into a greased and floured Bundt pan. Add chocolate syrup and soda to remaining batter; mix well. Spoon chocolate batter over white batter, but do not mix up. Bake 60–70 minutes. Let cool in pan 10 minutes before removing cake.

My Grandmother Lamar's Pound Cake

PEGGY MCDONALD | BIG SPRING, CAP ROCK EC

10 eggs, separated
1 pound margarine (not butter)
1 pound (2½ cups) sugar
1 pound (4¼ cups) flour
¼ cup whiskey (a must)

Preheat oven to 300 degrees. In a large bowl, beat egg whites until stiff; set aside. In a mixing bowl, cream margarine and sugar. Add egg yolks. Add flour and whiskey. Fold in egg whites, then beat on low speed for 10 minutes. This is a must. Divide batter evenly between 2 loaf pans. Bake 2 hours.

COOK'S NOTE: This has been in our family for over 75 years. My grandma won a $1,500 prize over 60 years ago with this cake.

Coconut Pound Cake

LILLIE FAY HOPKINS | BERTRAM, PEDERNALES EC

2 cups sugar
1 cup shortening
1 teaspoon vanilla extract
1 teaspoon butter flavoring
6 eggs
2 cups flour
1 teaspoon salt
1 can (7 ounces) sweetened flaked coconut
COCONUT ICING:
1 cup sugar
½ cup water
2 teaspoons coconut flavoring

Preheat oven to 325 degrees. In a mixing bowl, cream sugar and shortening; add flavorings. Add eggs 1 at a time; mix well using high speed on an electric mixer. Sift flour and salt together in a separate bowl, then add to sugar mixture slowly. Fold in coconut. Pour into greased and floured 10-inch Bundt pan. Bake about 1 hour and 20 minutes, or until a toothpick inserted in center comes out clean. For Coconut Icing, mix all ingredients together in a saucepan. Bring to a boil and boil 1 minute. Make 5–10 minutes before cake is done. For hard glaze crust, remove cake from oven and brush or pour Coconut Icing over hot cake while still in the pan. Put cake back in the oven no more than 5 minutes. Remove cake from pan at once. For soft glaze, remove cake from pan immediately. Brush Coconut Icing on with pastry brush while cake is warm.

Butter Rum Pound Cake

MRS. G.W. MORRISON | GARRISON, DEEP EAST TEXAS EC

2 cups sugar
1 cup shortening or butter
4 eggs
1 teaspoon vanilla extract
1 teaspoon rum extract
3 cups cake flour
½ teaspoon baking soda
½ teaspoon salt
½ teaspoon baking powder
1 cup buttermilk
RUM GLAZE:
½ cup sugar
¼ cup water
2 teaspoons rum extract, or to taste
1 tablespoon butter

Preheat oven to 325 degrees. Cream sugar and shortening. Add eggs 1 at a time, beating after each addition. Blend in extracts. Sift flour, soda, salt and baking powder and add alternately with buttermilk. Bake in a well-greased and floured Bundt pan about 1 hour. For Rum Glaze, mix all ingredients in saucepan; boil 1 minute. Brush on hot cake with pastry brush.

Prunella Cake

MOZELLE BEHANNON | CORPUS CHRISTI, JASPER-NEWTON EC

½ cup butter, softened, or shortening
2 eggs
1 cup sugar
⅔ cup chopped prunes (approximately 18)
⅔ cup buttermilk
1⅓ cups flour
½ teaspoon baking soda
½ teaspoon salt
½ teaspoon baking powder
½ teaspoon nutmeg
½ teaspoon cinnamon
½ teaspoon allspice
½ cup chopped pecans
ICING:
2 cups powdered sugar, divided use
2 tablespoons prune juice
1 tablespoon lemon juice
½ tablespoon cinnamon
½ teaspoon salt
2 tablespoons butter

Preheat oven to 350 degrees. In a large bowl, blend butter with eggs and sugar; add prunes. Stir in buttermilk. In separate bowl, sift together dry ingredients and add pecans; pour into butter mixture and beat thoroughly. Bake in 2 greased and floured layer pans about 30 minutes. Test for doneness at 20–25 minutes. When cool, add Icing: In a bowl, mix 1 cup powdered sugar with prune juice and lemon juice. In a separate bowl, mix cinnamon, salt and butter with remaining cup of sugar. Blend the 2 mixtures; stir until creamy. Spread on cake.

COOK'S NOTE: This recipe was given to me in 1932, when the Depression was still on.

Praline Pumpkin Cake

SHIRLEY MORTON | FLOYDADA, LIGHTHOUSE EC

1 yellow cake mix
½ cup vegetable oil
1 cup canned pumpkin
¾ cup brown sugar
¼ cup water
1 teaspoon cinnamon
½ teaspoon allspice
¼ teaspoon nutmeg
4 eggs
PRALINE MIX:
½ cup chopped nuts
⅓ cup brown sugar
⅓ cup butter, softened
ICING:
½ cup butter, softened
8 ounces cream cheese
1 box (16 ounces) powdered sugar
1 teaspoon vanilla extract

Preheat oven to 350 degrees. In a mixing bowl, combine cake mix, oil, pumpkin, brown sugar, water and spices. Beat 1 minute. Add eggs, 1 at a time beating 1 minute after each. Pour half of batter into Bundt pan. Combine Praline Mix ingredients and put over batter in Bundt pan. Add remaining half of batter. Bake 1 hour. For Icing, mix together all ingredients and spread on cooled cake.

Great Depression Cake

ROSEMARY TAMEZ | HOUSTON, COLEMAN COUNTY EC

2 cups sugar
2 cups strong coffee
½ cup shortening
2 cups raisins
1 apple, peeled and grated
1 cup chopped walnuts
2 cups flour
1 teaspoon baking soda
2 teaspoons baking powder
1 teaspoon cinnamon
1 teaspoon allspice
1 teaspoon ground cloves
1 teaspoon nutmeg
Powdered sugar (optional)

Preheat oven to 350 degrees. In a large saucepan, simmer the first 5 ingredients 10 minutes, stirring occasionally. Cool 10 minutes. In a large bowl, combine remaining ingredients, then stir in coffee mixture. Pour batter into well-greased and floured 9-by-13-inch pan. Bake 25–30 minutes, or until toothpick comes out clean. Cool and dust with powdered sugar, if desired.

COOK'S NOTE: This recipe is Sun-Maid raisin's version of what I grew up calling "Poor Devil Cake." My cousin loved to tell about the time she made it. It seems that the cake never rose, or "squatted to rise and stayed in the squat." She couldn't afford to throw out all those ingredients and start afresh, so she salvaged it and served it to her family as "pudding." To this day, they swear that was the tastiest "cake" she ever made.

Mother's Spice Cake

GLADYS SAEGERT | PAIGE, BLUEBONNET EC

⅓ cup butter, softened
1⅓ cups dark brown sugar
2 eggs, lightly beaten
½ cup buttermilk
2 cups flour
⅛ teaspoon salt
2 teaspoons baking soda
¾ teaspoon cinnamon
¼ teaspoon nutmeg (optional)
⅛ teaspoon ground cloves (optional)
1 cup raisins, tossed in a little flour
1 cup pecans, or more
½ cup candied fruits
CARAMEL ICING:
2½ cups sugar, divided use
Water
½ teaspoon baking soda
1 cup milk
1 tablespoon butter
1 teaspoon vanilla extract

Preheat oven to 325 degrees. In a large bowl, cream butter and sugar; add beaten eggs, alternating with buttermilk. Add dry ingredients, raisins, nuts and fruit. Bake 45 minutes in loaf or Bundt pan. For Caramel Icing, put ½ cup sugar into a thick skillet (such as cast iron) over low heat, and cook until sugar is just melted. Cover with water and add soda, milk and remaining 2 cups sugar. Raise to medium heat and cook to soft-ball stage. Remove from heat; add butter and vanilla. Beat until thick enough to spread.

Spice Cake With Sour Cream

PHYLLIS A. HURLEY | RIO FRIO, BANDERA EC

¾ cup butter, softened
1½ cups sugar
3 eggs, separated
2 cups flour
1 teaspoon baking soda
1 teaspoon salt
1 teaspoon ground cloves
1 teaspoon allspice
1 teaspoon nutmeg
1 teaspoon cinnamon
1 cup sour cream
1 teaspoon vanilla extract

Preheat oven to 350 degrees. In a large bowl, cream butter, sugar and egg yolks. In a separate bowl, sift flour with soda, salt and spices. In a mixing bowl, beat egg whites until stiff. Add sifted ingredients to creamed mixture, alternating with sour cream. Then, add vanilla and fold in stiffly beaten egg whites. Pour into 2 well-greased and floured 9-inch cake pans. Bake 35 minutes, or until cake tests done. When cool, frost with frosting of your choice.

Strawberry Cake

JUDY HOWARD | BONHAM, FANNIN COUNTY EC

1 box white cake mix
3 tablespoons flour
½ cup water
½ cup vegetable oil
1 small box (3 ounces) strawberry Jell-O
½ package frozen strawberries, thawed but not
    drained (5 ounces total)
4 eggs
ICING:
¼ cup butter, softened
1 box powdered sugar
½ pint fresh strawberries (or other ½ package,
    thawed and drained)

Preheat oven to 350 degrees. In a large bowl, mix all ingredients well. Pour into a greased and floured 9-by-13-inch pan. Bake 35–40 minutes. For Icing, mix ingredients and spread on cooled cake.

Strawberry Angel Food Cake

MRS. JACK COOK | SHALLOWATER, SOUTH PLAINS EC

1 box Betty Crocker Angel Food cake mix
    (plus ingredients on box)
Heavy whipping cream
Sugar, to taste
Vanilla extract, to tste
4 egg whites
2 packages (10 ounces each) frozen strawberries,
    thawed and drained, or 2 pints fresh

Prepare cake mix according to directions. Using toothpicks as guide, slice cake into 3 layers. Whip cream until stiff and sweeten to taste with sugar and vanilla; set aside. Beat egg whites as you would for meringue. Fold egg whites into whipped cream. Spread strawberries on bottom layer of cake and top with cream mixture. Add next cake layer, berries and cream. Add top layer. Spread top and sides with cream mixture. Garnish with strawberries and refrigerate.

COOK'S NOTE: Can use homemade angel food cake. This cake is made for most all birthdays in my family, especially for grandchildren. The cream and meringue mixture tastes like cream but stands up better. My mother called it her cream-stretcher when she did not have enough cream—it was needed to make our butter—but we always had plenty of eggs.

Rum Cake

SALLY SCROGHAM | GARRISON, RUSK COUNTY EC

2 cups sugar
1 cup shortening
4 eggs
3 cups flour
½ teaspoon baking soda
½ teaspoon baking powder
¼ teaspoon salt
1 cup buttermilk
1 teaspoon rum extract
SAUCE:
1½ cups sugar
¾ cup water
1½ teaspoon rum extract

Preheat oven to 350 degrees. In a large bowl, cream sugar and shortening; add eggs. Add dry ingredients, buttermilk and extract. Pour into a greased and floured Bundt pan and bake 60–65 minutes. Remove cake from oven. Make Sauce in last few minutes while cake is baking: Bring all ingredients to boil in a saucepan, then pour over hot cake.

Bohemian Pound Cake

NELDA F. WILCOXEN | ABILENE, TAYLOR EC

2 cups sugar
½ cup brown sugar
1 cup shortening
4 eggs
2½ cups flour
1 teaspoon baking powder
1 teaspoon salt
1 large can (12 ounces) evaporated milk
1 teaspoon vanilla extract
1 cup chopped pecans
1 cup sweetened flaked coconut

Preheat oven to 350 degrees. In a large bowl, cream sugars and shortening until fluffy. Add eggs, flour, baking powder and salt; beat lightly between each addition. Add milk, vanilla, pecans and coconut, beating together as you add. Pour into large Bundt pan. Bake 1½ hours.

Walnut Dream Cake

KATHY SCHULZE | DRIFTWOOD, PEDERNALES EC

½ cup butter, softened
1½ cups packed brown sugar
1 teaspoon maple flavoring
2 eggs
2⅓ cups sifted flour
1 teaspoon salt
1 teaspoon baking soda
1 cup buttermilk
1 cup chopped walnuts
MAPLE FROSTING:
⅓ cup butter, softened
3 cups powdered sugar, sifted
3 tablespoons cream or milk
1 teaspoon maple flavoring
Walnut halves or pieces, for decoration

Preheat oven to 350 degrees. In a mixing bowl, cream butter. Gradually beat in sugar, creaming until light and fluffy. Beat in flavoring and eggs, 1 at a time. Re-sift flour with salt and soda. Blend into creamed mixture, alternating with buttermilk. Stir in chopped walnuts. Pour into a greased and floured 9-inch Bundt pan. Bake about 1 hour, or until cake tests done. Let stand 10 minutes. Invert onto wire rack to cool before frosting. For Maple Frosting, beat together butter, sugar, cream and maple flavoring until smooth and creamy. Frost cake. Decorate with walnut halves or pieces.

Roll Cake

MRS. ADAM BRUNKENHOEFER | HALLETTSVILLE, FAYETTE EC

4 eggs, separated
¾ cup sugar
1 teaspoon vanilla extract
¾ cup sifted cake flour
¾ teaspoon baking powder
¼ teaspoon salt
Strawberry or other jam or jelly

Preheat oven to 375 degrees. In a mixing bowl, beat egg yolks, slowly adding sugar and vanilla. Sift flour and baking powder and add to sugar mixture; beat until smooth. In a separate bowl, whip egg whites with salt until stiff. Fold into flour mixture. Spread dough evenly on 10-by-15-inch jellyroll pan lined with waxed paper. Bake 15 minutes. Invert onto damp towel and roll up. When cool, unroll and spread with strawberry or other fruit jam, reroll and slice to serve.

Kentucky Wonder Cake

MRS. A.D. CROWDER | ROSCOE, LONE WOLF EC

2½ cups sifted flour
1½ cups vegetable oil
2 tablespoons hot water
2 cups sugar
4 egg yolks
1 cup crushed pineapple, undrained
2½ teaspoons cinnamon (optional)
1½ teaspoons nutmeg (optional)
1 cup chopped pecans, tossed in flour
4 egg whites

Preheat oven to 350 degrees. In a large bowl, mix all ingredients except pecans and egg whites. Fold in pecans. In a separate bowl, lightly beat egg whites. Fold into main mixture. Pour into ungreased Bundt pan. Bake about 1 hour and 10 minutes.

Best-Ever Fruit Cake

MRS. B.A. PATTERSON | SANTA ROSA, MAGIC VALLEY EC

2½ cups sugar
2 cups butter, softened
10 eggs
1 pound box graham crackers, crushed
1 pound green candied cherries
1 pound red candied cherries
1 pound raisins, soaked in hot water 5 minutes
    and drained
2 tablespoons vanilla extract
2 tablespoons lemon juice
1 pound pecans

Preheat oven to 275 degrees. In a large bowl, cream sugar and butter. Add eggs, 1 at a time, and stir well. Add graham crackers and mix well. Add remaining ingredients and mix. This makes 4 loaf-size cakes. Grease pans, and line bottom and ends with waxed paper. Bake 2½ hours.

COOK'S NOTE: This is the best fruit cake I have ever eaten. Try it.

Magic Fruit Cake

MRS. V.G. FRENZEL | ROUND TOP, FAYETTE EC

1 pound candied cherries
1 pound candied pineapple
1 pound pitted dates
1 pound (4 cups) pecans
1 can (14 ounces) sweetened condensed milk
1 large bag (14 ounces) sweetened flaked coconut

Preheat oven to 325 degrees. Cut up fruit, and chop pecans coarsely. Combine with milk and coconut, mixing with your hands. Pack into loaf pans lined with waxed paper. Bake 1 hour. Remove cake from oven, and turn out of pan. Peel off paper and cool cake on rack. Wrap in aluminum foil and store.

Caramel Icing

ROBERT AND SUE BURRIS | ALVARADO, JOHNSON COUNTY EC

1 cup sugar
½ cup brown sugar
⅔ cup milk
Pinch of salt
1 teaspoon vanilla extract
2–3 tablespoons butter

In a saucepan, boil sugars and milk to soft-ball stage. Boil 1 minute more. Remove from heat; add vanilla and butter. Stir to cool. Spread on cooled cake.

COOK'S NOTE: I cook this in an iron skillet, and it works great. It's delicious on any cake, especially spice cake. My grandmother gave me this one.

Shiny Chocolate Glaze

MRS. JAMES CAVE | ROBY, MIDWEST EC

2 squares (1 ounce each) semisweet baking chocolate
¼ cup butter
⅓ cup sugar
2 teaspoons cornstarch
¼ cup milk
1 teaspoon vanilla extract

Melt chocolate and butter in saucepan over low heat. In a small bowl, mix sugar and cornstarch; stir in milk. Add to chocolate mixture. Cook over medium heat to boiling, stirring constantly. Cook 2 minutes. Remove from heat and add vanilla. Drizzle over warm cake.

Cream Cheese Icing

PAULA MAYS | SEGUIN, GUADALUPE VALLEY EC

½ cup butter, softened
8 ounces cream cheese
1 teaspoon vanilla extract
1 box (16 ounces) powdered sugar
Chopped pecans

Cream together butter and cream cheese; add vanilla, and beat in sugar a little at a time, until of spreading consistency. Sprinkle top with chopped pecans.

Good Quick Frosting

GLADYS M. WILLIAMS | DEKALB, BOWIE-CASS EC

1 cup sugar
1 carton (8 ounces) sour cream
1 small container (8 ounces) whipped topping
1 teaspoon vanilla extract
1 can (7 ounces) sweetened flaked coconut

Blend all ingredients and spread on cooled cake. Refrigerate cake with this frosting on it.

Chocolate Cream Cheese Frosting

MRS. J.W. DAY JR. | FLOYDADA, LIGHTHOUSE EC

2 packages (4 ounces each) sweet baking chocolate squares
6 ounces cream cheese
2 tablespoons half-and-half
2 cups sifted powdered sugar
¼ teaspoon salt
1 teaspoon vanilla extract

Place chocolate in top of double boiler and set over hot water until melted. Cool slightly. Blend in cream cheese and cream. Add powdered sugar. Then add salt and vanilla. Blend until spreading consistency. Spread on tops and sides of cake. Makes about 2 cups.

Lemon Icing

MRS. C.W. VOELKEL | NORDHEIM, DE WITT COUNTY EC

5 level tablespoons flour
1 cup sugar
1 egg, beaten
⅓ cup lemon juice
⅔ cup water
2 teaspoons butter
1 teaspoon grated lemon zest
½ cup heavy whipping cream

Boil all ingredients except cream over low heat in a saucepan or double boiler, stirring constantly. Cool. In mixing bowl, whip cream until stiff peaks form. Fold whipped cream into cooled mixture.

Marshmallow Icing

MRS. C.W. VOELKEL | NORDHEIM, DE WITT COUNTY EC

2 egg whites
½ teaspoon cream of tartar
¼ cup sugar
1 teaspoon vanilla extract
½ cup light corn syrup

In a mixing bowl, beat egg whites with cream of tartar. Add sugar, vanilla and corn syrup. Mix until fluffy and use on cake.

COOK'S NOTE: This is very easy; needs no cooking and turns out well.

Seven-Minute Icing

MRS. HERMAN HAYNER | KARNACK, PANOLA-HARRISON EC

2 egg whites
⅓ cup water
1½ cups sugar
½ teaspoon cream of tartar
Flavoring as desired

Mix all ingredients in top of double boiler. Place over boiling water and beat with rotary egg beater or hand mixer while cooking. Beat until stiff enough to put cake layers together, approximately 7 minutes.

Fluffy White Frosting

MRS. J.S. SPRAGUE | LANEVILLE, RUSK COUNTY EC

1 cup milk
3 tablespoons flour
½ teaspoon salt
1 cup shortening
1 cup sugar
2 teaspoons vanilla extract
¼ teaspoon butter flavoring

In a saucepan over medium heat, cook milk, flour and salt until thick; stirring constantly. Let cool. In a bowl, cream shortening and sugar very well, and add flavorings. Combine with first mixture, beat well.

COOK'S NOTE: Makes a delicious frosting that will frost up to 3 9-inch layers.

Cointreau Frosted Brownies

LESLIE HOWLAND | AQUILLA, HILL COUNTY EC

1 box brownie mix
⅓ cup Cointreau
2 eggs
½ cup chopped pecans
FROSTING:
¼ cup butter, softened
¼ teaspoon salt
2 cups sifted powdered sugar, divided use
2 squares unsweetened chocolate, melted
1 egg yolk
¼ cup Cointreau

Preheat oven to 350 degrees. In a large bowl, combine brownie mix with other ingredients. Mix well, pour into greased square pan. Bake 25–30 minutes. Wait for brownies to cool before frosting them. For Frosting, combine butter, salt and ⅔ cup powdered sugar and mix well. Add chocolate, remaining sugar, egg yolk and Cointreau. Beat until smooth.

Butterscotch Pecan Squares

MRS. LEVI A. DEIKE | HYE, PEDERNALES EC

1 pound brown sugar
4 eggs
2 cups chopped pecans
2 cups flour
2 teaspoons baking powder
Pinch of salt
2 teaspoons vanilla extract

Preheat oven to 350 degrees. Put brown sugar in top of a double boiler and break eggs over it. Put over hot water and stir. Add pecans. Stir in dry ingredients and vanilla. Pour into greased and floured 10-by-15-inch jellyroll pan. Bake 20 minutes. Cool slightly and cut into squares.

COOK'S NOTE: You could substitute old-fashioned rolled oats for the pecans.

Choco-Chip Bites

ESTELLE WINNINGHAM | MULESHOE, BAILEY COUNTY EC

¾ cup butter, softened
1½ cups packed brown sugar, divided use
½ cup sugar
3 eggs, separated
1 teaspoon vanilla extract
2 cups sifted flour
1 teaspoon baking powder
¼ teaspoon baking soda
¼ teaspoon salt
1 small package (6 ounces) chocolate chips
1 cup sweetened flaked coconut
¾ cup coarsely chopped nuts

Preheat oven to 350 degrees. Blend butter, ½ cup brown sugar, sugar, egg yolks and vanilla. Beat 2 minutes on medium speed with mixer or 300 strokes by hand, scraping bowl constantly. Sift in dry ingredients and stir into creamed mixture until thoroughly mixed. Spread or pat dough into greased 9-by-13-inch pan. Sprinkle with chocolate chips, coconut and nuts. In a separate bowl, beat egg white until frothy; add 1 cup brown sugar, and beat until stiff, but not dry. Spread on top of chocolate-coconut-nut mixture. Bake 35–40 minutes. Cool and cut into bars.

Easy Fudge Squares

MRS. DANIEL HEIDEKE | SEGUIN, GUADALUPE VALLEY EC

½ cup butter
2 squares unsweetened baking chocolate
1 cup sugar
2 eggs
¾ cup flour
1 teaspoon vanilla extract
½ cup chopped pecans

Preheat oven to 350 degrees. In an 8-by-8-inch pan, melt butter and chocolate. Add the sugar and mix. Cool slightly. Add the eggs and mix well. Stir in flour, vanilla and pecans. Bake 20–25 minutes. Cut into squares and serve topped with ice cream or whipped cream, if desired.

COOK'S NOTE: You can substitute 8 tablespoons cocoa powder plus 4 teaspoons butter for the baking chocolate.

Apple Brownies

BELINDA VINKLAREK | FLATONIA, FAYETTE EC

⅔ cup butter, softened
1 cup brown sugar
1 cup sugar
2 eggs
1 teaspoon vanilla extract
1½ cups flour
2 teaspoons baking powder
¼ teaspoon salt
1 teaspoon cinnamon
1 cup chopped apples
½ cup chopped nuts (optional)

Preheat oven to 350 degrees. In a large bowl, mix butter, sugars, eggs and vanilla. Mix in flour, baking powder, salt and cinnamon. Stir in apples and nuts. Spread in greased 9-by-9-inch pan. Bake 35–40 minutes.

Simply Terrific Brownies

MRS. SAM HOUSTON | SPUR, DICKENS COUNTY EC

1 package chocolate buttercream frosting mix, divided use
2 cups graham cracker crumbs
¼ cup powdered sugar
½ cup butter, melted
1 can (14 ounces) sweetened condensed milk
2 cups sweetened flaked coconut
6 bars (1.55 ounces each) milk chocolate

Preheat oven to 350 degrees. In a 9-by-13-inch pan, combine ⅓ cup firmly packed dry frosting mix, graham cracker crumbs, sugar and butter. Stir with fork until well mixed. Press firmly onto bottom of pan. Combine remaining frosting mix, milk and coconut in bowl and blend well. Spread over crumb mixture. Bake 22–27 minutes, until edges begin to pull from sides of pan. Remove from oven; place candy bars over top at once. Let stand 5 minutes, until candy melts, then spread evenly over top. Cool completely. Cut into bars. Makes about 40 bars.

COOK'S NOTE: Milk chocolate frosting mix may be substituted if desired. Walnuts or pecans may also be added, if desired.

Fig Squares

MRS. BRYAN A. ERICKSON | CLIFTON, ERATH COUNTY EC

½ cup butter, softened
1¾ cups brown sugar
4 eggs, well beaten
1 teaspoon grated orange zest
1 teaspoon grated lemon zest
2 cups chopped figs or dates
1 cup chopped nuts
1½ cups sifted flour
1 teaspoon baking powder
½ teaspoon salt

Preheat oven to 325 degrees. In a large bowl, cream butter with brown sugar. Add eggs; mix well. Stir in lemon and orange zest, figs and nuts. Sift together dry ingredients, then blend into batter. Pour into greased 9-by-13-inch pan. Bake 50–55 minutes. Cut into squares and serve warm with ice cream or creamy hard sauce. It may also be iced with cream frosting.

Banana Squares

MRS. TED SORRELLS | SILVER, LONE WOLF EC

1 cup butter, softened
1 cup light brown sugar
1 egg
1 teaspoon vanilla extract
1 cup mashed bananas
1 teaspoon baking powder
¼ teaspoon salt
¾ cup sweetened flaked coconut
1¼ cups flour
TOPPING:
1 tablespoon sweetened flaked coconut
1 tablespoon butter, melted

Preheat oven to 325 degrees. In a large bowl, blend butter, sugar, egg and vanilla. Add mashed bananas. Sift dry ingredients; add to other mixture. Stir in coconut. Turn into greased 9-by-13-inch pan. For Topping, toss coconut in melted butter and sprinkle over batter. Bake about 45 minutes. Cut into bars.

Double-Chocolate Crumble Bars

THERESA MADDUX | LOVELADY, HOUSTON COUNTY EC

½ cup butter, softened
¾ cup sugar
2 eggs
1 teaspoon vanilla extract
¾ cup flour
½ cup chopped pecans
2 tablespoons unsweetened cocoa powder
¼ teaspoon baking powder
¼ teaspoon salt
2 cups miniature marshmallows
TOPPING:
1 small package (6 ounces) semisweet chocolate chips
1 cup creamy peanut butter
1½ cups crispy rice cereal

Preheat oven to 350 degrees. In a mixing bowl, cream butter and sugar. Beat in eggs and vanilla; set aside. In a separate bowl, stir together flour, pecans, cocoa, baking powder and salt. Stir into butter mixture. Spread in bottom of a greased 9-by-13-inch pan. Bake 15–20 minutes, or until bars test done. Sprinkle marshmallows evenly on top; bake 3 minutes more. Cool. For Topping, combine chocolate chips and peanut butter in a small saucepan. Cook and stir over low heat until chocolate is melted. Stir in cereal. Spread mixture on top of cooled bars and chill. Cut in bars and refrigerate. Makes 3–4 dozen bars.

Caramel Chocolate Chip Brownies

BRIAN DYER | CONROE, MID-SOUTH EC

35 caramels (about a 10-ounce bag), unwrapped
1 small can (5 ounces) evaporated milk, divided use
1 box German chocolate cake mix
¾ cup butter, melted
1 small package (6 ounces) chocolate chips
1 cup chopped pecans

Preheat oven to 350 degrees. Melt caramels in ⅓ cup evaporated milk in microwave. In a bowl, stir together dry cake mix with remaining milk and butter. Grease a 9-by-13-inch glass pan. Spread half the batter in the pan and bake 6 minutes. Remove from oven and spread with melted caramels. Sprinkle on chocolate chips and chopped nuts. Top with remaining batter and bake 20 minutes more. Cool and cut into squares. Makes 32 brownies.

COOK'S NOTE: This recipe was Reserve Champion Homemaking at 1988 Montgomery County Fair and sold at auction for $1,050.

Coconut Squares

MRS. CLYDE SELJOS | CLIFTON, ERATH COUNTY EC

½ cup butter, softened
1 cup flour
½ cup brown sugar
TOPPING:
1 cup brown sugar
2 eggs
½ teaspoon salt
2 tablespoons flour
½ teaspoon baking powder
1 teaspoon vanilla extract
1 can (7 ounces) sweetened flaked coconut
1½ cups chopped pecans

Preheat oven to 375 degrees. In a bowl, combine butter, flour and brown sugar and pat into an 8-by-12-inch pan. Bake 10 minutes. For Topping, mix all ingredients and pour over first mixture. Bake an additional 15 minutes.

Pecan Torte Cookies

DELORES NEVERS | SAN ANTONIO, BANDERA EC

1 cup butter, softened
2 cups flour, divided use
1 pound brown sugar, divided use
4 eggs
2 teaspoons baking powder
2 cups chopped pecans
1 teaspoon vanilla extract

Preheat oven to 350 degrees. In a bowl, combine butter, 2 cups flour (less 4 tablespoons) and ½ cup brown sugar. Pat into well-greased jellyroll pan and bake 15 minutes. In a separate bowl, mix eggs, rest of brown sugar, baking powder, 4 tablespoons flour, pecans and vanilla. Spread on top of first mixture and bake 25 minutes more.

Honey Bars

MRS. DELVIN BEUTNAGEL | SEGUIN, GUADALUPE VALLEY EC

1 cup brown sugar
2 egg whites
1 cup pecans
¾ cup flour
½ teaspoon baking powder
2 teaspoons vanilla extract

Preheat oven to 350 degrees. In a mixing bowl, beat brown sugar and egg whites together until shiny. Fold in the rest of the ingredients. Line a 9-by-13-inch pan with waxed paper, and put batter in. Bake about 20–25 minutes.

Lemon Squares

MRS. ERNEST E. LOCKLAR | MIDLAND, CAP ROCK EC

CRUST:
1 cup flour
½ cup butter, softened
¼ cup sugar
TOPPING:
2 eggs, beaten
2 tablespoons flour
½ tablespoon baking powder
1 cup sugar
2 tablespoons lemon juice
Zest of 1 lemon

Preheat oven to 350 degrees. Grease bottom and sides of 9-by-9-inch pan. For Crust, mix flour, butter and sugar in a small bowl, and spread into bottom of pan. Bake 15 minutes. In a separate bowl, stir eggs with flour, baking powder, sugar, lemon juice and zest. Pour over crust. Bake 25 minutes longer or till light brown. Dust with powdered sugar. Cut in squares.

Orange Slice Squares

MRS. LANELL NEUMANN | BIG FOOT, MEDINA EC

4 eggs, well beaten
2 cups brown sugar
1 tablespoon cold water
2 cups flour
¼ teaspoon cinnamon
⅛ teaspoon salt
1 cup chopped nuts
1 cup chopped candy orange slices

Preheat oven to 350 degrees. In a mixing bowl, beat eggs until fluffy. Add brown sugar, then cold water. In a separate bowl, sift flour, cinnamon and salt, then add to first mixture and mix well. Fold in nuts and orange slices. Pour into a greased, 9-by-13-inch pan. Bake 18 minutes, or until done.

Mexican Chews

MRS. E.J. GROSSMAN | NEDERLAND, JASPER-NEWTON EC

4 eggs
1 pound brown sugar
1 teaspoon salt
4 teaspoons baking powder
2 cups flour
2 cups pecans
1 teaspoon vanilla extract
Powdered sugar

Preheat oven to 350 degrees. Beat eggs and brown sugar over low heat in a saucepan until thin, like syrup, about 15 minutes. Remove from heat; stir in dry ingredients, pecans and vanilla. Bake in greased and floured 9-by-13-inch pan about 35 minutes. Cool and sprinkle powdered sugar on top.

Coffee Bars

MRS. A.K. WYBORNY | MABANK, NEW ERA EC

1 cup golden raisins
½ teaspoon cinnamon
⅔ cup hot coffee
1 cup sugar
⅔ cup butter, softened
2 eggs, beaten
1½ cups flour
½ teaspoon baking powder
½ teaspoon baking soda
½ teaspoon salt
GLAZE:
Coffee
1 cup powdered sugar

Preheat oven to 350 degrees. Combine raisins, cinnamon and coffee; let stand. In a mixing bowl, cream sugar and butter; add eggs and mix well. In a separate bowl, combine flour, baking powder, soda and salt. Gradually add to creamed mixture. Add raisin mixture and blend. Spread batter in greased 10-by-15-inch jellyroll pan. Bake 20–25 minutes. While warm, spread with Glaze: Add enough coffee to powdered sugar for a thin consistency. Cut when cool.

COOK'S NOTE: Always use golden raisins.

Pecan Pie Bars

SHIRLEY LATHAM | EVADALE, JASPER-NEWTON EC

2 cups flour
1 cup brown sugar
½ cup butter
½ cup margarine
1 cup light corn syrup
5 eggs
¾ cup sugar
Dash of salt
1 teaspoon vanilla extract
1 cup pecan pieces

Preheat oven to 350 degrees. In a large bowl, combine flour and brown sugar. Cut in butter and margarine until it makes coarse crumbs. Press into a 9-by-13-inch pan. Bake 10 minutes, until golden. Remove from oven and reduce heat to 275 degrees. Combine syrup, eggs, sugar, salt, vanilla and pecans. Pour over baked crumb mixture. Bake 50 minutes, or until center sets.

Easy-Cheesy Lemon Bars

MRS. ROGER FOUSE | DOUGLASSVILLE, BOWIE-CASS EC

1 box lemon cake mix
½ cup butter, melted
3 eggs, divided use
1 package lemon frosting mix
8 ounces cream cheese

Preheat oven to 350 degrees. Grease bottom only of 9-by-13-inch pan. In a large bowl, combine cake mix, butter and 1 egg. Stir until moist. Pat into pan. In a separate bowl, blend frosting mix into cream cheese; reserve ½ cup for frosting baked bars. Add 2 eggs to remaining frosting mixture. Beat 3–5 minutes at high speed. Spread over cake mix. Bake 30–40 minutes. Cool and frost. Cut into bars. Refrigerate leftovers. Makes about 36 bars.

Scotchies

WENDY HENDERSHOT | ROGERS, BARTLETT EC

½ cup butter, melted
1¼ cups brown sugar
2 eggs
1 cup flour
1 teaspoon baking powder
½ teaspoon salt
1 teaspoon vanilla extract
1 cup chopped nuts
Raisins (optional)
Chocolate chips (optional)

Preheat oven to 350 degrees. In a large bowl, mix together the butter, brown sugar and eggs. In a separate bowl, sift together flour, baking powder and salt, then stir into the sugar mixture. Blend in the vanilla and nuts. Add raisins and/or chocolate chips, if desired. Spread in greased 9-by-9-inch pan. Bake 30 minutes.

Apricot Bars

MRS. R.H. SCHMUCK | MONTGOMERY, MIDWEST EC

8 ounces dried apricots
1 cup butter, softened
½ cup sugar
2⅔ cup flour, divided use
1 teaspoon baking powder
½ teaspoon salt
4 eggs
2 cups brown sugar
3 teaspoons vanilla extract
1 cup chopped nuts

Preheat oven to 350 degrees. Cover dried apricots with water in a pan and cook 8 minutes; drain, chop and set aside. In a bowl, mix butter, sugar and 2 cups flour. Press into a 9-by-13-inch pan. Bake 25 minutes. In a separate bowl, mix together ⅔ cup flour, baking powder and salt. In a mixing bowl, beat eggs and then stir in brown sugar plus flour mixture, vanilla and chopped nuts. Mix well and fold in the cooked, chopped apricots. Pour over the baked layer and bake at least 30 minutes longer (test for firmness). Cut into squares. Also freezes well and stays moist.

Pumpkin Bars

MRS. MILBURN CARROLL | CROWELL, SOUTHWEST RURAL EA

4 eggs, beaten
1 cup vegetable oil
2 cups sugar
1 cup canned pumpkin
2 cups flour
½ teaspoon salt
2 teaspoons cinnamon
1 teaspoon baking soda
1 teaspoon baking powder
1 teaspoon vanilla extract
FROSTING:
8 ounces cream cheese
½ cup plus 1 tablespoon butter, softened
3 cups powdered sugar
1 teaspoon vanilla extract
2 teaspoons milk
1 cup chopped nuts

Preheat oven to 350 degrees. In a large bowl, mix eggs, oil, sugar and pumpkin together. In a separate bowl, combine dry ingredients, then add to first mixture. Stir in vanilla. Pour into a greased and floured 9-by-13-inch pan. Bake 20 minutes. For Frosting, mix all ingredients except nuts in a large bowl until smooth. Frost bars while warm and sprinkle nuts over Frosting.

Aunt Frankie's Old-Time Tea Cakes

JANIE W. BEST | AUSTIN, PEDERNALES EC

2 cups sugar
1 cup shortening
2 eggs, beaten, plus whole milk to equal 1 cup
2 teaspoons vanilla extract
4–5 cups flour, divided use
2 heaping teaspoons baking powder
Pinch of salt

Preheat oven to 350 degrees. In a mixing bowl, beat sugar and shortening together. Add egg-milk mixture and vanilla; set aside. Blend 2 cups flour with baking powder and salt. Combine with creamed mixture and add more flour, enough to make a soft dough. Refrigerate dough until chilled, about 1 hour. Roll out to ¼-inch thick and cut with biscuit cutter. Sprinkle with sugar. Place on greased cookie sheet and bake 12–15 minutes.

COOK'S NOTE: These are the cookies Aunt Frankie baked for everyone in town. Everyone remembers her for her tea cakes.

Seven-Layer Cookies

MARY MCCREIGHT | HILLSBORO, HILL COUNTY EC

½ cup butter
1 cup graham cracker crumbs
1 cup sweetened flaked coconut
1 small package (6 ounces) chocolate morsels
1 small package (6 ounces) butterscotch morsels
1 can (14 ounces) sweetened condensed milk
1 cup finely chopped pecans

Preheat oven to 325 degrees. Melt butter in a 9-by-13-inch baking dish. Add other ingredients in layers in order listed. Bake about 30 minutes. Let cool in pan and cut into squares.

COOK'S NOTE: Pecans stay on better if you press them down lightly just before baking.

Olga's Icebox Cookies

ELIZABETH HOWARD | BAY CITY, JACKSON EC

1 cup butter, softened
½ cup brown sugar
2 cups sugar
2 eggs
1 tablespoon vanilla extract
4 cups flour
3 teaspoons baking powder
½ teaspoon salt
Beaten egg for top

Preheat oven to 425 degrees. In a mixing bowl, cream butter, brown sugar and sugar. Add eggs and beat well; add vanilla. In a separate bowl, sift together flour, baking powder and salt. Add to egg mixture and beat well. Shape into rolls about 1½ inches in diameter. Wrap in waxed paper. Chill until firm enough to slice. Brush tops with beaten egg and decorate as desired with sprinkles, colored sugars, nuts, etc. Bake 6 minutes.

COOK'S NOTE: I grew up with this cookie; the recipe was given to my mother in Lakeport, California, by Olga Gruwell. We wrapped them in cellophane, tied with curling ribbon, and hung as ornaments from the tree (packages of 4 or 5 cookies). I include them as gifts to friends and always leave a plateful for Santa.

Chinese New Year Cookies

MRS. JOHN GALLAHER | CIBOLO, GUADALUPE VALLEY EC

1 small package (6 ounces) chocolate chips
1 small package (6 ounces) butterscotch chips
1 small can (5 ounces) crispy chow mein noodles
¾ cup cocktail peanuts

Melt chips in double boiler over hot water. Remove from heat; add noodles and nuts. Mix thoroughly and drop by the teaspoonful on waxed paper. Let cool. Another package of butterscotch chips may be used instead of chocolate chips.

Oatmeal Cookies

MRS. EDWIN MOELLER | ROWENA, COLEMAN COUNTY EC

1 cup shortening
1 cup sugar (or ¼ cup honey and ¾ cup sugar)
2 eggs
1½ cups flour
Pinch of salt
¾ teaspoon baking soda
2 cups old-fashioned rolled oats
1 cup raisins
1 cup pecans

Preheat oven to 375 degrees. In a large bowl, mix all ingredients until stiff. Drop by the spoonful on greased cookie sheet and bake 12–15 minutes.

Vanilla Wafers

JEANNIE OWENS | COVINGTON, HILL COUNTY EC

1 cup shortening
2 cups sugar
3 eggs
3 cups flour
1 teaspoon salt
½ cup milk
1 teaspoon vanilla extract

Preheat oven to 350 degrees. In a large bowl, mix shortening, sugar and eggs. Add remaining ingredients and mix well. Drop by the teaspoonful onto a greased cookie sheet. Bake until brown on bottom and around edge.

West Texas Peanut Butter Cookies

MRS. MARVIN STIEWERT | HASKELL, STAMFORD EC

1 box yellow cake mix
1 cup peanut butter
½ cup vegetable oil
2 tablespoons water
2 eggs

Preheat oven to 350 degrees. In a large bowl, combine all ingredients and mix well. Drop by the teaspoon onto an ungreased cookie sheet. Press a crisscross on each cookie with fork prongs that have been dipped in water. Bake 10–12 minutes, until golden. Cool on cookie sheet for about 1 minute, then remove to rack to finish cooling. Makes 4–5 dozen 2½-inch cookies.

Peanut Butter Cookies

MRS. WAYNE TAYLOR | CLYDE, TAYLOR EC

1 cup peanut butter
1 cup shortening
2½ cups flour
2 teaspoons baking soda
2 eggs
1 cup brown sugar
1 cup sugar
1 teaspoon vanilla extract

Preheat oven to 375 degrees. In a large bowl, mix all ingredients. Drop by the spoonful onto cookie sheet and mash down with a fork. Bake 12 minutes. Yields 6½ dozen 2-inch cookies.

Peanut Butter and Jelly Cookies

H. TICE | LUBBOCK, SOUTH PLAINS EC

1 cup shortening
1 cup sugar
1 cup peanut butter
1 cup jelly
2 eggs
1 teaspoon vanilla extract
2 teaspoons baking soda
¼ teaspoon salt
3¼ cups flour

In a large bowl, cream shortening and sugar. Add peanut butter, jelly, eggs and vanilla, then add dry ingredients and mix well. Chill dough. Drop by spoonfuls onto a cookie sheet. Cookies may be pressed flat with a fork dipped in water. Bake 12 minutes, or until brown.

Peanut Brittle Cookies

MRS. FANTON HOEHN | VALLEY VIEW, DENTON COUNTY EC

1 cup light corn syrup
1 cup brown sugar
½ cup sugar
1½ cups peanut butter
5 cups whole grain cereal flakes
½ cup salted peanuts

In a large saucepan, heat sugars with syrup until sugars melt. Remove from heat. Add peanut butter, cereal and peanuts. Stir together. Drop by spoonfuls on wax paper. Makes 5 dozen.

Grandma's Brown Sugar Cookies

JOY LOHMER | CLIFTON, ERATH COUNTY EC

1 pound light brown sugar
1 cup shortening
2 eggs
2 cups flour
1 teaspoon baking soda
1 teaspoon cinnamon
½ teaspoon allspice
½ teaspoon nutmeg

Preheat oven to 325 degrees. In a large bowl, cream brown sugar and shortening. Add eggs. In a separate bowl, sift all dry ingredients together, then add them to creamed mixture. Drop dough by the tablespoonful onto cookie sheet and flatten. Bake 15 minutes.

COOK'S NOTE: These cookies were always in grandma's cookie jar. Whenever the grandchildren and great-grandchildren visited, my grandma would bake a fresh batch. They are great for dunking in milk or coffee.

No-Bake Cookies

MRS. T.W. ETCHISON | MERIDIAN, ERATH COUNTY EC

½ cup butter
¾ cup sugar
1 cup chopped dates
2 eggs
1 cup chopped nuts
1 teaspoon vanilla extract
1 cup crispy rice cereal
Sweetened flaked coconut

In a large pan, melt butter. Add sugar, dates and well-beaten eggs and cook 10 minutes or until thick, stirring often. Remove from heat and add nuts, vanilla and cereal. Spread coconut onto a plate. Drop dough by spoonfuls onto coconut and roll in balls.

COOK'S NOTE: The coconut may be colored to carry out a color scheme.

No-Bake Quick Chocolate Cookies

MRS. J.W. HOWARD | HASKELL, STAMFORD EC

2 cups sugar
½ cup butter
5 tablespoons cocoa powder
½ cup milk
½ cup peanut butter
3 cups quick-cooking oats

In a large pan over low heat, cook sugar, butter, cocoa and milk slowly until sugar is melted. Bring to boil and boil 1 minute. Remove from heat and add peanut butter, stirring until melted, and then add oats. Mix until all oats are coated. Drop while hot by the teaspoonful on waxed paper. Cookies will set firmly when cool. Makes approximately 4 dozen.

COOK'S NOTE: My kids call them "candy-cookies."

Oatmeal Crispies

MRS. FRANK POPLAWSKI | ENNIS, NAVARRO COUNTY EC

1 cup shortening
1 cup brown sugar
1 cup sugar
2 eggs
1 teaspoon vanilla extract
1 teaspoon baking soda
3 cups quick-cooking oats
1½ cups flour
½ cup chopped pecans

In a large bowl, cream shortening and sugars. Add eggs and vanilla. Add dry ingredients and mix. Form dough into rolls 2 inches in diameter. Wrap in foil. Chill thoroughly. Cut into ¼-inch thick slices. Bake at 350 degrees 10 minutes.

Almond Crescents

MRS. JAMES A. NOEL | BAY CITY, JACKSON EC

1 cup butter
½ cup sugar
1 tablespoon milk
1 teaspoon vanilla extract
2 cups flour
½ cup chopped almonds
Powdered sugar

Preheat oven to 350 degrees. In a large bowl, cream together butter and sugar. Add milk and vanilla. Mix in flour and chopped almonds. Shape into crescents on ungreased cookie sheet and bake 18 minutes. Roll in powdered sugar. Makes 4 dozen.

Pecan Ice Box Cookies

MRS. E.D. MCDOWELL | PEACOCK, DICKENS EC

2 cups brown sugar
1 cup butter
2 eggs
3¾ cups flour
1 teaspoon salt
1 teaspoon baking soda
1 cup pecans
1 teaspoon vanilla extract

In a large bowl, mix together all ingredients and work into a stiff dough. Make into oblong rolls and wrap with waxed paper. Put into refrigerator and let set 2–3 hours before baking. Slice into ½-inch slices. Flatten with fork dipped in flour. Bake at 350 degrees 10 minutes.

Fudge Cookies

HELEN F. MUMS | LA GRANGE, FAYETTE EC

1 large package (12 ounces) chocolate chips
¼ cup butter
1 can (14 ounces) sweetened condensed milk
1 cup flour
1 teaspoon vanilla extract
2 cups chopped nuts

Preheat oven to 350 degrees. Combine chocolate chips, butter and milk in a saucepan. Heat until the chocolate chips are melted. Add flour, vanilla and nuts; mix well. Drop by the teaspoonful onto ungreased cookie sheet. Bake 10 minutes.

COOK'S NOTE: A favorite with children of all ages! Quick and easy and as near to actual "fudge" as you can get in a cookie!

Aunt Ada's Old-Time Raisin Cookies

LONITA KUNKEL | OLNEY, FORT BELKNAP EC

¾ cup butter
1½ cups brown sugar
3 eggs
2 tablespoons molasses
1 tablespoon baking soda
2½ cups sifted flour
1 cup raisins
1 cup chopped nuts

Preheat oven to 350 degrees. In a large bowl, cream butter and brown sugar. Add the eggs and mix well. In a small bowl, stir together molasses and soda. Combine with first mixture. Add the flour. Stir in the raisins and nuts. Drop by the teaspoonful onto greased cookie sheet. Bake 12 minutes.

Doc's Molasses Cookies

MRS. J.W. DAY | FLOYDADA, LIGHTHOUSE EC

⅓ cup shortening
⅓ cup packed brown sugar
⅔ cup molasses
2 eggs
2¾ cups sifted flour
1 teaspoon baking soda
1 teaspoon salt
1 teaspoon ginger
2 teaspoons cinnamon

In a large bowl, mix shortening, brown sugar, molasses and eggs thoroughly. In a separate bowl, sift together flour, soda, salt, ginger and cinnamon. Add to sugar mixture. Chill dough. Preheat oven to 375 degrees. Roll out dough and cut into desired shapes. Place cookies 1 inch apart on lightly greased cookie sheet. Bake 8–10 minutes or until no impression remains when touched lightly with a finger. Makes about 5 dozen.

Bake While You Sleep Cookies

KAY KOCH | BLANCO, PEDERNALES EC

2 egg whites
⅔ cup sugar
1 cup chocolate chips
1 teaspoon vanilla extract

Preheat oven to 350 degrees. In a mixing bowl, beat egg whites until foamy. Add sugar gradually and beat until stiff. Fold in chips and vanilla. Put foil over a cookie sheet and drop by the teaspoonful onto the foil. Put cookies in oven and IMMEDIATELY turn off oven. Leave in oven overnight, or 4 hours.

Breakfast in a Cookie

FRANCES MALAER | ABBOTT, HILL COUNTY EC

⅓ cup whole bran cereal
¼ cup orange juice
¾ cup butter, softened
¼ cup sugar
1 egg
¼ cup honey
1½ teaspoons vanilla extract
1 cup unbleached flour
1 teaspoon baking powder
½ teaspoon baking soda
½ teaspoon salt
⅓ cup nonfat dry milk
2 teaspoons grated orange zest
1 cup old-fashioned rolled or quick-cooking oats
   (not instant)
1 cup finely chopped walnuts, or other nuts
1 cup raisins

Preheat oven to 350 degrees. In a small bowl, combine bran cereal and orange juice; set aside. In another bowl, cream butter and sugar. Add egg and beat until light. Blend in honey, vanilla and orange-bran mixture. In a separate bowl, combine flour, baking powder, baking soda, salt, dry milk, orange zest, oats, nuts and raisins. Stir dry mixture into creamed mixture. Drop by the level teaspoonful onto greased cookie sheets, about 2 inches apart. Bake 10–12 minutes. Makes 3½–4 dozen.

COOK'S NOTE: This cookie is excellent for breakfast for people who are in a hurry; just grab a few and eat on the way to work or school. May also be eaten crumbled in bowl with milk. If you have any left, freeze them.

Monster Chip Cookies

LANELLE KASPER | SHINER, GUADALUPE VALLEY EC

3 squares (1 ounce each) semisweet baking chocolate
1¼ cups pecan halves, divided use
1 cup plus 2 tablespoons flour
½ teaspoon baking powder
½ cup butter, softened
⅓ cup peanut butter
½ cup sugar
½ cup firmly packed brown sugar
1 egg
1 teaspoon vanilla extract

Preheat oven to 325 degrees. Lightly grease 2 large cookie sheets. Chop chocolate into thumbnail-sized chunks; set aside. Chop 1 cup pecan halves and set aside remaining ½ cup. In a small bowl, stir flour and baking powder together. In a mixing bowl, beat together butter, peanut butter and sugars until light and fluffy. Beat in egg and vanilla. Stir in flour mixture and pecans. Using ¼-cup measure, shape dough into 12 evenly spaced mounds. Push chocolate chunks and pecan halves into mounds. Bake 15–17 minutes. Let cool on cookie sheets to firm up. Place on racks to cool completely.

Graham Cracker Cookies

PENNY NICHOLS | PICKTON, FARMERS EC

1½ cups butter
1 cup sugar
1 egg
½ cup milk
1½ cups crushed graham crackers
Whole graham crackers
1 teaspoon vanilla extract
1 cup sweetened flaked coconut
1 cup chopped nuts
ICING:
¼ cup butter
2 tablespoons evaporated milk
8 ounces powdered sugar (½ of a 16-ounce box)
½ teaspoon vanilla extract

In a large saucepan over medium heat, mix the butter, sugar, egg and milk and boil 2 minutes, stirring constantly. Remove from heat and add the crushed graham crackers, vanilla, coconut and chopped nuts. Cover the bottom of a 9-by-13-inch (or larger) pan with whole graham crackers. Cover the crackers with the above filling. Add another layer of crackers and press down. Cover with Icing. For Icing, mix all ingredients together, spread over cookies, cover with foil and refrigerate overnight before cutting into bars.

Chewy Oatmeal Cookies

CARMEN MUNIZ | FLOYDADA, LIGHTHOUSE EC

1 cup butter, softened
2 eggs
1 cup sugar
½ cup packed brown sugar
2 teaspoons vanilla extract
1½ cups flour
1 teaspoon baking soda
1 teaspoon salt
1 cup chopped nuts
2 cups quick-cooking oats
1½ cups raisins

Preheat oven to 375 degrees. Place butter, eggs, sugars and vanilla in a large mixing bowl. Beat until light and fluffy. Add the flour, baking soda, salt, nuts, oats and raisins. Blend all ingredients well. Drop by the teaspoonful onto an ungreased cookie sheet, 2 inches apart. Bake 8–10 minutes. Makes about 4 dozen cookies.

Chocolate Chip Oatmeal Cookies

HELEN HOLTZEN | BURKBURNETT, SOUTHWEST RURAL EA

1 cup shortening
1 cup brown sugar
1 cup sugar
2 eggs
1 teaspoon vanilla extract
2 cups flour
½ teaspoon baking powder
½ teaspoon salt
1 teaspoon baking soda
2 cups old-fashioned rolled oats
1 cup chocolate chips
1 cup chopped pecans

Preheat oven to 350 degrees. In a large bowl, cream shortening and sugars; add eggs and mix well. Add vanilla. In a separate bowl, sift flour, baking powder, salt and soda together, and add to first mixture. Mix in oats, chips and pecans. Drop by the teaspoonful onto a greased cookie sheet. Bake 12–15 minutes.

COOK'S NOTE: The secret to good cookies is not to overbake them. Boys from 7 to 70 love these cookies.

Opal's Oatmeal Spice Cookies

PEGGY ROLLANS | SAN ANGELO, CONCHO VALLEY EC

1 cup shortening
1½ cups brown sugar
2 eggs, beaten
2 cups flour
½ teaspoon baking soda
1 teaspoon cinnamon
½ teaspoon ground cloves
1½ cups old-fashioned rolled oats
¼ cup buttermilk
½ cup pecan pieces
½ cup raisins

Preheat oven to 350 degrees. In a large bowl, cream shortening and sugar. Add eggs and mix well. In a separate bowl, sift flour, soda, cinnamon and cloves together. Stir dry ingredients into creamed mixture. Add oats and buttermilk. Stir in pecans and raisins. Drop by the teaspoonful onto a cookie sheet. Bake 11–12 minutes.

COOK'S NOTE: This recipe has been in our family for over 50 years.

Ginger Crisps

PAT CARROLL | PORT LAVACA, VICTORIA COUNTY EC

⅔ cup shortening
1⅓ cups sugar, divided use
1 egg
¼ cup molasses
2 cups sifted flour
1 teaspoon baking soda
1 teaspoon cinnamon
½ teaspoon ground cloves
1¼ teaspoons ground ginger
½ teaspoon salt
½ cup finely chopped nuts

Preheat oven to 350 degrees. In a mixing bowl, cream shortening and 1 cup sugar. Add egg and molasses. Beat well. In a separate bowl, sift together flour, soda, cinnamon, cloves, ginger and salt. Add sifted dry ingredients to creamed mixture. Add nuts. Mix well. Shape dough into balls about the size of a walnut and roll in the remaining ⅓ cup sugar. Place about 2 inches apart on greased cookie sheet. Do not flatten balls. Bake 15 minutes. Yields about 4½ dozen.

Texas Teatime Tassies

NEVA BOX | LONGVIEW, RUSK COUNTY EC

½ cup butter
3 ounces cream cheese
1 cup sifted flour
FILLING:
1 egg
1 cup brown sugar
1 tablespoon butter, softened
1 teaspoon vanilla extract
Dash of salt
1 cup pecan pieces

In a bowl, cream together cream cheese and butter; blend in flour. Chill about 30 minutes. Preheat oven to 325 degrees. Shape dough into 2 dozen 1-inch balls. Place in small muffin cups. Press dough onto bottom and sides of cups. For Filling, beat together egg, sugar, butter, vanilla and salt in a bowl until smooth. Place half the pecan pieces on top of dough in muffin cups. Divide Filling between muffin cups and top with remaining pecans. Bake about 25 minutes, or until Filling is set.

Peanut Blossoms

MRS. HOUSTON BARTLETT | BOVINA, DEAF SMITH COUNTY EC

½ cup shortening
½ cup peanut butter
½ cup brown sugar
1 egg
2 tablespoons milk
1 teaspoon vanilla extract
1¾ cups flour
1 teaspoon baking soda
½ teaspoon salt
36 Hershey's Kisses

Preheat oven to 375 degrees. In a large bowl, cream shortening, peanut butter and brown sugar. Add egg, milk and vanilla. In a separate bowl, sift together flour, soda and salt; blend dry ingredients into first mixture. Shape into balls; roll in sugar and place on an ungreased cookie sheet. Bake 5 minutes. Remove from oven and press a candy kiss on top of each ball. Return to oven for 2–5 minutes. Makes 3 dozen.

Pine Nut Cookies

MRS. HARRY A. TUBBS | POST, LYNTEGAR EC

4 large eggs
1½ cups sugar
¼ teaspoon grated lemon zest
3–4 drops anise oil
2½ cups flour, sifted
¼ teaspoon salt
¼ cup powdered sugar
1 cup pine nuts

Put eggs and sugar in top of a double boiler over hot water. Beat with hand mixer or whisk, stirring constantly until mixture is lukewarm. Remove from water, beat until foamy, and cool. Preheat oven to 325 degrees. Add lemon zest and anise oil to the cooled mixture; fold in flour and salt. Drop by the teaspoonful onto greased and floured cookie sheets. Sprinkle cookies with powdered sugar and lightly press pine nuts into them. Let stand 10 minutes. Bake about 10 minutes. Makes 5 dozen.

COOK'S NOTE: This is a good cookie for gift giving.

Ranger Cookies

MRS. WALTER NESLONEY | ROBSTOWN, NUECES EC

1 cup shortening
1 cup sugar
1 cup brown sugar
2 eggs
2 cups flour
1 teaspoon baking soda
½ teaspoon baking powder
½ teaspoon salt
2 cups old-fashioned rolled oats
1 cup sweetened flaked coconut
1 cup chopped dates
1 cup chopped nuts

Preheat oven to 350 degrees. In a large bowl, cream shortening, sugars and eggs. Add other ingredients. Mix and roll into small balls. Bake 15 minutes.

Sand Tarts

MRS. DANIEL HEIDEKE | SEGUIN, GUADALUPE VALLEY EC

1 cup butter, softened
¼ cup powdered sugar
2 cups sifted flour
1 teaspoon baking powder
1 teaspoon vanilla extract
1 cup finely chopped pecans

In a large bowl, cream butter and sugar until creamy. In a separate bowl, sift together flour and baking powder; stir into creamed mixture, blending thoroughly. Gradually stir in vanilla and pecans. Chill dough overnight or for several hours until firm. Preheat oven to 350 degrees. Shape dough into small roll-shaped cookies, about 2 inches long and ½ inches thick, and place on lightly greased cookie sheets. Bake 10–12 minutes, until golden brown. Roll baked cookies in additional powdered sugar for a frosted look. Makes about 5 dozen.

Molasses Crinkle Cookies

MRS. FRED MUEHLBRAD | BURTON, BLUEBONNET EC

¾ cup shortening
1 cup brown sugar
1 egg, beaten
¼ cup light molasses
2¼ cups flour
¼ teaspoon salt
2 teaspoons baking soda
1 teaspoon cinnamon
1 teaspoon ground ginger
½ teaspoon ground cloves
¼ cup sugar

In a large bowl, thoroughly cream shortening and brown sugar. Add egg and molasses; beat well. Add sifted dry ingredients except sugar and mix well. Chill thoroughly or overnight. Preheat oven to 350 degrees. Shape in balls the size of walnuts and dip 1 side in sugar. Place sugared side up on an ungreased cookie sheet, 2–3 inches apart. Bake 15 minutes. Makes about 3 dozen big cookies.

Coconut Drop Cookies

PAT CARROLL | PORT LAVACA, VICTORIA COUNTY EC

¼ cup butter, softened
½ cup sugar
1 egg
2 teaspoons baking powder
1 cup sifted flour
Pinch of salt
1½ cups sweetened flaked coconut

Preheat oven to 350 degrees. In a large bowl, cream butter and sugar together. Add egg and dry ingredients. Mix well. Stir in coconut. Drop by the teaspoonful onto a greased cookie sheet. Bake 8–10 minutes.

Cowboy Cookies

MRS. W.R. WIMBERLEY | YOAKUM, DEWITT COUNTY EC

1 cup shortening
1 cup sugar
1 cup firmly packed brown sugar
2 eggs
2 cups flour
1 teaspoon baking soda
½ teaspoon salt
½ teaspoon baking powder
1 teaspoon vanilla extract
2 cups old-fashioned rolled oats
1 small package (6 ounces) chocolate chips, or
    ½ cup sweetened flaked coconut, nuts or raisins

Preheat oven to 350 degrees. In a large bowl, cream shortening and sugars; add eggs and continue beating until fluffy. Add flour, soda, salt, baking powder and vanilla. Mix until well blended; stir in oats and chocolate chips (or coconut, nuts or raisins, by preference). Drop by the teaspoonful on a cookie sheet about 2 inches apart. Bake 12–13 minutes.

Mexican Wedding Cookies

REBA FINCH | CEE VEE, GATE CITY EC

1 cup butter, softened
¾ cup powdered sugar
2 cups sifted flour
1 teaspoon vanilla extract
1 cup finely chopped pecans
Powdered sugar

Preheat oven to 325 degrees. In a mixing bowl, beat butter until fluffy. Gradually add sugar, flour and vanilla. Mix well. Blend in pecans. Shape dough into 1-inch balls or crescents. Place on an ungreased cookie sheets about 1 inch apart. Bake 25 minutes, or until pale golden brown. Roll each cookie in additional powdered sugar 2 times while hot (first layer will soak in). Cool. Makes about 4 dozen cookies.

Sugar Cookies

MRS. W.W. RUMAGE | JACKSBORO, J-A-C EC

½ cup butter, softened
½ cup shortening
½ cup sugar, plus more for rolling
½ cup brown sugar
1 egg, beaten
1 teaspoon vanilla extract
2¼ cups flour
½ teaspoon salt
2 teaspoons cream of tartar
1 teaspoon baking soda

Preheat oven to 350 degrees. In a large bowl, cream butter, shortening and sugars together. Add the egg and vanilla. In a separate bowl, sift together the flour, salt, cream of tartar and soda; then sift two more times. Mix into creamed mixture. Roll into balls 1 inch or less. Roll in sugar and place on an ungreased cookie sheet. Press down with fork or flat-bottomed glass. Bake until lightly browned.

Sugar 'n Spice Cookies

MRS. HOUSTON BARTLETT | BOVINA, DEAF SMITH COUNTY EC

¾ cup shortening
1 cup sugar
1 egg
¼ cup molasses
2 cups sifted flour
2 teaspoon baking soda
¼ teaspoon salt
2 teaspoon cinnamon
¾ teaspoon ground cloves
¾ teaspoon ground ginger

Preheat oven to 375 degrees. In a large bowl, mix shortening, sugar, egg and molasses; then add dry ingredients. Mix thoroughly. Form into balls the size of walnuts. Place about 2 inches apart on a cookie sheet. Bake 10–12 minutes. Roll in powdered sugar while still warm. Makes 4–5 dozen.

Drop Sugar Cookies

MRS. J.W. DAY JR. | FLOYDADA, LIGHTHOUSE EC

1 cup butter, softened
⅔ cup packed brown sugar
⅔ cup sugar
2¼ cups flour
2 teaspoons baking soda
1 egg
½ teaspoon salt
2 tablespoons hot water
1 teaspoon vanilla extract

Preheat oven to 350 degrees. In a large bowl, mix all ingredients well and drop on a greased cookie sheet. Bake until golden brown.

Petticoat Tails

FRANCENE BROUN | TAHOKA, LYNTEGAR EC

5 cups flour
1 cup powdered sugar
1 pound (4 sticks) butter, softened (not margarine)

Into a large bowl, sift flour and sugar together several times. Knead in butter. Shape into 2 rolls and refrigerate overnight. Preheat oven to 350 degrees. Slice thinly and bake until lightly browned.

COOK'S NOTE: You can add nuts, cherries, orange peel and different flavors. This is a very versatile cookie.

Bourbon Balls

MINNIE N. MOORE | SPICEWOOD, PEDERNALES EC

2 cups finely crushed vanilla wafers
1 cup finely chopped nuts
1 cup powdered sugar, sifted, plus more for rolling
2 tablespoons cocoa powder
2 tablespoons light corn syrup
¼–½ cup bourbon or rum

In a large bowl, mix vanilla wafers, nuts, powdered sugar and cocoa. Work corn syrup into mixture. Add enough bourbon so that balls can be formed. Mold into balls with hands and roll in a generous amount of sifted powdered sugar.

COOK'S NOTE: These keep well in a tightly closed container in the refrigerator and make good Christmas gifts.

Fruit Cake Balls

MARY CARTER | CHANDLER, NEW ERA EC

1 can (14 ounces) sweetened condensed milk
1 pound dates, chopped
4 ounces candied cherries, chopped
4 cups coarsely chopped pecans
1 cup sweetened flaked coconut
2 teaspoons vanilla extract

Preheat oven to 300 degrees. Put all ingredients in a large mixing bowl. Mix together by hand. Roll into balls the size of a walnut. Bake on a greased cookie sheet 25 minutes.

COOK'S NOTE: You have to work with this to learn to make balls. If 1 should fall apart in baking, let it cool. It can easily be rolled again at that stage. A friend, Addie Martin, brought these to a Christmas luncheon in the early '70s. I've made them since for Christmas in preference to a fruitcake.

Walnut Sour Cream Fudge

JOANN ATCHLEY | TEAGUE, NAVASOTA VALLEY EC

2 cups sugar
½ cup sour cream
⅓ cup light corn syrup
2 tablespoons butter
¼ teaspoon salt
2 tablespoons vanilla extract,
    or rum or brandy extract
¼ cup candied cherries
1 cup coarsely chopped walnuts

Combine sugar, sour cream, corn syrup, butter and salt in saucepan. Bring to boil slowly, stirring until sugar dissolves. Boil, without stirring, over medium heat to 236 degrees on a candy thermometer or to soft-ball stage. Remove from heat and let stand 15 minutes. Do not stir. Add extract. Beat until mixture starts to lose its gloss, about 8 minutes. Stir in cherries and walnuts, and quickly pour into greased shallow pan. Cool and cut into squares.

Toasted Pecan Clusters

GWEN ELLIOTT | HUNTSVILLE, MID-SOUTH EC

3 tablespoons butter
3 cups pecan pieces
12 ounces chocolate or white almond bark
    candy coating

Preheat oven to 300 degrees. Melt butter in a 10-by-15-inch jellyroll pan. Add pecans to pan and toss in butter, then spread pecans evenly in pan. Bake 30 minutes, stirring and turning pecans every 10 minutes. Place candy coating in top of a double boiler; bring water to a boil. Reduce heat to low; cook until coating melts. Cool 2 minutes, add pecans and stir until coated. Drop by the rounded teaspoonful onto waxed paper. Cool completely. Makes 4 dozen.

COOK'S NOTE: My two daughters (ages 4 and 2) love helping make this candy at Christmas and delivering it to family, friends and neighbors as gifts.

Mexican Candy

SIBYL SEARS | RISING STAR, COMANCHE COUNTY EC

2 cups sugar
1 teaspoon baking soda
1 cup buttermilk
Pinch of salt
3¼ cups pecans, divided use

In a large kettle, cook first 4 ingredients briskly to 210 degrees on a candy thermometer. Stir and add 2½ cups pecans. Stir continuously until the thermometer reads 230 degrees. Remove from heat, cool slightly and add remaining pecans. Beat until thickened and creamy. Drop by the teaspoonful onto foil and cool.

COOK'S NOTE: This has been my favorite food gift at Christmastime.

Chocolate Bon-Bons

HELEN MAJORS | CLEBURNE, JOHNSON COUNTY EC

2 boxes (16 ounces each) powdered sugar
1 can (14 ounces) sweetened condensed milk
1 small package (7 ounces) sweetened flaked coconut
½ cup butter, melted
2 cups chopped pecans
¼ pound paraffin
1 small package (6 ounces) chocolate chips

In a large bowl, mix first 5 ingredients, roll into balls and place on a cookie sheet in refrigerator for 15–20 minutes. Melt paraffin and chocolate chips in double boiler. Dip balls of candy in this mixture and replace on the cookie sheet. Use toothpicks to dip candy. Reheat if mixture gets too thick.

Corn Cookies

LILLY F. BISKUP | BAY CITY, WHARTON COUNTY EC

1 cup sugar
1 cup corn syrup
1 cup crunchy peanut butter
10 cups corn flakes

Put sugar and corn syrup in saucepan and bring to boiling point. Add the peanut butter and stir until mixture is smooth. Pour over corn flakes and toss gently, then press into buttered pan. Allow to cool and then cut into squares.

Kisses

CHARLOTTE HELLESON | AQUILLA, HILL COUNTY EC

3 egg whites
1 cup sugar
1 teaspoon vanilla extract
Pinch of salt
1 cup chopped pecans

Preheat oven to 300 degrees. In a mixing bowl, beat egg whites until stiff. Add sugar, vanilla and salt. Then fold in nuts. Put by spoonfuls on greased foil over a cookie sheet. Bake until browned.

Date Loaf

LINDA FULLER | CALL, JASPER-NEWTON EC

8 ounces dates
Pinch of baking soda
3 cups sugar
1 cup milk
3 cups chopped pecans
Pinch of salt
1 teaspoon vanilla extract

Cut up dates and toss with soda. Put dates, sugar and milk in a saucepan over medium heat and cook to soft-ball stage, stirring constantly. Remove from heat and add pecans, salt and vanilla. Beat until smooth. Wrap in wet cheese cloth and roll into a log. Chill until firm enough to slice.

Nut Log

MRS. CHARLES ATCHLEY | WINDTHORST, J-A-C EC

½ cup butter
1 small package (6 ounces) chocolate chips
1 package (10 ounces) miniature marshmallows
1 box (18 ounces) crispy rice cereal
2 cups Spanish peanuts
2 cups chopped pecans
1 cup raisins
3 cups popped popcorn

Melt butter, chocolate chips and marshmallows together in top of double boiler. Mix rice cereal, Spanish peanuts, pecans, raisins and popcorn in a large bowl. Pour melted mixture over dry ingredients and mix thoroughly. Spoon the mixture into a used ½-gallon milk carton that has been cleaned and dried thoroughly. Pack tightly and put in refrigerator. When cool, peel carton off and slice.

Microwave Caramel Corn

CAROLYN CUNNINGHAM | LOCKNEY, LIGHTHOUSE EC

½ cup butter
1 cup firmly packed brown sugar
¼ cup dark corn syrup
¼ teaspoon salt
½ teaspoon vanilla extract
¼ teaspoon baking soda
10 cups popped popcorn
Peanuts (optional)

Combine butter, sugar, syrup and salt in 1½- to 2-quart microwavable dish. Bring the mixture to a boil in the microwave and cook on full power for 2 minutes. Remove from microwave; stir in vanilla and soda. Put popcorn in a paper grocery bag. Peanuts may be added. Pour syrup mixture over popcorn. Close bag and shake. Cook in bag on high in microwave for 1½ minutes. Shake bag and cook another 1½ minutes. May need another 1½ minutes, depending on microwave. Pour onto aluminum foil to let cool. Store in a tightly covered container.

Peanut Brittle

E.F. KOENIG | SAN ANTONIO, DEWITT COUNTY EC

2 cups sugar
1 cup light corn syrup
½ cup boiling water
3 cups raw peanuts
3 tablespoons butter
1 teaspoon vanilla extract
1 heaping teaspoon baking soda

Boil sugar, syrup and water until it spins a thread. Add peanuts and stir until nuts smell parched and syrup turns slightly dark. Add butter, vanilla and soda. Stir 1 minute and pour on buttered sheets to cool. Crack into pieces when cooled.

Nutty Noodle Clusters

PAMELA MONTGOMERY | AQUILLA, HILL COUNTY EC

1 large package (12 ounces) butterscotch chips
    or chocolate chips
2 cans (5 ounce each) chow mein noodles
2 cans (6 ounces each) cashews

Put chips in a pan to melt. When melted, quickly fold in noodles and nuts. Drop by the tablespoonful onto waxed paper. Put in refrigerator to chill.

Peanut Butter Fudge

MRS. S.G. APPLING | FLOYDADA, LIGHTHOUSE EC

2 cups sugar
⅔ cup milk
1 jar (7 ounces) marshmallow cream
1 cup peanut butter

In a saucepan over medium heat, combine sugar and milk. Cook, stirring constantly, to soft-ball stage. Remove from heat and stir in marshmallow cream and peanut butter. Pour into well-buttered dish and let set until firm.

Peanut Patties

MRS. EMMETT D. KING | TIPTON, SOUTHWEST RURAL EC

3 cups sugar
1 cup light corn syrup
1 cup water
1 pound raw Spanish peanuts
6 or more drops red food coloring
¼ cup butter
¼ teaspoon salt

Combine sugar, syrup and water in saucepan. Bring to boil over medium heat. Add peanuts and food coloring. Cook to hard-ball stage (260 degrees). Remove from heat and add butter and salt. Beat until mixture begins to thicken. Pour onto a greased cookie sheet or greased muffin tins. Cool, cut or break candy into pieces. Makes 2 dozen 2-inch patties, ¼-inch thick.

Pecan Clusters

MRS. CLYDE SELJOS | CLINTON, ERATH COUNTY EC

½ cup sugar
½ cup evaporated milk
1 tablespoon light corn syrup
1 package chocolate chips
1 cup pecans

Put sugar, milk and syrup in saucepan and bring to a boil. Let ingredients boil 2 minutes. Remove from heat and add chocolate chips and pecans; stir until chocolate melts. Drop by the teaspoonful onto waxed paper. Chill in refrigerator about 30 minutes, until firm.

Easy-Do-Pralines

MRS. V.G. FRENZEL | ROUND TOP, FAYETTE EC

1 small box (3.4 ounces) butterscotch instant
    pudding mix
1 cup sugar
½ cup brown sugar
½ cup evaporated milk
1 tablespoon butter
1½ cups chopped pecans

In a saucepan over low heat, combine first 5 ingredients and cook slowly until dissolved. Add pecans and boil slowly until candy reaches soft-ball stage. Remove from heat and beat until mixture thickens. Drop by the teaspoonful on waxed paper.

Butterscotch Candy

SHARON SIMPSON | VAN ALSTYNE, GRAYSON-COLLIN EC

3 small packages (6 ounces each) butterscotch chips
2 heaping tablespoons peanut butter
1 can peanuts (about 1½ cups)
1 can shoestring potatoes (about 4 ounces)

Melt butterscotch chips and peanut butter in double boiler; add peanuts and shoestring potatoes. Drop by the spoonful onto waxed paper.

Coconut Kisses

SHARON SIMPSON | VAN ALSTYNE, GRAYSON-COLLIN EC

½ cup butter
2 cups powdered sugar
3 cups sweetened flaked coconut
Hershey's Kisses

In a large saucepan, melt butter. Remove from heat and add sugar and coconut; mix well. Shape into balls. Make a little hole in the top of each ball and put a Kiss in the hole. Chill until firm.

Toffee

BETTY BOYD | BIVINS, BOWIE-CASS EC

1 cup butter (not margarine)
1 cup sugar
1 tablespoon light corn syrup
1 tablespoon water
5 Hershey's milk chocolate bars (1.55 ounces each)
Sliced almonds

Put butter, sugar, syrup and water into a cast iron skillet. Cook bubbling mixture, stirring constantly, until golden brown, approximately 12 minutes (300 degrees on candy thermometer). Spread out on a cookie sheet with a wooden spoon. Break Hershey's bars and spread on mixture while it's hot. Sprinkle almonds over this and press into mixture.

COOK'S NOTE: This is so simple, and it tastes as good as the bought version.

Stuffed Dates

DOROTHY CHAMBERLAND | WHITNEY, HILL COUNTY EC

Large whole dates
Pecan or other nut halves
Powdered sugar
Cherry halves

Remove seeds from dates. Insert nut halves. Roll in powdered sugar. Arrange on shallow dish. Place slice of cherry on each date.

Divinity

YVETTE RENÉE HAMETT | YOAKUM, COMANCHE COUNTY EC

2 egg whites
3 cups sugar
½ cup light corn syrup
½ cup water
1 teaspoon vanilla extract
½ cup pecans (optional)
½ cup cherries (optional)

In a large bowl, beat egg whites until stiff. In a saucepan over medium heat, cook sugar, syrup and water until soft-ball stage. Add ½ of cooked mixture to egg whites. Cook the remainder to crack or hard-ball stage. Add this to egg white mixture, and add vanilla, pecans and cherries. Beat until creamy. Drop by tablespoonfuls onto waxed paper and cool.

Easy Divinity

MRS. W.C. DAVIS | KOPPERL, JOHNSON COUNTY EC

2 cups sugar
⅔ cup water
1 jar (7 ounces) marshmallow cream
1 teaspoon vanilla extract
2 cups nuts (optional)

In a saucepan over medium heat, boil sugar and water until firm soft ball. Remove from heat and add marshmallow cream, vanilla and nuts, if desired. Blend well. Drop by the teaspoonful onto waxed paper or pour into buttered platter and cut into squares when cool.

Apricot Divinity

CYNTHIA THIGPEN | FARWELL, DEAF SMITH EC

4 cups sugar
1 cup light corn syrup
¾ cup water
⅛ teaspoon salt
3 egg whites
1 box (3 ounces) apricot Jell-O
1 teaspoon vanilla extract
½ cup chopped pecans

Combine sugar, corn syrup, water and salt in a 2-quart saucepan. Cook over medium heat until mixture reaches hard-ball stage (260 degrees). While syrup cooks, beat egg whites with apricot gelatin until whites become very stiff. Gradually pour hot syrup over egg whites. Continue beating at a high speed until mixture is thick and candy starts to gloss, about 12 minutes. Add vanilla and nuts to candy, and drop by the teaspoonful onto waxed paper. Makes 7 dozen pieces.

Easy Pecan Fudge

MRS. A.C. MINZENMAYER | WINTERS, COLEMAN COUNTY EC

3 small packages (6 ounces each) semisweet
    chocolate chips
1 teaspoon vanilla extract
1 can (14 ounces) sweetened condensed milk
¾ cup chopped pecans

Butter an 8-inch pan. Melt chocolate chips in a saucepan. Stir in remaining ingredients. Pour into buttered pan. Refrigerate 2 hours, or until firm. Makes 25 squares.

Puppy Chow

BILLIE JAKUBICEK | SEYMOUR, B-K EC

1 large package (12 ounces) semisweet
    chocolate chips
1 cup butter
¾ cup peanut butter
1 box (12 ounces) Rice Chex cereal
4 cups powdered sugar

In a saucepan over low heat, melt chocolate chips, butter and peanut butter. Pour over Rice Chex and mix gently. In large paper grocery bag, pour powdered sugar and Rice Chex mixture; shake well to coat.

Mamie Eisenhower Fudge

LINDA FAY ELDERS | WEATHERFORD, TRI-COUNTY EC

4½ cups sugar
½ teaspoon salt
2 tablespoons butter
1 large can (12 ounces) evaporated milk
1 jar (7 ounces) marshmallow cream
1 large package (12 ounces) semisweet
    chocolate chips
3 bars (4 ounces each) German's sweet baking
    chocolate, coarsely chopped
2 cups chopped pecans

Combine the sugar, salt, butter and milk in a large saucepan, and cook over medium heat. Stir and boil 6 minutes. Remove from heat. Stir in the marshmallow cream, chocolate chips, sweet chocolate and pecans; stir until chocolate is melted. Pour into greased pans. Cool and slice into small squares.

COOK'S NOTE: This is my favorite candy recipe for fudge, which I first sampled in the early 1950s. A neighbor in the rural Dennis community in Parker County served this wonderful fudge to my family when we visited her, and it was love at first bite. This candy has become a Christmas tradition for us since then. It represents the ultimate in rich chocolate goodness and has the calories to prove it!

Old-Way Family Fudge

CHRIS COKER | NAPLES, BOWIE-CASS EC

2 cups sugar
½ cup cocoa powder
1 cup whole milk
1 teaspoon vanilla extract
2 tablespoons melted butter

Mix sugar and cocoa in a saucepan over medium heat. Pour in milk, a little at a time, until all ingredients are mixed. Add vanilla and butter. Cook until soft-ball stage, or thick. Cool and stir until thick. Pour onto greased platter. Cool well before cutting.

COOK'S NOTE: Leslia Cross of Jamestown, Texas, taught all her four girls to make fudge with this recipe. We all passed it to our children all over Texas. We would "swipe" sugar when it was rationed during the war (had to have stamps to get sugar then) and make this fudge.

Microwave Peanut Brittle

SHERRY NICHOLS | JASPER, JASPER-NEWTON EC

1 cup raw peanuts
1 cup sugar
½ cup light corn syrup
⅛ teaspoon salt
1 teaspoon butter
1 teaspoon vanilla extract
1 teaspoon baking soda

Stir raw peanuts, sugar, syrup and salt in a microwave-safe 1½-quart casserole dish. Cook 8 minutes on high, stirring well after 4 minutes. Add butter and vanilla to syrup, beating well. Return to microwave and cook 2 minutes longer on high. Peanuts will be lightly browned and syrup very hot. Add soda and gently stir until light and foamy. Pour onto a slightly greased cookie sheet to cool. Break into pieces when cool. Makes 1 pound.

Sugared Nuts

VIRGINIA ZILLMANN | SAN ANTONIO, KARNES EC

1 cup brown sugar
¼ teaspoon salt
¼ teaspoon cinnamon
6 tablespoons milk
1 teaspoon vanilla extract
2½–3 cups pecans or peanuts

In a saucepan, mix and cook sugar, salt, cinnamon and milk to 235 degrees on a candy thermometer. Remove from heat; add vanilla and nuts. Stir until sugary. Turn onto waxed paper and separate nuts to dry.

Crispy Cinnamon Pecans

MRS. EDWARD H. BURKE | LAKE HILLS, BANDERA EC

1 egg white
Dash of salt
2 cups pecans
1½ cups sugar
1½ teaspoon cinnamon

Preheat oven to 200 degrees. In a 2-quart bowl that has a fitted cover, beat the egg white with a fork until frothy. Add salt and pecans, cover bowl and shake until pecans are coated. Mix sugar and cinnamon, and add to pecans. Cover bowl again and shake until pecans are coated. Place pecans in single layer on a cookie sheet and bake approximately 1½ hours. About every 20 minutes, stir them around.

COOK'S NOTE: This makes a nice gift when placed in a clear plastic bag and tied with a pretty ribbon.

Almond Rocha

CINDY BRASHEAR | LUBBOCK, SOUTH PLAINS EC

1 package sliced almonds
1 cup sugar
1 cup less 2 tablespoons butter
½ teaspoon salt
6 Hershey's milk chocolate bars (1.55 ounces each)

Spread thin layer of almonds onto waxed paper. In a saucepan over medium heat, cook sugar, butter and salt, stirring constantly, until consistency of peanut butter. Pour over the almonds. Lay Hershey's bars on top and, after a couple of minutes, spread melted bars. Put in refrigerator to set. Break into pieces.

Walnut Spice Kisses

MRS. ROBERT SCHWAB | MCALLEN, MAGIC VALLEY EC

1 egg white
2 dashes of salt
¼ cup sugar
1 teaspoon cinnamon
⅛ teaspoon ground nutmeg
⅛ teaspoon ground cloves
1 cup finely chopped walnuts
Walnut halves (optional)

Preheat oven to 250 degrees. In a mixing bowl, beat egg white with salt until stiff. Mix sugar with spices and gradually beat into egg. Fold in chopped walnuts. Drop from a teaspoon onto a well-greased cookie sheet. Top with walnut halves, if desired. Bake 35–40 minutes. Makes about 2 dozen.

Apple Pie Surprise

PAT PAINTER | EDMONSON, SWISHER EC

PASTRY:
2½ cups flour
¼ cup sugar
1½ teaspoons salt
½ cup butter
¼ cup oil
¼ cup water
1 egg
FILLING:
6 cups peeled, sliced apples
1 cup sugar
⅓ cup flour
2 teaspoons grated lemon zest
2 tablespoons lemon juice
CARAMEL SAUCE:
28 light-colored candy caramels, unwrapped
½ cup evaporated milk
TOPPING:
8 ounces cream cheese, softened
⅓ cup sugar
⅓ cup chopped nuts, plus more for top
1 egg

Preheat oven to 375 degrees. For Pastry, put flour, sugar and salt in a large bowl. Cut in butter with a pastry blender until particles are the size of small peas. In a separate bowl, combine oil, water and egg; mix until smooth and creamy, then blend this mixture into the flour mixture. Pat evenly into the bottom and sides of an ungreased jelly-roll pan. For Filling, combine the apples, sugar, flour, lemon zest and lemon juice. Toss lightly and spoon into the Pastry-lined pan. Make Caramel Sauce by melting caramels in milk in a saucepan over medium heat, stirring until smooth. Drizzle this over the Filling. For Topping, combine cream cheese, sugar, nuts and egg in a large bowl, and beat until smooth. Spoon this over top of all. Sprinkle with additional nuts. Bake 30–35 minutes, or until light brown.

Paper Bag Apple Pie

SYBLE MOORE | ODESSA, HAMILTON COUNTY EC

6 cups peeled and sliced tart apples
1 cup sugar
2 tablespoons plus ½ cup flour, divided use
1 teaspoon lemon juice
½ teaspoon cinnamon
½ teaspoon ground nutmeg
⅛ teaspoon salt
1 9-inch pie crust, unbaked
½ cup packed brown sugar
3 tablespoons butter

Preheat oven to 400 degrees. In a large bowl, toss apples with sugar, 2 tablespoons flour, lemon juice, spices and salt until well coated. Spoon into crust. Combine ½ cup flour and brown sugar. Cut in butter until crumbly. Spread evenly over apples. Place pie in large, heavy-duty, brown paper bag. Fold over twice and seal with a paper clip. Bake 45–50 minutes, or until topping is golden.

COOK'S NOTE: I sometimes put pastry strips on top of topping before baking. It is very good to freeze before baking. I make up several during apple season.

Blush Apple Pie

MRS. EDWIN MOELLER | ROWENA, COLEMAN COUNTY EC

5 large apples, peeled and sliced
3 slices pineapple (cubed or use
    ½ cup crushed pineapple)
¼ cup red cinnamon drops
1 teaspoon grated lemon zest
2 tablespoons melted butter
½ cup sugar
⅛ teaspoon salt
2 tablespoons flour
2 9-inch pie crusts, unbaked

Preheat oven to 425 degrees. In a large bowl, combine all ingredients except pie crusts; mix well and let stand 5 minutes. Line pie pan with 1 crust, pour in apple mixture, then make top crust (full or criss-cross) with second crust. Bake until golden brown.

Apple Pecan Shoo-Fly Pie

MARY E. JUNG | PIPE CREEK, BANDERA EC

1½ cups flour
½ cup sugar
½ teaspoon baking soda, divided use
¼ cup butter
1 cup Simple Maple Syrup (see below)
¼ teaspoon baking soda
1 9-inch pie crust, unbaked
2 cups sliced apples
¼ cup raisins
1 cup chopped pecans
SIMPLE MAPLE SYRUP:
½ cup sugar
½ cup brown sugar
2 cups water
1 teaspoon maple flavoring

In a large bowl, thoroughly stir together flour, sugar and ¼ teaspoon baking soda. Cut in butter until mixture is crumbly; set aside. Make Simple Maple Syrup: Butter sides of medium-sized, heavy saucepan. Boil sugar and water 5 minutes, stirring occasionally; add maple flavoring. Measure out 1 cup of syrup and reserve the rest for other use. To 1 cup syrup, add ¼ teaspoon soda and stir. Preheat oven to 375 degrees. Line pie crust with half of apples; sprinkle with half of raisins and pecans. Cover with ⅓ of crumb mixture. Dribble ½ cup syrup over crumbs. Repeat layers and top with remaining ⅔ of crumb mixture. Bake 40–45 minutes, until golden brown. Eat hot or cold with whipped cream.

COOK'S NOTE: This syrup is excellent over pancakes and waffles. A wet cloth wrapped around a fork may be used to wipe sides of pan while cooking to keep from crystallizing. One cup maple syrup or ½ cup molasses and ½ cup water may be substituted for the Simple Maple Syrup.

Apricot Pie

ANITA BOYD | BROWNWOOD, COMANCHE COUNTY EC

1 package dried apricots
2 cups water
1¾ cups sugar
2 tablespoons flour
2 9-inch pie crusts, unbaked

Boil apricots in water until tender. Preheat oven to 425 degrees. Mash apricots and add sugar and flour. Pour into unbaked pie crust and cover with other pie crust. Bake until golden brown.

Blueberry Delight

JENELL MCKINNEY | KAUFMAN, KAUFMAN COUNTY EC

CRUST:
1½ cups flour
2 tablespoons sugar
½ cup butter, softened
1 cup chopped pecans
TOPPING:
8 ounces cream cheese
1 cup powdered sugar, sifted
1 small container (8 ounces) whipped topping
1 can (21 ounces) blueberry pie filling

Preheat oven to 350 degrees. In a bowl, mix flour and sugar together. Cut in butter and pecans until crumbly and press into 9-by-13-inch pan. Bake 10–15 minutes. While baking, prepare Topping: In a bowl, combine cream cheese, sugar and whipped topping, stirring until smooth. Spread on top of cooled crust. Pour pie filling on top of this. Refrigerate until ready to serve.

Blackberry Jam Pie

MRS. CARL CURRY | IVANHOE, FANNIN EC

3 egg yolks
1 cup sour cream
1 tablespoon butter
⅛ teaspoon salt
1 cup blackberry jam
1 9-inch pie crust, unbaked

Preheat oven to 425 degrees. In a mixing bowl, beat egg yolks until light. Add other ingredients and mix well. Pour into pie. Cook until filling is thick and crust is crisp. Top with meringue, if desired.

Cherry Pie

MRS. R.L. CLARK | TULIA, SWISHER COUNTY EC

1 can (14 ounces) pitted tart cherries
1 small can (8 ounces) crushed pineapple
Water
2 cups sugar
7 tablespoons cornstarch
½ teaspoon salt
1 teaspoon vanilla extract
1 tablespoon red food coloring
4 bananas
1 cup chopped nuts
2 9-inch pie crusts, baked

Into a large measuring cup, drain juice from cherries and pineapples. Add enough water to make 2 cups of liquid. Pour into a saucepan over medium heat, add sugar and cornstarch, and stir until dissolved. Add vanilla and food coloring, and cook until thick. Cool; add cherries, pineapple, bananas and nuts. Pour into pie crusts. Serve with whipped cream on top, if desired.

Cherry Pie

ELAINE PEARSON | O'DONNELL, LYNTEGAR EC

2½ tablespoons tapioca
⅛ teaspoon salt
1 cup sugar
Red food coloring (enough to make a pretty red)
1 can (14 ounces) sour cherries, drained and chopped
½ cup cherry juice
¼ teaspoon almond extract
2 9-inch pie crusts, unbaked
Ground nutmeg
2 tablespoons butter, cut into small chunks
Cinnamon
Sugar

Preheat oven to 325 degrees. Mix first 7 ingredients together and let stand for a few minutes. Pour into an unbaked pie crust that has been lightly dusted with nutmeg. Dot with butter. Cut second crust into strips and make lattice-type top crust. Sprinkle generously with cinnamon and sugar. Bake at 325 degrees until bubbly and nicely browned.

COOK'S NOTE: This recipe has been a family favorite. I have added and taken away until it is just right for us. Chopping the cherries was my last change.

Cherry-O Cream Cheese Pie

BETTY MCCLURE | SHALLOWATER, SOUTH PLAINS EC

8 ounces cream cheese
1 can (14 ounces) sweetened condensed milk
⅓ cup lemon juice
1 teaspoon vanilla extract
1 9-inch graham cracker crust
1 can (21 ounces) cherry pie filling

In a bowl, soften cream cheese and whip until fluffy. Add milk, lemon juice and vanilla. Blend well and pour into crust. Chill 2–3 hours before topping with cherry pie filling.

COOK'S NOTE: This is fast and simple to make.

Dewberry Cream Pie

MRS. REX LEE WILKES | BROWNFIELD, LYNTEGAR EC

PIE:
1 9-inch pie crust, unbaked
Dewberries
½ cup sugar
2 eggs
½ cup flour
½ cup sour cream
Pinch of salt
TOPPING:
8 tablespoons flour
8 tablespoons sugar
4 tablespoons butter

Preheat oven to 325 degrees. Fill an unbaked pie crust with dewberries. Mix next 5 ingredients in a bowl and pour over berries. Make Topping: In a bowl, mix ingredients with a fork until crumbly and sprinkle over pie. Bake 30 minutes, then reduce heat to 350 for 15 minutes.

Green Grape Pie

LYNDA LENAMON | CRAWFORD, MCLENNAN COUNTY EC

1 egg, beaten
1½ cups sugar
3 tablespoons flour
¼ teaspoon salt
1 cup heavy whipping cream
½ teaspoon lemon juice
¼ teaspoon vanilla extract
2 cups green grapes (wild mustang,
    size of English peas)
2 9-inch pie crusts, unbaked

Preheat oven to 350 degrees. In a large bowl, mix first 8 ingredients together and pour into unbaked pie crust. Cut second crust into strips and make a lattice-type top crust. Bake 45 minutes, or until done.

COOK'S NOTE: This is an old family recipe that can only be made if you have access to wild mustang grapes, which we have in abundance around here. The grapes should be about the size of an English pea or they will explode. The tartness of the grapes is enhanced by the sweetness of the custard.

Date Nut Pie

MRS. REX LEE WILKES | BROWNFIELD, LYNTEGAR EC

CRUST:
3 ounces cream cheese
½ cup butter
1 cup flour
Pinch of salt
FILLING:
3 eggs
1½ cups sugar
¾ tablespoons flour
¼ cup buttermilk
½ tablespoon vanilla extract
¼ cup (½ stick) butter, melted
¾ cup pecans
½ cup chopped dates

For Crust, bring cream cheese and butter to room temperature in a bowl. Mix in flour and salt until smooth. Press into pie plate. Preheat oven to 425 degrees. For Filling, slightly beat eggs in a mixing bowl; add sugar, flour, buttermilk and vanilla; mix well. Stir in melted butter, nuts and dates. Put in Crust. Bake 10 minutes; then reduce heat to 350 degrees 30–40 minutes more.

Millionaire Pie

MARVIN L. CAMPBELL JR. | FORT WORTH, TRI-COUNTY EC

8 ounces cream cheese
1½ cups powdered sugar
1 small can (8 ounces) crushed pineapple, drained
1 small container (8 ounces) whipped topping
1 cup chopped nuts
1 9-inch graham cracker crust

In a mixing bowl, whip cream cheese and powdered sugar together. Fold in pineapple, whipped topping and nuts. Pour into graham cracker crust. Refrigerate at least 1 hour before serving.

Plentiful Pear Pie

KITTY BAUCOM | SAN ANGELO, CONCHO VALLEY EC

4 large pears
1 large apple
1 teaspoon lemon juice
1 small can (8 ounces) crushed pineapple
1 cup sugar
1 teaspoon cinnamon
⅛ teaspoon salt
2 tablespoons flour
3 tablespoons butter, cut into small chunks
2 9-inch pie crusts, unbaked

Preheat oven to 400 degrees. Peel, core and slice pears and apple. Place in pie pan lined with 1 crust; sprinkle with lemon juice and crushed pineapple. In a bowl, mix sugar, cinnamon, salt and flour; sprinkle on top of pears, apple and pineapple. Dot with butter. Cover with second crust and slice in several places to vent. Moisten edges of crust with water and seal. Bake 30–40 minutes.

Pineapple Coconut Pie

BOBBIE PEAK | COMFORT, BANDERA EC

1 cup sugar
3 eggs
6 tablespoons butter, melted
1 teaspoon vanilla extract
1 small can (8 ounces) crushed pineapple
⅔ cup sweetened flaked coconut
1 9-inch pie crust, unbaked

Preheat oven to 350 degrees. In a mixing bowl, beat first 4 ingredients thoroughly. Add pineapple and coconut. Pour into an unbaked pie crust. Bake until center is completely set.

Pineapple Pie

MINNIE JO SCHMELTEKOPJ | KYLE, PEDERNALES EC

1 small can (8 ounces) crushed pineapple, drained
½ cup butter, melted
3 eggs, beaten
1 cup sugar
1 9-inch pie crust, unbaked

Preheat oven to 350 degrees. Mix all ingredients together in a bowl and pour into pie crust. Bake 40 minutes.

COOK'S NOTE: This pie tastes so wonderful; it reminds you of buttermilk pie. The real wonder is how easy it is!

Raisin Pie

MRS. CHARLES W. HAEDGE | BELLVILLE, BLUEBONNET EC

2 cups raisins
Water
1 cup plus 2 tablespoons sugar, divided use
4 tablespoons flour
4 eggs, separated
¼ cup butter
Pinch of salt
1 teaspoon vanilla extract
2 9-inch pie crusts, baked

In a saucepan, cook raisins, with water to cover, and ½ cup sugar over medium heat until slightly thickened. In a mixing bowl, beat egg yolks with ½ cup sugar, butter, salt and flour until the mixture turns a light yellow; then, pour into the raisins. Cook, stirring constantly, until mixture thickens; pour into baked pie crusts. Preheat oven to 300 degrees. In a separate bowl, whip egg whites and 2 tablespoons sugar to make meringue. Top pies with meringue. Bake 12 minutes. Makes 2 pies.

Hawaiian Pie

MRS. EDWARD HALE | DAWSON, NAVARRO EC

1 cup sugar
4 tablespoons flour
1 large can (20 ounces) crushed pineapple
2 eggs
½ cup butter
1 can (7 ounces) sweetened flaked coconut
2 bananas
1 9-inch pie crust, baked

Sift together sugar and flour into a saucepan. Add crushed pineapple and eggs and cook over low heat until thick. Stir in butter and coconut until butter is melted and combined. Pour mixture into bowl and cool in refrigerator. When cool, remove from refrigerator and beat well, then fold in sliced bananas. Put mixture in pie crust.

Strawberry Pie Alaska

MARGARET KUNZ | COLUMBUS, SAN BERNARD EC

1 box (3.4 ounces) strawberry Jell-O
⅔ cup boiling water
1 cup vanilla ice cream
1 small container (8 ounces) whipped topping
1 cup diced fresh strawberries
1 9-inch graham cracker crust

Dissolve Jell-O in boiling water. Add ice cream by spoonfuls. Stir until melted and smooth. Blend in whipped topping and strawberries. Chill, if necessary, until mixture will mound. Spoon into crust. Chill about 3 hours, or freeze until firm. Makes 8 servings.

COOK'S NOTE: I cut additional strawberries in halves and turn cut sides up around edge on top for trim.

Quick Strawberry Ice Box Pie

SARA COURSEY | FLOYDADA, LIGHTHOUSE EC

1 can (14 ounces) sweetened condensed milk
⅓ cup lemon juice
1 large container (16 ounces) whipped topping
1 cup chopped pecans
1 package (10 ounces) frozen strawberries, thawed
2 9-inch graham cracker crusts

Combine milk, lemon juice and whipped topping in bowl and mix well. Fold in pecans and strawberries. Pour into pie crusts. Chill until ready to serve. Other fruits may be substituted for the strawberries.

Toasted Coconut Pie

PAULINE WALLACE | LOTT, BELFALLS EC

3 eggs, beaten
1½ cups sugar
½ cup butter, melted
1 teaspoon vanilla extract
3½ tablespoons lemon juice
1 cup packed sweetened flaked coconut
1 9-inch pie crust, unbaked

Preheat oven to 350 degrees. In a mixing bowl, thoroughly combine eggs, sugar, butter, vanilla and lemon juice; stir in coconut. Pour into unbaked crust. Bake 40–45 minutes.

Old-Time Buttermilk Pie

JANIE WILSON-AMESCUA | LEANDER, PEDERNALES EC

⅓ cup butter, softened
2 cups sugar
3 rounded tablespoons flour
3 eggs
1 cup buttermilk
1 teaspoon vanilla extract
1 9-inch pie crust, unbaked

Preheat oven to 350 degrees. Place butter, sugar, flour, eggs, buttermilk and vanilla in blender. Blend at medium speed until thoroughly blended. (A mixer may also be used.) Pour into unbaked pie crust. Bake 45–50 minutes. Test by inserting toothpick into center; if it comes out clean, it is done. Place on rack to cool completely before serving.

COOK'S NOTE: This recipe is a favorite from a recipe booklet by Borden containing 20 buttermilk recipes.

Buttermilk Pie

MRS. D.L. ALFORD | WAELDER, BLUEBONNET EC

3 eggs, separated
1½ cups sugar
3 tablespoons flour
½ teaspoon salt
2 cups buttermilk
1 teaspoon lemon extract
1 9-inch pie crust, unbaked

Preheat oven to 350 degrees. In a large bowl, beat egg yolks well, then mix in sugar, flour, salt, buttermilk and lemon extract. In a separate bowl, whip egg whites until stiff. Fold these into first mixture. Pour into unbaked crust and bake about 40 minutes, until firm in center.

Philadelphia Cream Cheese Pie

MRS. A.B. MIDDLETON | LAMESA, LYNTEGAR EC

CRUST:
1½ cups crushed chocolate wafers
⅓ cup butter, melted
FILLING:
8 ounces cream cheese
½ cup sugar, divided use
1 teaspoon vanilla extract
2 eggs, separated
1 small package (6 ounces) chocolate chips, melted
1 cup heavy whipping cream, whipped
¾ cups chopped nuts

Preheat oven to 325 degrees. Combine crushed wafers with butter and press into bottom of pie pan. Bake 10 minutes. Make Filling: In a mixing bowl, combine cream cheese, ¼ cup sugar and vanilla. Blend until smooth. Stir in beaten egg yolks and melted chocolate chips. In a separate bowl, beat egg whites until peaks form. Gradually beat in remaining ¼ cup sugar, and fold into chocolate mixture. Fold in whipped cream and nuts. Place in the refrigerator until set before serving.

COOK'S NOTE: If desired, a plain pie crust can be used instead of the chocolate wafer crust. This is a rich and delicious pie and is easy to prepare.

No-Crust Fudge Pie

JUNE DONNELLY | DONIE, NAVASOTA VALLEY EC

½ cup butter, softened
1 cup sugar
2 eggs, well beaten
1 teaspoon vanilla extract
2 tablespoons cocoa powder
½ cup sifted flour
Nuts, for garnish
Whipped cream (optional)

Preheat oven to 350 degrees. In a bowl, cream butter and sugar; then add eggs and vanilla. In a separate bowl, mix cocoa with flour and stir into butter mixture. Pour into greased pie plate. Sprinkle on a few nuts before baking, if desired. Bake 25 minutes. Serve with whipped cream.

Ausgood Pie

MRS. STACY ABERNATHY | HUGHES SPRINGS, BOWIE-CASS EC

1 tablespoon butter
1 tablespoon vinegar
2 eggs, separated
1 cup sugar
1 tablespoon flour
⅓ teaspoon ground allspice
½ cup pecans
½ cup raisins
1 9-inch pie crust, unbaked
Whipped cream (optional)

Preheat oven to 400 degrees. In a small saucepan, melt butter and vinegar. In a mixing bowl, beat egg whites until stiff. In a separate bowl, beat egg yolks and add sugar, flour and allspice, then add butter mixture. Fold in egg whites, pecans and raisins. Put in unbaked pie crust. Bake 10 minutes, then reduce heat to 350 degrees and bake 20–25 minutes more, until done. Serve with whipped cream on top, if desired.

Annie's Chocolate Pie

ANNIE DUDLEY | CONROE, SAM HOUSTON EC

4 tablespoons flour
1 cup plus 3 tablespoons sugar, divided use
¼ teaspoon salt
½ cup cocoa powder
2 cups milk
1 tablespoon butter
3 eggs, separated
1 teaspoon vanilla extract
1 9-inch pie crust, baked

Preheat oven to 375 degrees. In the top of a double boiler, mix together flour, 1 cup sugar, salt and cocoa. Add milk, butter, egg yolks and vanilla. Cook over boiling water until mixture thickens. Pour into baked pie crust. In a bowl, beat egg whites with 3 tablespoons sugar until stiff. Top pie with meringue and brown in oven, 10–12 minutes.

German Chocolate Pie

MELBA COWSERT | BLANCO, PEDERNALES EC

1 9-inch pie crust, unbaked
¼ cup butter
¼ cup firmly packed brown sugar
¼ cup chopped pecans
¼ cup sweetened flaked coconut plus more for garnish
2½ cups milk
1 large box (5.9 ounces) vanilla instant pudding mix
1 box (4 ounces) German's sweet baking chocolate, broken into pieces
1 cup whipped topping

Preheat oven to 425 degrees. Prick pie crust with fork. Bake shell until it begins to brown. Remove from oven, but leave oven on. Meanwhile, combine butter, brown sugar, pecans and coconut in a saucepan. Heat until butter and sugar are melted. Spread in bottom of pie crust. Bake 5 minutes, or until bubbly. Cool. Combine milk, pudding mix and chocolate in a saucepan. Cook and stir over medium heat until mixture comes to a full bubbling boil. Remove from heat; cool 5 minutes, stirring occasionally. Pour over coconut mixture in crust; cover surface with plastic wrap. Chill at least 4 hours before serving. Remove plastic wrap and garnish pie with whipped topping. Sprinkle with additional coconut.

Old-Fashioned Egg Custard Pie

WANDA M. ODNEAL | FRANKLIN, NAVASOTA VALLEY EC

4 eggs
1 cup sugar
1 cup whole milk
1 teaspoon vanilla extract
Cinnamon and ground nutmeg, to taste
1 9-inch pie crust, unbaked

Preheat oven to 375 degrees. In a bowl, combine eggs and sugar; beat well. Add milk and vanilla, and beat. Pour into unbaked pie crust. Sprinkle with cinnamon and nutmeg. Bake until firm, about 40 minutes.

Caramel Pie

MRS. RUFUS DILL | BROWNFIELD, LYNTEGAR EC

PIE:
2 cups sugar, divided use
2 cups milk
2 tablespoons flour
1 teaspoon vanilla extract
5 egg yolks
2 9-inch pie crusts, baked
MERINGUE:
5 egg whites
5 tablespoons sugar
1 teaspoon vanilla extract

Caramelize 1 cup sugar in a cast iron skillet. Add milk and stir until caramel is melted. In a bowl, combine remaining sugar, flour, vanilla and egg yolks. Gradually stir egg mixture into milk on stove. Cook until thick. Pour into pie crust and top with Meringue. Preheat oven to 375 degrees. To make Meringue, beat egg whites until foamy in a mixing bowl. Beat in sugar, 1 tablespoon at a time. Continue beating until stiff and glossy. Add vanilla. Spread half of meringue over each pie, sealing to edges of crusts. Bake 10–12 minutes until browned. Makes 2 pies.

Chocolate Pecan Pie

SHERHONDA GINN | LUBBOCK, SOUTH PLAINS EC

3 eggs, slightly beaten
1 cup light corn syrup
1 large package (12 ounces) semisweet chocolate chips, melted and cooled slightly
½ cup sugar
2 tablespoons butter, melted
1 teaspoon vanilla extract
1½ cups pecan halves
1 9-inch unbaked pie crust

Preheat oven to 350 degrees. In a large bowl, combine eggs, syrup, chocolate, sugar, butter and vanilla. Mix well. Stir in pecans. Pour into pie crust. Bake 50–60 minutes, or until set in the center. Can be frozen.

O-So-Good Pie

DEBBIE MASTERSON | DAWSON, NAVARRO COUNTY EC

2 cups sugar
4 eggs, separated
1 cup raisins
1 cup nuts
½ teaspoon cinnamon
½ teaspoon ground cloves
½ teaspoon allspice
2 teaspoons vinegar
Butter, size of walnut
1 9-inch pie crust, unbaked

Preheat oven to 350 degrees. In a mixing bowl, cream sugar and egg yolks. Add raisins, nuts, spices, vinegar and butter. In a separate bowl, whip egg whites and fold into sugar mixture. Pour into pie crust and bake about 40 minutes.

COOK'S NOTE: This recipe was given to me by my neighbor, Annie Beatrice Jordan, who is 75 years old. She said the recipe was her grandmother's. I had to ask her about the "butter size of walnut," and she said that was their way of measuring—by comparing the amount to the size of something. It was new to me!

Old-Way Chess Pie

CHRIS COKER | NAPLES, BOWIE-CASS EC

3 eggs, beaten
1½ cups sugar
½ cup butter, melted
1 tablespoon cornmeal
1 tablespoon flour
1 tablespoon vinegar
1 9-inch pie crust, unbaked

Preheat oven to 350 degrees. In a bowl, mix first 6 ingredients well and pour into pie crust. Bake 1 hour, or until brown.

COOK'S NOTE: This is an Erna Cross Dunn recipe from Whitney. This pie was used to serve to cotton gin workers and farm families in the Hill Country.

Lemon Chess Pie

BETTYE J. HUCKABEE | SEGUIN, GUADALUPE VALLEY EC

4 eggs, beaten
2 cups sugar
1 tablespoon cornmeal
1 tablespoon flour
¼ cup whole milk
¼ cup lemon juice
Grated zest of ⅓ lemon
½ cup butter, melted
1 9-inch pie crust, unbaked

Preheat oven to 325 degrees. In a mixing bowl, beat eggs thoroughly. In another bowl, mix together sugar, cornmeal and flour, then mix with eggs. Add milk, lemon juice and zest, then stir in butter and pour into pie crust. Bake 45 minutes.

COOK'S NOTE: Delicious holiday dessert!

Toddy Pie

BILLIE ROLLINS | CORPUS CHRISTI, BANDERA EC

PIE:
1½ cups eggnog
½ cup sugar
½ cup baking mix
4 eggs
2 tablespoons rum, or 1 teaspoon rum extract
Ground nutmeg
SPICED WHIPPED CREAM:
½ cup chilled heavy whipping cream
1 tablespoon sugar
¼ teaspoon ground nutmeg

Preheat oven to 350 degrees and grease a pie plate. Place all ingredients, except nutmeg, in blender. Cover and blend on high for 15 seconds. Pour into pie plate. Sprinkle with nutmeg. Bake until knife inserted in center comes out clean, about 40 minutes. This pie makes its own crust. Serve with Spiced Whipped Cream: Beat all ingredients in chilled bowl until stiff.

Lemon Chiffon Pie

MRS. MONROE FLOYD | AMARILLO, SOUTH PLAINS EC

1 cup boiling water
1 tablespoon butter
1 teaspoon grated lemon zest
5 eggs, separated
⅔ cup plus 5 scant tablespoons sugar, divided use
3½ tablespoons cornstarch
½ cup lemon juice (3–4 lemons)
1 9-inch pie crust, baked

Preheat oven to 350 degrees. Mix water and butter in top of double boiler. In a bowl, add lemon zest to egg yolks and beat well. In a separate bowl, mix ⅓ cup sugar and cornstarch; then add to egg yolk mixture, along with lemon juice; beat well. Add this mixture to boiling water mixture and cook until thickened. Set aside to cool. In another bowl, beat egg whites with 5 scant tablespoons sugar until stiff. Add half this mixture to the cooked mixture, folding in carefully. Pour into pie crust. Cover pie with remaining egg white mixture and brown in oven.

COOK'S NOTE: This is my mother's recipe from years ago.

Pink Lemonade Pie

FAMMIE HILL | HENDERSON, RUSK COUNTY EC

6 ounces frozen pink lemonade concentrate, thawed
1 can (14 ounces) sweetened condensed milk
1 container (8 ounces) whipped topping
1 9-inch graham cracker crust

Pour lemonade in mixing bowl. Add condensed milk and blend. Fold in whipped topping. Put in graham cracker crust. Chill until firm.

COOK'S NOTE: Makes a very big pie. You could use 2 smaller pie crusts.

Lemon Sour Cream Pie

ANGIE WALKER | MONTGOMERY, MID-SOUTH EC

3 egg yolks
¾ cup sugar
3 tablespoons cornstarch
1 tablespoon grated lemon zest
¼ cup lemon juice
¼ cup butter, melted
½ cup half-and-half
½ cup milk
1 cup sour cream
1 9-inch pie crust, baked
Whipped cream or meringue (optional)

Combine egg yolks, sugar, cornstarch, lemon zest and lemon juice, butter, half-and-half and milk in a saucepan; cook over low heat, stirring constantly, until thick. Remove from heat and cool. When cool, fold in sour cream. Pour into pie crust and top with whipped cream or meringue, if desired. Chill completely before cutting.

COOK'S NOTE: This pie will keep for days in the refrigerator, if not eaten first!

French Lemon Pie

MRS. GORDON SHOOK | PEARL, HAMILTON COUNTY EC

1 cup sugar
4 eggs
1 tablespoon flour
2 tablespoons butter, softened
1 cup light corn syrup
Grated zest and juice of 1 lemon
1 9-inch pie crust, unbaked

Preheat oven to 350 degrees. In a mixing bowl, combine sugar, eggs, flour and butter; beat until fluffy. Add syrup, lemon zest and juice. Put in pie crust and bake 45 minutes, or until firm.

Lemon-Banana Pie

MRS. QUINTON MCCAGHREN | SUDAN, LAMB COUNTY EC

1 small can (8 ounces) crushed pineapple, drained
⅓ cup lemon juice
1 can (14 ounces) sweetened condensed milk
2 bananas
1 9-inch pie crust, baked, or graham cracker crust
Whipped cream

In a bowl, mix together pineapple, lemon juice and milk. Slice two bananas into cooked pie crust or graham cracker crust; pour pineapple mixture over them and top with whipped cream.

Yummy Mince Pie

D. MCKINNEY | KINGSBURY, GUADALUPE VALLEY EC

1½ cups chopped apples
1 cup chopped green tomatoes
1 teaspoon cinnamon
½ teaspoon salt
½ teaspoon allspice
½ teaspoon ground cloves
1½ cups sugar
½ pound raisins
⅛ cup vinegar
4 9-inch pie crusts, unbaked
Milk
Sugar

Put apples and tomatoes in saucepan with cinnamon, salt, allspice and cloves. Add sugar, raisins and vinegar. Cook about 10 minutes. Preheat oven to 375 degrees. Pour cooked mixture into 2 pie pans with crusts. Cut remaining crusts into strips for lattice-type crusts. Lay over filling and sprinkle tops with a little milk and sugar. Bake about 35 minutes. Makes 2 pies.

COOK'S NOTE: People who never liked mince pie usually love this!!

Mincemeat Pie

LANELLE ROBISON | ATLANTA, BOWIE-CASS EC

MINCEMEAT:
1 gallon pears
1 large apple
1 orange
1 lemon
1 pound raisins
6 cups brown sugar
1 cup vinegar
6 ounces frozen grape juice concentrate
1 tablespoon salt
1 tablespoon cinnamon
1 tablespoon ground allspice
1 tablespoon ground cloves
PIE:
1 tablespoon flour
2 9-inch pie crusts, unbaked
1 cup chopped nuts
¼ cup butter, melted

Prepare homemade Mincemeat: Core pears and apples, grate the zest from the orange and lemon, and grind these together. Mix in remaining ingredients. In a large saucepan, bring mixture to a boil and simmer 2 hours. Process for canning, if desired, or store in sealed containers in refrigerator up to 2 weeks or freezer for 6 months. For Pie: Preheat oven to 350 degrees. In a bowl, mix flour into 2 cups Mincemeat. Pour into bottom crust. Sprinkle with nuts of your choice. Pour butter over pie. Cover with top crust and bake until crust is brown, about 40 minutes.

COOK'S NOTE: This has been a favorite in my family for years. In October, when pears are ready, I can my own mincemeat. One cup in pound cake is great.

Oatmeal Pie

MARY H. PETERSON | KLONDIKE, FARMERS EC

3 eggs, well beaten
⅔ cup sugar
⅔ cup quick-cooking oats
⅔ cup sweetened flaked coconut
2 tablespoons butter
½ cup chopped nuts (optional)
1 9-inch pie crust, unbaked

Preheat oven to 375 degrees. In a bowl, combine filling ingredients and mix well. Pour into pie crust. Bake 30 minutes, or until done.

COOK'S NOTE: Mix in all the love that's needed to share with others. You will never be hungry after this. I remember when we didn't have the nuts and coconut to go in it. This brings back loving memories.

Creamy Pecan Pie

ELAINE HAMBRECHT | WESLACO, MAGIC VALLEY EC

⅓ cup butter, softened
¾ cup brown sugar
2 eggs, slightly beaten
½ cup corn syrup
1 teaspoon vanilla extract
1¼ cups chopped pecans
1 cup sour cream
1 9-inch, deep dish pie crust, unbaked
Pecan halves
Whipped topping

Preheat oven to 375 degrees. In a mixing bowl, cream butter and sugar. Add eggs, syrup and vanilla; mix well. Stir in the pecans and sour cream until blended. Pour into pie crust. Garnish with pecan halves. Bake 40–45 minutes. Chill and garnish with whipped topping before serving.

COOK'S NOTE: My family votes this one "super."

Crustless Pecan Pie

RUBY FLENTGE | ROSEBUD, BELFALLS EC

2 eggs
½ cup flour
1 cup sugar
¾ cup butter, melted
1⅓ cups sweetened flaked coconut
1 cup chopped pecans
1 teaspoon vanilla extract

Preheat oven to 350 degrees. In a mixing bowl, beat eggs, and add flour and sugar. Mix in other ingredients. Pour into greased and floured pie pan. Bake 25–30 minutes, or until light brown.

Pecan Pie

MRS. W.A. HENRICHSEN | EDINBURG, MAGIC VALLEY EC

1 egg
½ cup sugar
⅓ pound chopped pecans
1 9-inch pie crust, unbaked
1 tablespoon butter, melted
1 tablespoon flour
½ cup light corn syrup
½ cup whole milk

In a bowl, mix beaten egg with sugar and pecans. Pour into unbaked crust. In a separate bowl, mix butter, flour, syrup and milk. Beat well and pour over pecan mixture. Place in cold oven and turn to 300 degrees. Bake slowly until set, about 1 hour.

COOK'S NOTE: The success of this pie depends upon the beating and slow baking. Brown sugar may be used in place of white to make a darker, richer-looking pie.

Maysell Pie

IDA S. KOLL | SEGUIN, GUADALUPE VALLEY EC

3 egg whites
½ teaspoon baking powder
1 cup sugar
11 graham crackers, crushed
1 cup chopped pecans
1 cup whipped cream

Preheat oven to 300 degrees. In a mixing bowl, beat egg whites and baking powder until stiff. Add sugar and mix well. Add graham crackers and pecans, and mix well. Pour into a well-greased pie pan and bake 40 minutes. After pie has cooled, cover with whipped cream. Refrigerate at least 4 hours, or overnight.

Deluxe Pecan Pie

DOROTHY RHEINLAENDER | NEW BRAUNFELS, GUADALUPE VALLEY EC

3 eggs
1 cup light or dark corn syrup
1 cup sugar
2 tablespoons butter, melted
1 teaspoon vanilla extract
½ teaspoon salt
2 cups pecans
1 9-inch pie crust, unbaked

Preheat oven to 350 degrees. In mixing bowl, beat eggs slightly, then add corn syrup, sugar, butter, vanilla and salt, beating until well blended. Stir in pecans. Pour filling into pie crust. Bake 55–65 minutes, or until knife inserted halfway between center and edge comes out clean. Cool. If desired, serve with whipped cream.

COOK'S NOTE: This is the best pecan pie you'll ever eat.

Honey Pecan Pie

VIRGINIA J. HOOD | MURCHISON, NEW ERA EC

½ cup sugar
1 cup honey
3 tablespoons butter, melted
1 teaspoon vanilla extract
3 eggs, beaten
1 cup finely chopped pecans
1 9-inch pie crust, unbaked

Preheat oven to 375 degrees. In a mixing bowl, combine all filling ingredients in order given. Pour into pie crust. Bake 45 minutes, or until firm in center.

Lemon Pecan Pie (With Cream Cheese Pastry)

ANN JOHNSON | BRADY, MCCULLOCH EC

CRUST:
3 ounces cream cheese
¼ teaspoon butter flavoring
½ cup butter, softened
1 cup flour, sifted
FILLING:
3 eggs
1 cup light brown sugar
1 cup light corn syrup
⅓ cup butter, melted
Pinch of salt
1 teaspoon vanilla extract
1 tablespoon lemon extract
1 teaspoon butter flavoring
1 cup pecan halves

Preheat oven to 350 degrees. For Crust, blend all ingredients thoroughly in a bowl. Chill dough, then press into a 9-inch pie plate. Trim and flute dough. For Filling, slightly beat eggs in medium-size bowl. Blend in sugar, corn syrup and butter. Blend in salt, extracts and flavoring. Arrange pecan halves on bottom of crust. Pour Filling over them. Bake 50–60 minutes, until center of pie is almost set but still soft. Do not overbake—filling will set as it cools. Cool on wire rack at least 1 hour before cutting.

Surprise Pecan Pie

MRS. E.J. GROSSMAN | NEDERLAND, JASPER-NEWTON EC

⅔ cup butter, softened
⅔ cup sugar
1 tablespoon brown sugar
⅔ cup light corn syrup
2 eggs, beaten
1 teaspoon vanilla extract
½ teaspoon salt
⅔ cup quick-cooking oats
⅔ cup pecans
⅔ cup sweetened flaked coconut
1 9-inch deep dish pie crust, unbaked

Preheat oven to 350 degrees. In a mixing bowl, cream butter, sugars and corn syrup. Add eggs, vanilla, salt and oats. Fold in pecans and coconut. Pour into pie crust and bake 45 minutes.

Fast Holiday Pie

JEANNITTA LOPEZ | DONIE, NAVASOTA VALLEY EC

2 bananas
1 9-inch pie crust, baked
1 can (14 ounces) sweetened condensed milk
1 large can (20 ounces) crushed pineapple, well drained
1 small container (8 ounces) whipped topping
½ cup colored miniature marshmallows
½ cup maraschino cherry halves
½ cup chopped pecans

Slice bananas into baked pie crust, arranging slices to line bottom and sides. In a bowl, mix milk and pineapple. Pour into pie crust. Put whipped topping in peaks on top. Garnish with marshmallows, cherries and pecans. Refrigerate until ready to serve.

Peppermint Swirl Pie

WANDA GRANT | WEATHERFORD, HAMILTON COUNTY EC

CRUST:
1 cup flour
6 tablespoons butter
½ cup finely chopped nuts
FILLING:
8 ounces cream cheese
1 cup powdered sugar
1 small box (3.4 ounces) instant vanilla pudding mix
2 cups milk, divided use
1 teaspoon peppermint extract
2 cups whipped topping, plus more for garnish
½ cup chocolate chips
3 tablespoons butter
Maraschino cherries

Preheat oven to 275 degrees. For Crust, mix all ingredients and spread in bottom of a 7-by-12-inch Pyrex baking dish. Cook until light brown. For Filling, beat cream cheese and powdered sugar together in a mixing bowl until fluffy; pat into bottom of crust. Mix pudding mix, 1½ cups milk, and peppermint extract together. Pour over cream cheese. Spread whipped topping over pudding layer. Melt chocolate chips with butter and lightly marbleize whipped topping. To garnish, add whipped topping flowerets around edge of pie. Place a maraschino cherry in each flower.

COOK'S NOTE: This recipe was concocted by myself, Wanda Grant, and my sister, Pat Holt.

Blessing Pie

SARAH SCALISE | PRINCETON, GRAYSON-COLLIN EC

22 ginger snaps, crushed
5 tablespoons butter, melted
1 large container (16 ounces) whipped topping
1 small box (3.4 ounces) pistachio instant pudding
    mix
1 small can (8 ounces) crushed pineapple, drained
½ cup slivered almonds
¾ cup sweetened flaked coconut

Preheat oven to 300 degrees. Blend ginger snaps and melted butter and pat into a 9-inch pie pan. Bake 10 minutes. Mix whipped topping, pistachio pudding mix and crushed pineapple. Pour into cooled crust. Top with slivered almonds and flaked coconut.

COOK'S NOTE: Wrap in your love and deliver with the following blessing card: "Hidden in its ingredients are my prayers for you: a spicy crust, signifying the many treasures of a giving and receiving relationship (I Kings 10:10 and 10:13); a cool green filling, symbol of serenity (Psalm 23:2); pineapple, coconut and almonds, to represent the fruits of the Spirit (Galatians 5:22). Serve with a generous helping from the blessing passage in Deuteronomy 28:2-6."

Yam Pie

MRS. CLYDE LANGLEY | KILGORE, RUSK COUNTY EC

2 cups cooked, mashed sweet potatoes
2 cups sugar
½ cup heavy whipping cream
½ cup butter, softened
1 egg
½ teaspoon vanilla extract
1 9-inch pie crust, unbaked

Preheat oven to 350 degrees. In a bowl, mix all filling ingredients. Pour into pie crust. Bake about 50 minutes.

Sweet Potato Pie

MRS. R.T. LOVELADY | SNYDER, MIDWEST EC

2 cups cooked, mashed sweet potatoes
½ cup butter, softened
2 egg yolks
1 cup packed brown sugar
¼ teaspoon salt
½ teaspoon ground ginger
½ teaspoon cinnamon
½ teaspoon ground nutmeg
½ cup milk
2 egg whites
¼ cup sugar
1 9-inch pie crust, unbaked

Preheat oven to 400 degrees. In a large bowl, mix first 9 ingredients together. In a separate bowl, beat egg whites until foamy; add sugar and beat until stiff. Fold into first mixture and pour into crust. Bake 10 minutes, then reduce temperature to 350 degrees and bake 30 minutes more.

Spiced Pumpkin Pie

MARY PHILLIPS | FLOYDADA, LIGHTHOUSE EC

3 eggs
½ cup evaporated milk
1½ cups sugar
2 cups canned pumpkin
1 teaspoon ground ginger
1 teaspoon cinnamon
1 teaspoon ground cloves
1 teaspoon allspice
¼ teaspoon salt
1 teaspoon vanilla extract
2 tablespoons butter, softened
1 9-inch pie crust, unbaked

Preheat oven to 400 degrees. In a mixing bowl, beat eggs, milk and sugar together until well mixed. Add remaining ingredients and blend thoroughly. Pour into crust and bake approximately 1 hour, or until knife inserted in center comes out clean.

Pumpkin Chiffon Pie

MRS. TOMMIE (ANITA) DE HAY | BROWNWOOD, COMANCHE COUNTY EC

1 envelope unflavored gelatin
¼ cup cold water
1½ cups canned pumpkin
1 cup brown sugar
2 teaspoons cinnamon
½ teaspoon ginger
¼ teaspoon allspice
½ teaspoon salt
2 tablespoons butter
½ cup milk
3 eggs, separated
2 tablespoons sugar
1 9-inch deep dish pie crust, baked
Whipped cream (optional)

Soften gelatin in cold water 5 minutes. Combine next 8 ingredients in double boiler. Add egg yolks and cook, stirring often, until thickened. Remove from heat and add gelatin to pumpkin mixture; stir until dissolved. Cool until beginning to congeal. In a bowl, beat egg whites until frothy; then add sugar gradually and continue beating until mixture is stiff. Fold into pumpkin mixture. Pour into crust and chill until firm. Serve with whipped cream, if desired.

Never-Fail Pie Crust

MRS. HENRY BECHTHOLD | BOOKER, NORTH PLAINS EC

3 cups flour
1 teaspoon salt
1 cup shortening
1 egg, beaten
1 tablespoon vinegar
½ cup cold water

Into a mixing bowl, sift together flour and salt; add shortening and cut in until mixture resembles cornmeal. In a small bowl, combine egg, vinegar and water, and add to flour mixture. Stir lightly with a fork until dough follows fork in the bowl. Form into 4 balls and chill. Makes 4 9-inch crusts.

Grandma's Pumpkin Pie

DORIS LEMOND | ABILENE, TAYLOR EC

2 eggs
1½ cups canned pumpkin
1 cup brown sugar
2 tablespoons molasses
1 cup milk
1 teaspoon cinnamon
1 teaspoon ground ginger
½ teaspoon salt
1 9-inch pie crust, unbaked
Whipped cream (optional)

Preheat oven to 350 degrees. In a bowl, beat eggs well and mix in pumpkin and sugar. Add molasses, milk and spices, and mix well. Pour into crust and bake 30 minutes, or until filling is solid. Cool and serve with whipped cream, if desired.

Corn Flake Pie Crust

ETHEL MAY | AMARILLO, GREENBELT EC

4 cups corn flakes
¼ cup sugar
⅓ cup butter, melted

Crush corn flakes into fine crumbs. Combine with sugar and melted butter. Mix and press over bottom and sides of a 9-inch pie pan. Chill several hours before adding filling.

Mixer Pie Crust

SETHIENA ENGLISH | DEKALB, BOWIE-CASS EC

3 cups flour
1 teaspoon salt
1 cup shortening
5 tablespoons cold water

Into a mixing bowl, sift the flour and salt together. Cut shortening into this mixture with mixer, beating until mixture looks like coarse cornmeal. Add cold water and mix until mixture clings to beaters. Roll out on a floured surface. Makes crusts for 2 pies.

Easy, Easy Pie Crust

MRS. JAKE C. WALKER | CARTHAGE, RUSK COUNTY EC

¾ cup shortening
½ cup boiling water
2 cups flour
1 teaspoon salt or less, as desired

Put shortening in a bowl and pour boiling water over it; blend. Stir in flour and salt. Set in refrigerator until cool. Divide into thirds; roll out and fit into 3 8-inch or 9-inch pans. May be frozen in pie pans.

Hurry-Up Pie Crust

BILLIE BOEHME | PARIS, LAMAR COUNTY EC

½ cup butter
2 tablespoons powdered sugar
1 cup plus 2 tablespoons flour

Preheat oven to 350 degrees. Melt butter in an 8-inch or 9-inch pie pan. In a bowl, combine sugar and flour, then place in pie pan. Mix with fork until well blended. Pat out mixture with hand and crimp edges. Bake 8–12 minutes, or until lightly browned.

COOK'S NOTE: Watch carefully, as it scorches easily. This recipe is for cream pies only.

Meringue

DOROTHY M. MALLEY | MOULTON, FAYETTE EC

3 egg whites
¼ teaspoon cream of tartar
6 tablespoons sugar
1 teaspoon vanilla extract

In a mixing bowl, beat egg whites until frothy. Add cream of tartar. Continue beating while adding sugar. Add vanilla and beat until stiff and glossy. When pie is ready, preheat oven to 400 degrees and spread meringue over pie filling. Bake 8–10 minutes, until delicately browned.

Apple Turnovers

NARCISA P. GARZA | SANTA ELENA, MEDINA EC

3 cups flour
3 tablespoons sugar
½ teaspoon cinnamon
1 cup shortening
5–6 tablespoons water
1 can (21 ounces) apple pie filling
   (Comstock preferred)

Preheat oven to 425 degrees. In a bowl, mix flour, sugar and cinnamon well; then cut shortening into flour mixture until it is crumbly. Add water and form into a ball. Divide dough into small balls. Roll into small rounds, fill half, and fold and seal edges with a fork. Place on an ungreased cookie sheet and bake 10–15 minutes.

Little Pecan Pies

BILLIE ASHBY | LEILIAN, JOHNSON COUNTY EC

PASTRY:
3 ounces cream cheese
½ cup butter
1 cup flour
PECAN FILLING:
¾ cup brown sugar
1 tablespoon butter
2 tablespoons dark corn syrup
1 teaspoon vanilla extract
1 egg, beaten
Pinch of salt
⅔ cup finely chopped pecans

In a bowl, cut cream cheese and butter into flour with pastry blender. Refrigerate 2 hours; then, make into 24 balls. Press into miniature muffin tins and make a hole in center, forming tiny crusts. Preheat oven to 350 degrees. Fill crusts with Pecan Filling: In a saucepan, heat sugar, butter and syrup until butter is melted. Let cool and add vanilla, egg, salt and pecans. Fill pastry shells. Bake 30 minutes.

COOK'S NOTE: We had a good laugh when my grandmother, Grace Huff, God rest her soul, made cornbread using my tart pans by mistake. She said, "Your muffin pans sure make tiny cornbread muffins."

Mocha Swirl Cheesecake

LOIS NEUMANN FERGUSON | BIG FOOT, MEDINA EC

2 cups graham cracker crumbs
½ teaspoon cinnamon
½ cup butter, melted
2 squares (1 ounce each) semisweet baking chocolate
16 ounces cream cheese, softened
1 cup sugar
6 eggs
¼ cup plus 1 tablespoon flour
1½ teaspoons grated lemon zest
3 tablespoons lemon juice
1 teaspoon vanilla extract
1 cup heavy whipping cream, whipped
Grated chocolate (optional)

Preheat oven to 300 degrees. In a bowl, combine graham cracker crumbs, cinnamon and butter; mix well. Firmly press onto bottom and sides of a 9-inch springform pan. Refrigerate. Bring water to a boil in the bottom of double boiler. Place chocolate in top of double boiler and melt on low. Set aside to cool. In a mixing bowl, beat cream cheese with mixer until light and fluffy. Gradually add sugar and mix well. Add eggs, 1 at a time, beating after each addition. Stir in flour, lemon zest, lemon juice and vanilla. Combine 1 cup cheesecake mixture and melted chocolate. Pour remaining cheesecake filling into prepared crust. Pour chocolate mixture over top and gently swirl with a knife. Bake 1 hour. Turn heat off and let cheesecake stand in closed oven 1 hour. Open oven door and allow cheesecake to cool 2–3 hours. Chill in refrigerator before serving. Serve with whipped cream and garnish with grated chocolate, if desired.

Pomodora Cheesecake

CHARLENE SLIGER | ANTON, STAMFORD EC

CRUST:
1½ cups graham cracker crumbs
2 tablespoons sugar
¼ cup unsalted butter, melted
FILLING:
16 ounces cream cheese, softened
2 eggs, slightly beaten
½ cup sugar
1 teaspoon vanilla extract
1 small carton (8 ounces) sour cream
TOPPING:
1 package (10 ounces) frozen raspberries, thawed, juice reserved
1 tablespoon cornstarch

For Crust, thoroughly combine graham cracker crumbs, sugar and butter in a bowl. Press mixture into the bottom and sides of greased 9-inch springform pan. Chill 15–30 minutes. Preheat oven to 375 degrees. For Filling, mix cream cheese, eggs, sugar, vanilla and sour cream. Pour into chilled crust. Bake 25 minutes. Cool on wire rack to room temperature, then refrigerate 8 hours, or overnight. For Topping, strain juice from the thawed berries into a small saucepan. Set fruit aside. Add cornstarch to the juice and stir until smooth. Cook over medium heat, stirring constantly, until bubbling and thickened. Remove sauce from heat, and gently stir in fruit. Cool, if necessary, then spread on chilled cake. Return cake to refrigerator until topping is set.

Rich Chocolate Cheesecake

EVELYN WHITEHURST | FRANKSTON, NEW ERA EC

3 cups graham cracker crumbs
1 cup butter, melted
1 large package (12 ounces) semisweet chocolate
  chips
32 ounces cream cheese, softened
2 cups sugar
4 eggs
1 tablespoon cocoa powder
2 teaspoons vanilla extract
1 large carton (16 ounces) sour cream
Whipped cream

Preheat oven to 300 degrees. In a bowl, combine graham cracker crumbs and butter, mixing well. Firmly press onto bottom and sides of a 10-inch springform pan. Place chocolate chips in top of double boiler; bring water to a boil. Reduce heat to low and cook until chocolate melts. In another bowl, beat cream cheese with an electric mixer until light and fluffy; gradually add sugar and mix well. Add eggs, 1 at a time, beating well after each addition. Stir in melted chocolate, cocoa and vanilla; beat until blended. Stir in sour cream, blending well. Pour into prepared pan. Bake 1 hour and 40 minutes. Center may be soft but will firm when chilled. Let cool to room temperature on a wire rack; leave in pan and chill at least 5 hours in refrigerator. Remove from pan before serving. Garnish with whipped cream.

Party Cheesecakes

MRS. O.L. BLANTON | KAUFMAN, KAUFMAN COUNTY EC

12 ounces cream cheese, softened
⅔ cup sugar
2 eggs
1 teaspoon vanilla extract
1 box (12 ounces) vanilla wafers
16 foil-covered muffin papers
FROSTING:
½ cup sour cream
¼ cup sugar
Cherry pie filling

Preheat oven to 350 degrees. In a bowl, mix cream cheese, sugar, eggs and vanilla until fluffy. Place 1 wafer in bottoms of about 16 muffin liners and fill halfway with cream cheese mixture. Bake 15 minutes. Top with Frosting: Mix sour cream and sugar together, and spread on top of cheesecakes. Top each with pie filling.

COOK'S NOTE: Can be made several days ahead of time.

Sour Cream Cheesecake Supreme

MELINDA WOODS | CLEBURNE, JOHNSON COUNTY EC

CRUST:
1 box (12 ounces) vanilla wafers
2 tablespoons sugar
½ cup butter, melted
FILLING:
4 eggs
1¼ cups sugar
24 ounces cream cheese, room temperature
2 tablespoons lemon juice
2 teaspoons vanilla extract
TOPPING:
1 small carton (8 ounces) sour cream
2 teaspoons vanilla extract
¼ cup sugar

Preheat oven to 350 degrees. For Crust, crush wafers, and mix in a bowl with sugar and butter. Press crumbs into 2 pie pans. For Filling, beat eggs until fluffy in a mixing bowl. Add sugar and beat until creamy. Add cream cheese and beat 2 minutes, or until smooth. Add lemon juice and vanilla. Pour over Crust. Bake 30 minutes. While baking, make Topping: In a bowl, mix all ingredients together. Pour on top of baked cheesecake. Increase oven temperature to 450 degrees and bake 7 minutes more.

Blackberry Cobbler

FRANCES TAYLOR | HENDERSON, RUSK COUNTY EC

½ cup butter
2 9-inch pie crusts
2 cups blackberries
2 cups water
¼ teaspoon salt
¼ cup flour
1½ cups sugar

Preheat oven to 350 degrees. Melt butter in a round baking dish (about 9 inches across). Cut 1 crust into strips and lay strips on top of butter. In a microwave-safe bowl, mix together blackberries, water, salt, flour and sugar. Cook in microwave 5 minutes on high, then pour over strips of pie crust. Lay remaining pie crust on top. Bake 30 minutes, or until brown on top. Peaches or other fruit may be used instead of blackberries.

Cranberry Cobbler

MRS. HOWARD WHITWORTH | ROBY, MIDWEST EC

1 can (21 ounces) peach pie filling
1 can (16 ounces) whole cranberry sauce
1 box deluxe yellow cake mix
    (Duncan Hines preferred)
½ teaspoon cinnamon
¼ teaspoon ground nutmeg
1 cup butter, softened
½ cup chopped nuts
Ice cream or whipped cream (optional)

Preheat oven to 350 degrees. Combine peach pie filling and cranberry sauce in bottom of a 9-by-13-inch baking dish. In a bowl, combine cake mix and spices. Cut in butter and add nuts. Sprinkle over fruit evenly. Bake 45–50 minutes. Serve with ice cream, if desired. Makes approximately 16 servings.

COOK'S NOTE: Great for Thanksgiving. This recipe has been in our family over 20 years.

Peach Cobbler

A.J. ASSMAN | NEW ULM, SAN BERNARD EC

2 cups sliced, fresh peaches (peeled, if desired)
1 tablespoon lemon juice
1 cup plus 2 tablespoons sugar, divided use
2 tablespoons butter, melted
1 cup flour
½ teaspoon salt
2 tablespoons baking powder
2 tablespoons shortening
⅔ cup milk

Preheat oven to 350 degrees. In a baking dish, mix together peaches, lemon juice, 1 cup sugar and butter. In a mixing bowl, sift together flour, salt, remaining sugar and baking powder. Cut in the shortening, add milk and mix well. Spread over top of peaches. Bake 30 minutes, or until a little brown on top.

Curley Brown's Peach Cobbler

CURLEY BROWN | LAMPASAS, HAMILTON COUNTY EC

1 large can (29 ounces) sliced peaches with syrup
1 cup butter
1½ cups water
2 cups sugar
1 cup baking mix
1 9-inch pie crust, unbaked
Sugar and cinnamon, to taste

Preheat oven to 350 degrees. In a saucepan over medium heat, combine peaches with syrup, butter, water and sugar. Bring to a boil. Stir and remove from heat. Stir in baking mix. Pour all into a greased 9-by-13-inch baking dish. Lay strips of uncooked pie crust on top. Sprinkle on a little sugar and cinnamon. Bake until top is slightly browned, approximately 45–50 minutes, but no longer than 1 hour.

COOK'S NOTE: This is real good and I have never had a failure yet. Everyone loves it. This is my own worked-out recipe.

Surprise Peach Cobbler

GAIL ROHRBACH | HONDO, MEDINA EC

1 cup sugar
¾ cup flour
¼ cup vegetable oil
½ cup milk
1 teaspoon baking powder
Dash of salt
1 can (15 ounces) peaches with syrup
Grated nutmeg (optional)

Preheat oven to 350 degrees. Mix all ingredients, except peaches, in a large mixing bowl. Pour into greased 8-inch square baking dish. Pour peaches with syrup over batter. Bake 30 minutes. Add nutmeg on top, if desired.

Spicy Cherry Cobbler

IVY STURDIVANT | HERMLEIGH, MIDWEST EC

FILLING:
1 can (14 ounces) red sour pitted cherries
    (canned in water)
¼ cup sugar
¼ teaspoon cinnamon
¼ teaspoon almond extract
3 tablespoons butter, melted
4 drops red food coloring
TOPPING:
½ cup sugar
1 cup flour
½ teaspoon salt
1 teaspoon baking powder
½ cup milk
2 tablespoons butter, melted

Preheat oven to 350 degrees. Mix all Filling ingredients and pour into deep baking dish. For Topping, mix all ingredients and spread over Filling. Bake 45 minutes.

Quick Fruit Cobbler

MRS. VONA FISHER | POST, DICKENS COUNTY EC

FILLING:
1 can (16 ounces) or 2½ cups chopped fruit
  (apple, peach, plum or other)
¾ cup sugar
1 cup water
2 tablespoons butter
CRUST:
½ cup sugar
1 teaspoon baking powder
1 teaspoon salt
1 scant cup flour
½ cup milk

Preheat oven to 350 degrees. For Filling: In a saucepan, mix together fruit, sugar, water and butter. Bring to a boil, then remove from heat while making Crust: Mix all ingredients together in buttered baking dish. Pour Filling over Crust and bake until brown.

Apple 'n Cheese Tarts

MRS. KENT O. WATTS | LULING, GUADALUPE VALLEY EC

2 cups shredded cheddar cheese
2 cups sifted flour
½ teaspoon salt
½ cup butter (not margarine)
⅓ cup milk
FILLING:
1 cup canned apple pie filling
¼ cup raisins

Combine cheese, flour and salt in mixing bowl. Cut in butter until particles are fine. Sprinkle milk over mixture while stirring with fork until dough holds together. Form into a ball. Wrap and chill at least 2 hours. Preheat oven to 400 degrees. In a bowl, mix together Filling ingredients. Roll out dough on floured surface to ⅛-inch thickness. Cut into rounds with floured 3-inch cutter or other fancy shaped cutter. Place half of rounds on an ungreased cookie sheet. Place rounded teaspoonful of Filling in center of each. Cut a cross in remaining rounds and place over Filling. Seal edges. Bake 12–15 minutes, until light brown. Makes about 2 dozen.

Sweetheart Crescents

GERTRUDE KARCHER | LA GRANGE, FAYETTE EC

4 cups flour
½ teaspoon salt
1 cup butter
3 egg yolks
½ cup sour cream
1 teaspoon vanilla extract
1 packet active dry yeast
PECAN FILLING:
3 egg whites
1 cup sugar
½ cup ground nuts
1 teaspoon vanilla extract

Sift together flour and salt into large bowl. Cut in butter until particles are the size of small peas. Blend together egg yolks, sour cream, vanilla and yeast. Mix well and add to flour mixture. Stir to form dough. Divide dough into 8 parts and let stand at room temperature for 1 hour. While dough is rising, make Filling by beating egg whites until straight peaks form. Add remaining ingredients and mix until well blended. Preheat oven to 350 degrees. To make crescents, roll out dough on pastry cloth or board sprinkled with sugar. Roll each piece into an 8-inch circle about ⅛-inch thick. Cut into wedges like a pie. Spread wedges with Pecan Filling. Roll each wedge, starting with the wide side and rolling to a point. Place point-side down on a greased sheet. Bake 25–30 minutes, until light brown.

Fried Pies

MRS. REX LEE WILKES | BROWNFIELD, LYNTEGAR EC

3 cups sifted flour
½ cup sugar (optional)
½ teaspoon salt
½ cup butter
½ cup shortening
1½ teaspoons butter flavoring
½ teaspoon black walnut flavoring
½ cup milk
1 egg, beaten

In a mixing bowl, combine flour, sugar (if using) and salt. Cut in butter and shortening until mixture is uniform. In a separate bowl, add flavorings to cold milk, then mix with beaten egg and incorporate into flour mixture. Chill dough while preparing filling. Use favorite filling or prepared mincemeat. Roll dough on floured surface and use round cutter or cut into 5-inch squares. Place about 1 tablespoon filling into center of each square; moisten edges with water, fold over and pinch both sides with fork to seal. Fry in deep hot fat, 375 degrees approximately 2 minutes. Drain on paper towel.

Fresh Apple or Peach Strudel

CHERYL CARTER | DALHART, RITA BLANCA EC

Apples or peaches, sliced
1½ cups sugar, divided use
2 tablespoons cinnamon
2 tablespoons butter
1 teaspoon baking powder
1 cup flour
½ teaspoon salt
1 egg
Whipped cream or ice cream (optional)

Preheat oven to 350 degrees. Into the bottom of a buttered 9-by-13-inch baking dish, put thick layers of sliced fruit. Combine ½ cup sugar with cinnamon and sprinkle over fruit. Dot with lumps of butter. Into a mixing bowl, sift remaining sugar, baking powder, flour and salt. Into this, break egg. Mix until crumbly. Put over fruit. Bake until brown. Serve with whipped cream or ice cream, if desired.

Pumpkin Roll

SUE SIRMAN | FORESTBURG, WISE EC

¾ cup flour
1 teaspoon baking powder
2 teaspoons cinnamon
1 teaspoon pumpkin pie spice
½ teaspoon ground nutmeg
½ teaspoon salt
3 eggs, slightly beaten
1 cup sugar
⅔ cup canned pumpkin
1 cup chopped walnuts
CREAM CHEESE FILLING:
6 tablespoons butter, softened
8 ounces cream cheese, softened
1 cup sifted powdered sugar
1 teaspoon vanilla extract

Preheat oven to 375 degrees. Grease a 10-by-15-inch jellyroll pan. Line with waxed paper and grease and flour the waxed paper. Into a bowl, sift flour, soda, spices and salt. In a large bowl, beat eggs and sugar until thick and fluffy; beat in pumpkin. Stir in sifted ingredients all at once. Pour into prepared pan. Spread evenly with spatula. Sprinkle with walnuts. Bake 15 minutes. Loosen cake around edges with knife. Invert onto clean damp towel dusted with powdered sugar; peel off waxed paper. Trim ¼ inch from all sides. Roll up cake and towel together from short side. Place seam-side down on wire rack. Cool completely. Make Cream Cheese Filling: In a bowl, cream butter, cream cheese and powdered sugar together until fluffy. Add vanilla and blend. Unroll cake. Spread with Cream Cheese Filling. Re-roll cake. Refrigerate until ready to serve.

Cherry Tart

MRS. BRYAN MAXEY | POST, LYNTEGAR EC

3 egg whites
1 cup sugar
22 Ritz crackers, crushed
2 cups chopped pecans
1 teaspoon vanilla extract
1 can (21 ounces) cherry pie filling

Preheat oven to 325 degrees. In a mixing bowl, beat egg whites until stiff. Add sugar, Ritz crackers, pecans and the vanilla. Mix well. Bake in 9-by-9-inch pan for 40 minutes. Cool. Add cherry filling on top. Chill well and serve with whipped cream.

Butterscotch Apple Dumplings

THELMA BELL | BELLVILLE, SAN BERNARD EC

CRUST:
2 cups flour
2 teaspoons baking powder
Dash of salt
¼ cup shortening
FILLING:
4 apples, sliced
3 tablespoons butter, divided use
1 tablespoon lemon juice
½ cup chopped nuts
1 teaspoon cinnamon
6 tablespoons sugar, divided use
1 cup dark brown sugar
¾ cup water
1 teaspoon vanilla extract
½ cup butterscotch chips

Preheat oven to 375 degrees. For Crust, mix all ingredients in a bowl. Make dough stiff enough to handle, and roll out to ⅛-inch thick. Cut into 6 squares. For Filling, place apple slices in center of squares. Add small chunk of butter (using up 2 tablespoons total), lemon juice, nuts, cinnamon and 1 tablespoon sugar in each. Fold over and pinch together. Heat brown sugar, water and 1 tablespoon butter until sugar dissolves. Add vanilla. Pour over dumplings and bake 40 minutes, basting occasionally. Melt butterscotch chips and drizzle over warm dumplings. Serves 6.

Apple Crisp

MRS. W. BILLINGS | SEAGRAVES, LYNTEGAR EC

4 cups peeled and sliced apples
1 teaspoon cinnamon
1 teaspoon salt
¼ cup water
½ cup sugar
½ cup brown sugar
¾ cup flour
⅓ cup butter

Preheat oven to 350 degrees. Spray an 8-inch square pan with cooking spray and put apples in pan. Sprinkle with cinnamon, salt and water. In a bowl, mix sugars and flour together, and cut in butter with a pastry cutter. Drop mixture over apples. Bake about 40 minutes.

Apple Delight Dessert

PATSY ZANT | LAMESA, LYNTEGAR EC

1 box yellow cake mix
½ cup butter, melted
1 can (21 ounces) apple pie filling
1 small carton (8 ounces) sour cream
2 egg yolks
Cinnamon
Sugar

Preheat oven to 350 degrees. Mix cake mix and butter and press into bottom and about ½-inch up the sides of a 9-by-13-inch pan. Bake 10 minutes. Remove from oven. Top with apple pie filling. Mix sour cream and egg yolks, and pour on top of apples. Top sour cream with mixture of cinnamon and sugar, to taste. Bake 20–25 minutes, until sour cream mixture is set.

Apple Fritters

PATSY ATWOOD | GRAHAM, ERATH COUNTY EC

1¼ cups flour
1 teaspoon baking powder
½ teaspoon salt
¼ teaspoon ground nutmeg
5 chopped apples
½ cup milk
1 tablespoon vegetable oil
1 egg
1 tablespoon lemon juice
Sugar

In a large bowl, mix first 4 ingredients together. Add apples, milk, oil, egg and lemon juice, and mix well. Drop by the spoonful into hot oil. Drain briefly, and roll in sugar while warm.

COOK'S NOTE: My husband teaches Sunday school, and this is one of their favorites to fix in their home living centers.

Banana-Split Cake

LINDA KEY | ROBY, MIDWEST EC

2 cups graham cracker crumbs
½ cup butter, melted
5 bananas
2 cups powdered sugar
8 ounces cream cheese
1 large can (20 ounces) crushed pineapple, drained
10 large strawberries, cut into halves
1 medium container (12 ounces) whipped topping
½ cup crushed pecans
Cherries

Put graham cracker crumbs in a 9-by-13-inch pan. Pour melted butter over crumbs; mix, then spread over bottom of pan. Slice bananas lengthwise and arrange over crumbs. In a bowl, beat together powdered sugar and cream cheese, then spread over bananas. Spread pineapple over cream cheese mixture. Arrange strawberries over this. Cover pineapple and strawberries with whipped topping. Garnish with nuts and cherries. Chill 2–3 hours.

Czech Cake Bars

MILDRED PIETZSCH | ROSCOE, LONE WOLF EC

1 cup butter
1 cup sugar
2 egg yolks
2 cups flour
1 cup chopped pecans
Apricot preserves

Preheat oven to 325 degrees. In a bowl, cream together butter and sugar. Add egg yolks and blend in the flour and pecans. Wet or grease hands to handle dough. Spread half of dough in the bottom of a well-greased 8-inch square pan. Spread preserves on top of dough in pan. Spread rest of dough on top of fruit and bake 1 hour, or until done.

COOK'S NOTE: This is very good. I especially like it made with apricot preserves, but you can use any kind.

Cherry Dream Squares

BETTY HASTINGS | SEGUIN, GUADALUPE VALLEY EC

1 box lemon or pineapple cake mix
6 tablespoons butter, softened
1 cup old-fashioned rolled oats
1 egg
1 can (21 ounces) cherry pie filling
TOPPING:
¼ cup old-fashioned rolled oats
2 tablespoons butter, melted
¼ cup brown sugar
½ cup chopped pecans

Preheat oven to 350 degrees. Make a crumb mixture with cake mix, butter and oats. Reserve 1 cup of mixture for Topping; set aside. Add egg and blend well. Press into greased, 9-by-13-inch pan. Pour cherry pie filling over the crust. For the Topping, to the reserved 1 cup mixture, add oats, butter, brown sugar and pecans; mix until crumbly. Sprinkle over cherries. Bake 30–35 minutes.

Three-Layer Poppy Seed Torte

DIANNE BOWKER | GRANBURY, JOHNSON COUNTY EC

CRUST:
½ pound graham crackers, crumbled
½ cup butter, melted
¼ cup sugar
FILLING:
1 cup sugar
3 cups milk
3 tablespoons cornstarch
4 egg yolks, slightly beaten
½ cup poppy seeds
1 tablespoon vanilla extract
2 tablespoons butter
MERINGUE:
4 egg whites
4 tablespoons sugar

Preheat oven to 350 degrees. For Crust, mix ingredients together in a bowl. Reserve approximately ¼ cup for top; press the rest into a 9-by-13-inch pan. For Filling, mix sugar, milk and cornstarch in a saucepan. Stir in egg yolks. Cook over medium heat, stirring constantly, until thick. Stir in remaining ingredients and pour into Crust. For Meringue, beat egg whites until they hold a peak. Sprinkle sugar into egg whites before the end of beating process. Put on top of Filling and sprinkle on reserved Crust mixture. Bake 30 minutes. Serve chilled.

Pineapple Torte

MRS. EDWIN MOELLER | ROWENA, COLEMAN COUNTY EC

3 eggs, separated
½ cup sugar
1 cup graham cracker crumbs
½ cup chopped nuts
1 small can (8 ounces) crushed pineapple

Preheat oven to 350 degrees. In a mixing bowl, beat egg yolks until light and fluffy. Add sugar, crumbs, nuts and pineapple. In a separate bowl, beat egg whites until stiff peaks form. Then fold egg whites into sugar mixture. Pour into lightly buttered dish and bake until lightly browned.

Upside-Down Cake

DANNY M. GARRETT | JUSTIN, DENTON COUNTY EC

1 can (21 ounces) cherry pie filling
1 can (15 ounces) crushed pineapple
1 box yellow or white cake mix
1 cup butter, melted
1 cup pecans

Preheat oven to 350 degrees. Spread pie filling in bottom of 9-by-13-inch pan; add pineapple. Sprinkle cake mix evenly on top of fruit; pour butter evenly over cake mix. Finish with pecans on top of this. Cook 1 hour.

Surprise Sweet Potato Dessert

JUNE MCMURREY | LUBBOCK, COMANCHE COUNTY EC

6 medium sweet potatoes
2–4 tablespoons butter
¼–½ cup sugar
¼–½ cup milk
1 package (10 ounces) large marshmallows
1 large package (14 ounces) sweetened flaked
    coconut

Preheat oven to 350 degrees. Boil potatoes with skin on until tender. Drain and cool. Peel, mash and add butter, sugar and milk to make the potatoes stiff enough to make a ball. (If sweet potatoes are sweet enough, omit sugar.) Blend together until smooth. Grease hands, take a handful of sweet potato, and roll around marshmallow until a ball is formed. Roll ball in coconut and place in buttered dish. Place in oven until coconut is browned. Serve immediately!

COOK'S NOTE: Surprise! When you cut into the ball—melted, yummy marshmallow!

English Toffee Dessert

MRS. JIM BAXTER | FRIONA, DEAF SMITH EC

2 tablespoons powdered sugar
2 tablespoons cocoa powder
¼ teaspoon salt
½ cup butter, softened
2 egg yolks
½ cup chopped nuts
1 teaspoon vanilla extract
2 cups crushed vanilla wafers
Whipped cream

In a bowl, sift first three ingredients together. In a mixing bowl, beat butter, egg yolks, nuts and vanilla. Stir in dry ingredients. Place 1 cup crushed vanilla wafers in bottom of loaf pan. Fill with mixture; top with remaining wafers. Chill in refrigerator. Serve in slices with whipped cream.

COOK'S NOTE: This is delicious and tastes like Baby Ruth candy bars.

Creamy Banana Pudding

MRS. DENNIS MEYER | BELLVILLE, SAN BERNARD EC

1 can (14 ounces) sweetened condensed milk
1½ cups cold water
1 small box (3.4 ounces) vanilla instant pudding mix
1 small container (8 ounces) whipped topping
Vanilla wafers
3 bananas, sliced and dipped in lemon juice

In a large mixing bowl, combine condensed milk and water. Add pudding mix and beat until well blended. Chill 5 minutes. Fold in whipped topping. In a 2½-quart bowl, layer crumbled vanilla wafers, pudding and bananas. Chill thoroughly. Refrigerate leftovers. Serves 8–10.

COOK'S NOTE: You can substitute milk for the water. Chocolate or coconut cream pudding may be substituted for vanilla pudding.

Bread Pudding

THELMA NEW | HAWLEY, TAYLOR EC

1 small loaf dry bread, crusts removed, divided use
2 teaspoons baking powder
½ cup sugar
2 eggs, well beaten
½ teaspoon salt
1 teaspoon vanilla extract
1 quart milk
¼ cup butter, melted

Preheat oven to 350 degrees. Grate bread into 2 cups of crumbs and place in buttered casserole dish. In a small bowl, mix baking powder and sugar together. Crumble remaining bread into a large bowl; add baking powder mixture, eggs, salt, vanilla, milk and butter, mixing well. Pour mixture over bread in casserole dish and bake 30 minutes.

COOK'S NOTE: This recipe is from a 1912 cookbook. The book was given to my mother on her wedding day. She used the recipe many times, as I have also.

New Orleans-Style Bread Pudding

MS. W.E. DICKERSON | CARTHAGE, PANOLA-HARRISON EC

6 eggs
2½ cups sugar
1 tablespoon cinnamon
1 tablespoon ground nutmeg
1 tablespoon vanilla extract
½ cup butter, melted
1 quart milk
6 cups bread crumbs (preferably French bread)
1 cup chopped pecans
1 cup raisins
RUM SAUCE:
2 cups powdered sugar
2 tablespoons evaporated milk
2 tablespoons rum

Preheat oven to 350 degrees. In a large bowl, whip eggs until frothy. Add sugar, spices, vanilla and butter; mix well. Add milk and bread crumbs. Mix and let soak 15 minutes. Add pecans and raisins. Pour into greased pan. Bake 45 minutes, or until set. Mix all ingredients for Rum Sauce and serve over bread pudding.

Baked Pear Bread Pudding

PEGGY MULLINS | CLEBURNE, JOHNSON COUNTY EC

1 large can (15 ounces) pear halves,
    cut into 1-inch cubes
2 tablespoons raisins
½ teaspoon cinnamon
⅛ teaspoon ground nutmeg
3 slices white bread, crusts removed
2 tablespoons butter, softened
3 eggs, beaten
⅓ cup sugar
¼ teaspoon salt
2 cups milk, heated
½ teaspoon vanilla extract
2 tablespoons currant jelly
Powdered sugar

Preheat oven to 350 degrees. Lightly butter baking dish. Toss pears with raisins and spices. Spread in buttered dish. Spread bread generously with butter and cut slices in half diagonally; arrange overlapping in dish with buttered side up. In a bowl, beat eggs and gradually stir in hot milk and vanilla; add sugar and salt; stir to dissolve. Pour mixture over bread. Set dish in larger pan of hot water; bake 40–50 minutes. Remove pudding from water and cool at least 10 minutes before serving. Garnish with jelly and powdered sugar. Serve warm or cold.

COOK'S NOTE: Grandmother's Sunday special when I was growing up! Delicious!

Oneida's Coconut Custard Pudding

VONCILLE BALL | BOYD, WISE EC

1½ cups sugar
⅓ cup flour
Pinch of salt
3 eggs, beaten
¼ cup butter, softened
½ cup sweetened flaked coconut
l teaspoon coconut extract
1 cup milk

Preheat oven to 350 degrees. In a mixing bowl, mix sugar, flour and salt together. Add other ingredients. Turn into buttered baking dish. Bake 45 minutes.

Dirt Cake

PAT PAINTER | EDMONSON, SWISHER EC

1 package Oreo cookies
½ cup butter, softened
8 ounces cream cheese
1 cup sugar
1 medium container (12 ounces) whipped topping
3 cups milk
1 large box (5.9 ounces) vanilla instant pudding mix
1 teaspoon vanilla extract

Finely crush the entire package of cookies until creamy middle disappears. (This makes the "dirt" for the cake.) In a mixing bowl, cream butter and cream cheese together. Add sugar and whipped topping, mixing well. In a separate bowl, combine milk, pudding mix and vanilla. Chill. When set, fold this into the butter and cream cheese mixture. Pour half of the "dirt" mixture on the bottom of a 9-by-13-inch pan. Pour the filling mixture on top of this. Top the filling with the remaining "dirt." Freeze.

Brownie Pudding

MRS. TED SORRELLS | SILVER, LONE WOLF EC

BROWNIE:
½ cup sifted flour
1 tablespoon cocoa powder
1 tablespoon melted butter
1 teaspoon baking powder
¼ cup milk
½ cup sugar
1 teaspoon vanilla extract
¼ cup chopped nuts
TOPPING:
½ cup brown sugar
2 tablespoons cocoa powder
¾ cup boiling water

Preheat oven to 350 degrees. Mix all Brownie ingredients. Turn into greased casserole or small baking dish. For Topping, sprinkle brown sugar and cocoa mixture on top. Pour boiling water over mixture. (This makes chocolate sauce in bottom of pan after baking.) Bake 30–40 minutes.

Chocolate Delight

JANET HONEA | FRANKLIN, NAVASOTA VALLEY EC

¾ cup butter
1½ cups flour
¾ cup chopped nuts
8 ounces cream cheese
1 cup powdered sugar
1 medium container (12 ounces) whipped topping,
    divided use
1 small box (3.4 ounces) vanilla instant pudding mix
1 small box (3.4 ounces) chocolate instant pudding mix
3 cups milk
Chopped nuts, for garnish

Preheat oven to 375 degrees. Combine butter, flour and chopped nuts. Mix well and press into pan. Bake 15 minutes. Cool. In a bowl, combine cream cheese, powdered sugar and ½ cup whipped topping. Blend and spread on top of baked crust. Chill. In a mixing bowl, combine pudding mixes and milk; beat 3 minutes. Spread pudding on top of cream cheese layer, and then spread remaining whipped topping on top. Sprinkle with nuts and chill.

    COOK'S NOTE: This is a very refreshing dessert.

Pineapple Icebox Pudding

MRS. ELDON ROSSON | MILFORD, HILL COUNTY EC

1 can (14 ounces) sweetened condensed milk
2 tablespoons lemon juice
1 can (15 ounces) crushed pineapple, drained
1 box (12 ounces) vanilla wafers

In a bowl, mix milk with lemon juice; stir in pineapple. Alternate layers of vanilla wafers and pineapple mixture in a serving dish. Refrigerate. Serve cold. Serves 8.

Log Cabin Pudding

MRS. B.G. COTTON | HEREFORD, DEAF SMITH COUNTY EC

1 envelope unflavored gelatin
¼ cup cold water
1 cup whole milk, scalded
1 cup maple syrup
1¼ cups whipped cream
1 cup pecans
Vanilla wafers (enough to cover bottom of pan
    and top)

Dissolve gelatin in cold water. Let stand 5 minutes. Combine milk and gelatin mixture; stir in syrup. Let congeal. Then fold in whipped cream and pecans. Crush enough vanilla wafers to cover the bottom of pan. Then pour the mixture over wafers. Then put more crushed wafers on top. Place in refrigerator to chill.

Cherry Spoon-Up

MRS. FORD GREENHAW | LORENZO, SOUTH PLAINS EC

2 cans (21 ounces each) cherry pie filling
1 can (8 ounces) crescent rolls
1½ cups sour cream
1 cup firmly packed brown sugar
¼ teaspoon ground nutmeg
Cream or ice cream (optional)

Preheat oven to 375 degrees. Spread prepared pie filling in a 9-by-13-inch pan. Separate crescent roll dough into 4 rectangles and place over filling. In a bowl, combine sour cream, brown sugar and nutmeg. Spread over dough. Bake 45–50 minutes. May be topped with cream or ice cream.

Hello Dolly

MRS. LEE BEHANNON | CORPUS CHRISTI, JASPER-NEWTON EC

1½ cups crushed vanilla wafers
½ cup butter, melted
1 small bag (7 ounces) sweetened flaked coconut
1 cup chopped nuts
1 small package (6 ounces) chocolate chips
1 cup sweetened condensed milk

Preheat oven to 350 degrees. Put wafer crumbs in a loaf pan; pour butter over wafers and mix. Top with coconut, nuts and chocolate chips. Drizzle milk over all. Bake until light brown on top. Cut into squares to serve.

Fruit Torte

FRAULINE ROSENBERGER | NACOGDOCHES, DEEP EAST TEXAS EC

6 egg whites
¾ teaspoon cream of tartar
2 cups sugar
1 teaspoon vanilla flavoring
2 cups crushed soda crackers
1 cup chopped nuts (optional)
Whipped cream or whipped topping
1–2 cups prepared cherry, apricot or pineapple pie filling, to taste

Preheat oven to 350 degrees. In a mixing bowl, beat egg whites until stiff peaks form, adding cream of tartar slowly. Beat in sugar and vanilla. Fold in soda crackers and nuts, if desired. Spread in 9-by-13-inch pan and bake until lightly browned. Cool. Spread top with whipped cream or whipped topping. Dribble 1–2 cups prepared pie filling on top when serving. Serves 8–10.

COOK'S NOTE: Pineapple preserves or strawberries may be used instead of pie filling for this make-ahead dessert.

Lemon Angel Dessert

MRS. CHARLES MCCASLIN | TULIA, SWISHER COUNTY EC

1 envelope unflavored gelatin
¼ cup cold water
6 eggs, separated
Pinch of salt
1½ cups sugar, divided use
¾ cup lemon juice
½ prepared angel food cake
Whipped cream

Soften gelatin in cold water. Cook egg yolks, salt, ¾ cup sugar and lemon juice in double boiler until it coats the spoon. Add gelatin. In a mixing bowl, beat egg whites with remaining sugar. Fold into lemon mixture. Tear cake into pieces into a 9-by-13-inch pan and layer with lemon mixture. Top with whipped cream.

Lemon Dainty

MRS. W.W. RUMAGE | JACKSBORO, J-A-C EC

3 tablespoons shortening
⅛ teaspoon salt
¾ cup sugar
2 teaspoons flour
2 eggs, separated
1 cup milk
Juice of 1 lemon

Preheat oven to 350 degrees. In a mixing bowl, combine shortening, salt, sugar and flour; mix well and add lightly beaten egg yolks, milk and lemon juice, and beat until smooth. In a separate bowl, beat egg whites until stiff. Fold egg whites into other mixture. Pour into buttered baking dish, set in pan of hot water and bake 45 minutes. Serve warm.

COOK'S NOTE: When done, the pudding is a delicate sponge on top with a yellow gold sauce underneath.

Angel Chocolate Dessert

MRS. FRANK L. CERNOSEK | LUBBOCK, FAYETTE EC

2 large packages (12 ounces each) chocolate chips
4 eggs, separated
Salt
2 tablespoons sugar
1 pint heavy whipping cream
1 cup nuts
1 teaspoon vanilla extract
1 prepared angel food cake, torn into chunks

Melt chips in top of double boiler. Take off heat and stir in egg yolks, mixing well. In a mixing bowl, beat egg whites until stiff. Fold into chocolate mixture. Add salt and sugar. In a separate bowl, whip cream until stiff, and fold into chocolate mixture. Add chopped nuts. Make layers by lining 9-by-13-inch pan with half of cake chunks. Pour half the chocolate mixture over it. Make another layer with remainder of cake and pour remainder chocolate over that. Place in refrigerator overnight. Serves 18–20.

Baked Egg Custard

MRS. F.V. GARVIN | KERRVILLE, BANDERA EC

4 eggs
4 tablespoons sugar
3 cups milk
Grated or ground nutmeg

Preheat oven to 475 degrees. In a mixing bowl, beat eggs and sugar together, adding milk slowly until well mixed. Pour into baking dish, sprinkle nutmeg on the top and bake until custard pulls away slightly from side of baking dish.

Banana Split Gelatin Dessert

ELEANORE USTANIK | MCGREGOR, ERATH COUNTY EC

2 small boxes (3 ounces each) lemon Jell-O
10 large marshmallows, quartered
2 cups hot water
2 cups cold water
1 can (15 ounces) crushed pineapple, drained, juice reserved
4 bananas, diced
TOPPING:
2 tablespoons butter
2 tablespoons flour
½ cup sugar
Reserved pineapple juice (add water to make 1 cup)
2 eggs, beaten
1 cup heavy whipping cream, whipped
Pecans
Maraschino cherries

Dissolve Jell-O and marshmallows in hot water. Add cold water and fruit; mix well. Pour into 9-by-13-inch dish and refrigerate until firm. For Topping, mix first 5 ingredients thoroughly in a saucepan. Simmer until thick, stirring constantly. Let cool and then fold in whipped cream. Spread on top of first layer. Sprinkle with chopped pecans and decorate with Maraschino cherries.

COOK'S NOTE: This is a very pretty dessert, and it tastes absolutely scrumptious. The recipe was given to me by a friend many years ago. People always ask for the recipe whenever I take this dessert to a potluck dinner.

Cold Lemon Souffle

BILLIE CATHEY | WELCH, LYNTEGAR EC

1 envelope unflavored gelatin
¼ cup cold water
3 eggs, separated
1 cup sugar
⅓ cup lemon juice
Grated zest of 1 lemon
1 teaspoon vanilla extract
2 cups heavy whipping cream

In a small, heatproof dish, soak gelatin in cold water until firm. Place in larger container of hot water until dissolved and clear. In a mixing bowl, beat egg yolks until pale lemon colored; add sugar gradually and beat until light. Beat in lemon juice, lemon zest and vanilla. Add gelatin and blend well. Chill until it begins to congeal. While chilling, beat whipping cream until stiff; in a separate bowl, beat egg whites until stiff. Into slightly congealed gelatin, fold in whipped cream, then egg whites. Chill at least 2 hours.

Pretzel Dessert

MOLLIE WARREN | LONGVIEW, RUSK COUNTY EC

2 cups broken pretzels (not too fine)
1 cup plus 1 tablespoon sugar, divided use
¾ cup butter, melted
8 ounces cream cheese
1 small container (8 ounces) whipped topping
1 large box (6 ounces) raspberry Jell-O
2 packages (10 ounces each) frozen strawberries
2 cups boiling water

Preheat oven to 400 degrees. Combine pretzels, 1 tablespoon sugar and butter. Pat into 9-by-13-inch baking pan. Bake 6 minutes. Set aside to cool. In a mixing bowl, cream together cream cheese and remaining sugar. Fold in whipped topping and spread over pretzel layer. In a heatproof bowl, mix Jell-O, frozen strawberries and boiling water. Put bowl in refrigerator. When Jell-O has slightly thickened, spoon over cream cheese layer. Chill.

Biscuit Tortoni

EVA MEYER | HOUSTON AND MONTGOMERY, MID-SOUTH EC

½ cup whole almonds
1½ cups heavy whipping cream
½ cup powdered sugar
3 tablespoons rum or cognac
1 egg white

Preheat oven to 300 degrees. Blanch almonds; remove skins and chop (or used slivered almonds). Spread almonds on a cookie sheet and toast in oven until brown. Whip cream until it begins to thicken. Add sugar by sifting in a little at a time and beat until stiff. Stir in the rum. In a separate bowl, beat the egg white until stiff and fold into the whipped cream. Spoon into individual paper or foil cups about 2 inches in diameter. Sprinkle with the toasted almonds and freeze for about 5 hours. Serve in the cups. Serves 10.

Blueberries in the Snow

MRS. VERLIE KURETSCH | GANADO, JACKSON EC

PASTRY:
1 cup butter, softened
1½ cups flour
1 cup finely chopped pecans
TOPPING:
8 ounces cream cheese, softened
1 large container (16 ounces) whipped topping
2 cups powdered sugar
1 can (21 ounces) blueberry pie filling

Preheat oven to 350 degrees. In a bowl, mix butter, flour and pecans well and spread in a greased 9-by-13-inch pan. Press down gently, and bake until light brown. Cool. For Topping, mix the first 3 ingredients in a bowl, then spread on baked, cooled Pastry. Spoon blueberry pie filling on top of cream cheese mixture. Spread evenly and freeze. Take out of freezer 2 hours before serving (but keep in refrigerator). Cut into squares to serve.

COOK'S NOTE: Cherry pie filling is equally good.

Strawberry Yum Yum

HELEN JOHNSTON | BEDFORD, JOHNSON COUNTY EC

1 box (12 ounces) vanilla wafers
½ cup butter
1 box (16 ounces) powdered sugar
4 eggs
1 cup chopped nuts
2 large packages (16 ounces each) frozen
    strawberries, thawed and drained
1 medium container (12 ounces) whipped topping

Crush vanilla wafers and place in bottom of
8-by-12-inch pan. In a saucepan, combine butter
and powdered sugar, then add eggs. Mix well.
Cook in saucepan, stirring constantly, until thick;
pour over cookie crumbs. Add chopped nuts for
next layer. Add thawed strawberries for the next
layer and freeze. Spread with whipped topping
and return to freezer. Remove from freezer 1 hour
before serving.

COOK'S NOTE: Can be frozen for 1 week.

Summer Sundae Dessert

MARY J. KING | ATHENS, NEW ERA EC

Vanilla wafers
1 cup marshmallows
1 cup sweetened condensed milk
1 cup chocolate kisses
1 cup chopped pecans
Pinch of salt
Vanilla ice cream

Line a glass 9-inch pan with whole vanilla wafers.
In a saucepan, heat next 5 ingredients together
until melted. Stir together, then cool slightly. Place
dips of vanilla ice cream over vanilla wafer in pan.
Pour chocolate mixture over all. Chill several
hours, if possible. Serves 6–8.

COOK'S NOTE: This recipe is a best-ever summer
dessert. A friend brought this to me when I was ill. Her
husband was our district judge.

Voluptuous Butterfinger Ice Cream

JUNE HENDERSON | SULPHUR SPRINGS, FARMERS EC

2 cans (14 ounces each) sweetened condensed milk
2 cans water
6 eggs
Pinch of salt
1 quart heavy whipping cream
1 tablespoon vanilla extract
1 package Butterfinger candy bars, crushed
    (6 1.9-ounce bars)

In a saucepan, mix milk, water, eggs and salt
together, and cook over low heat until thickened,
stirring often. Scrape into a large bowl and refrigerate at least 4 hours. Stir in whipping cream,
vanilla and crushed Butterfinger candy. Freeze
according to directions on ice cream freezer.

COOK'S NOTE: I won first place in the candy divi-
sion of the National Homemade Ice Cream Contest of
Texas, 1988.

Fried Ice Cream

CALLIE EUDY FINLEY | CLARKSVILLE, LAMAR COUNTY EC

1 quart vanilla ice cream
½ teaspoon cinnamon
½ cup sugar
1 cup crushed corn flakes
Oil, for deep frying
¼ cup honey
Whipped cream
4 maraschino cherries

Let the ice cream stand at room temperature about
5 minutes to soften slightly. Combine the cinnamon, sugar and corn flake crumbs in a shallow pan.
Using an ice cream scoop, make 4 large, dense balls
of ice cream. Roll these balls in the crumb mixture
to cover completely. Wrap in pieces of aluminum
foil, and freeze 5 hours. Heat oil to 450 degrees in
a deep pan. Take the foil off of the ice cream ball
and deep fry very briefly, about 2 seconds. Drain
momentarily, and place in dessert dishes. Top
each ball with 1 tablespoon honey, a little whipped
cream and a cherry. Serve immediately.

Grandmother Hunter's Ice Cream

GRACIE M. SILLIMAN | SINTON, NUECES EC

4 eggs
2¼ cups sugar, divided use
1 can (14 ounces) sweetened condensed milk
2 teaspoons lemon extract
3 tablespoons vanilla extract
Whole milk to fill freezer container

In a large bowl, combine eggs and ½ cup sugar and beat until creamy. Add ½ cup sugar and beat thoroughly. Add sweetened condensed milk, remaining sugar, extracts and whole milk. Beat well. Pour into 4-quart ice cream freezer and freeze according to manufacturer's directions.

Apricot Ice Cream

MRS. REX LEE WILKES | BROWNFIELD, LYNTEGAR EC

4 eggs
1 teaspoon cream of tartar
2 tablespoons flour
¼ teaspoon salt
1 can (14 ounces) sweetened condensed milk
1 large can (12 ounces) evaporated milk
1 can (15 ounces) apricots
1 tablespoon vanilla extract

In a bowl, beat eggs with cream of tartar, gradually adding flour and salt. Add milks, fruit and vanilla. Pour into ice cream freezer, leaving room for cream to freeze and swell. Freeze according to manufacturer's directions.

Tutti Fruiti Ice Cream

MRS. ROY O'BRIAN | FRIONA, DEAF SMITH COUNTY EC

1 cup crushed drained pineapple
1 package frozen strawberries
2 chopped bananas
1 pint heavy whipping cream
2 pints half-and-half
5 eggs
2 cups sugar
1 tablespoon vanilla extract
½ cup chopped pecans
Milk

Blend fruits together in blender. In a bowl, beat eggs well, then add sugar and vanilla. Stir in whipping cream and half-and-half. Pour in fruit mixture and mix together. Pour mixture into a 4-quart ice cream freezer, and finish filling with milk. Freeze according to manufacturer's instructions.

COOK'S NOTE: You can just use 3 pints of half-and-half instead of the whipping cream and half-and-half in the ingredients list.

Lemon-Orange Sherbet

BILLIE CATHEY | WELCH, LYNTEGAR EC

1 can (12 ounces) frozen orange juice, undiluted
¾ cup lemon juice
4 cups sugar
1 pint heavy whipping cream
2 quarts milk
1 teaspoon vanilla extract

In a bowl, mix orange juice, lemon juice and sugar; let stand in refrigerator overnight. In a mixing bowl, whip cream to stiff peaks. Fold cream, milk and vanilla into juice mixture. Pour into 4-quart ice cream freezer and freeze according to manufacturer's directions

COOK'S NOTE: This is very smooth and rich. Stays easy to dip when stored in freezer. One dip makes a great light dessert.

SAUCES,
SPREADS
& MORE

Cheese Dressing for Sandwiches

MRS. WALTER MAHLOW | RAYMONDVILLE, MAGIC VALLEY EC

1 pound processed cheese (Velveeta preferred)
3 cups heavy whipping cream
4 boiled eggs, finely chopped
1 teaspoon finely chopped onion
1 small jar (4 ounces) pimientos

In a saucepan, heat cheese and cream, stirring until cheese is melted. Add remaining ingredients. Cool before spreading on sandwiches.

Salsa

CYNTHIA THIGPEN | FARWELL, DEAF SMITH EC

1 can (14.5 ounces) whole tomatoes
1½ cups chopped bell pepper
1½ cups chopped onions
1 small can (4 ounces) chopped green chiles
2 teaspoons granulated garlic
1 teaspoon salt
1 teaspoon black pepper
¼ cup Worcestershire sauce
¼ cup vegetable oil
¼ cup brown sugar

Mash tomatoes and mix in the remaining ingredients. Cover and let stand up to several hours for full flavor. Makes 2 quarts. Keep refrigerated, and it will stay good for a month.

Green Chile Sauce

MRS. T.F. HENSON | DUBLIN, ERATH COUNTY EC

4 medium tomatoes, chopped
1 medium onion, coarsely chopped
2 teaspoons garlic salt
1 small can (4 ounces) chopped green chiles
¼ teaspoon pepper

Mix all ingredients and chill.

Bell Pepper Relish

MRS. LYNDON S. KRAUSE | SAN ANTONIO, GUADALUPE VALLEY EC

12 large bell peppers
6 large onions
2 cups vinegar
2 cups sugar
3 tablespoons salt

Chop peppers and onions or put through a fine grinder. Put them in a heatproof bowl and cover with boiling water; let stand 5 minutes. Drain well. Place in a pot and add vinegar, sugar and salt; bring to a boil, and boil 5 minutes. Pour into glass containers and process for canning or store in refrigerator. Makes about 4 pints.

Chow Chow Relish

PAT ADCOX | SNYDER, MIDWEST EC

4 cups coarsely chopped cabbage
3 cups coarsely chopped cauliflower
2 cups coarsely chopped onion
2 cups seeded and coarsely chopped green pepper
1 cup seeded and coarsely chopped red pepper
2 cups coarsely chopped green tomatoes
2½ cups vinegar
1½ cups sugar
3 tablespoons coarse salt
2 teaspoons dry mustard
1 teaspoon ground turmeric
½ teaspoon ground ginger
2 teaspoons celery seed
1 teaspoon mustard seed

Mix all vegetables together in a bowl and chill 4–6 hours. Drain well. Combine vinegar, sugar, salt and spices in a large pot; bring to a boil and simmer 10 minutes. Add vegetables and bring back to a boil. Reduce heat slightly to a steady boil and cook 2 minutes, stirring frequently. Spoon into jars and process for canning or refrigerate.

COOK'S NOTE: If you prefer a spicy chow chow, add a few hot peppers to other vegetables. The coarse blade of a food grinder is good for chopping the vegetables.

Sweet Green Tomato Relish

MRS. ED CONRADY | WINDTHORST, J-A-C EC

8 cups chopped green tomatoes
2 tablespoons salt
2 cups vinegar
1 cup brown sugar
3 tablespoons dry mustard
1 teaspoon ground turmeric
1 cup sugar
½ tablespoon celery seed
3 cups chopped onions

Soak tomatoes in salt overnight. The next morning, drain. In a pot, bring vinegar to a boil, then boil 2 minutes. Add tomatoes and all other ingredients. Boil 5 minutes. Put in jars and process for canning or refrigerate.

Corn Relish

MRS. H.A. BRIGHT | GILMER, UPSHUR RURAL EC

12 ears corn
2 cups vinegar
12 large onions, finely chopped
12 sweet peppers (red and green), finely chopped
1¾ cup prepared mustard
3 cups sugar
6 hot peppers, finely chopped

Cut corn off cob and put in a pot. Add remaining ingredients and cook until thick, stirring constantly. Pack in jars and process for canning or refrigerate.

COOK'S NOTE: One medium head cabbage, finely chopped, may be added, if desired.

Onion Relish

JUDY LOGAN | HALE CENTER, LIGHTHOUSE EC

3½ cups chopped onions
½ cup chopped green peppers
½ cup chopped red peppers
1 cup vinegar
1 cup sugar
½ teaspoon salt

Mix onions and peppers in a large heatproof bowl. Pour boiling water over them. Let stand 5 minutes; drain. Put vinegar, sugar and salt in a large saucepan. Add drained mixture and let simmer 25 minutes. Put into jars and process for canning or refrigerate. Makes 3 pints.

End-of-Summer Relish

NATALIE LANGE | ROWENA, COLEMAN COUNTY EC

3 cups sugar
4 cups chopped green tomatoes
4 cups chopped cabbage
4 cups chopped green bell peppers
4 cups chopped onions
2 cups prepared mustard
2 tablespoons salt
2 tablespoons pepper
3 cups vinegar

Combine all ingredients in a large, heavy saucepan. Stir thoroughly. Bring to a boil slowly and boil 20 minutes. Pour into jars and process for canning or refrigerate. Makes 4 quarts.

COOK'S NOTE: This is good served with beef, pork or venison. This is an old recipe passed down to me from my mother. We have enjoyed it over the years. This is an excellent way to use all those green tomatoes left in the garden before the first frost.

Squash Relish

DOLORES WILLIS | JASPER, JASPER-NEWTON EC

12 cups chopped yellow squash
4 cups chopped onions
1 large green bell pepper, chopped
1 small jar (4 ounces) pimientos,
    drained and chopped
2½ cups white vinegar
5 cups sugar
5 tablespoons pickling spices
1 teaspoon ground turmeric
1 teaspoon celery seed
5 tablespoons salt

Place first 4 ingredients in a large, covered pot and cook over medium-high heat for 5–7 minutes, until vegetables release some liquid; strain. Mix remaining ingredients in a bowl. Pour vinegar mixture over squash mixture and mix. Bring to boil and boil about 2 minutes. Put in jars and process for canning or refrigerate. Makes 6 pints.

COOK'S NOTE: Squash relish mixed with a can of drained, flaked tuna and mayonnaise makes a good tuna salad. Squash relish is also good with beans.

Fire-and-Ice Tomatoes

MRS. T.F. HENSON | DUBLIN, ERATH COUNTY EC

¾ cup vinegar
1½ teaspoons celery salt
1½ teaspoons mustard seed
½ teaspoon salt
4½ teaspoons sugar
⅛ teaspoon red pepper
⅛ teaspoon black pepper
¼ cup cold water
6 tomatoes, quartered
1 green pepper, cut into strips
1 red onion, cut into rings
1 cucumber, peeled and sliced

In a saucepan, bring first 8 ingredients to a boil, and boil furiously 1 minute. Put the other ingredients in a heatproof bowl. While vinegar mixture is still hot, pour over remaining ingredients. Chill well before serving. Keeps well several days in refrigerator.

Pear Chutney

MRS. W.G. ROSSER | KARNACK, PANOLA-HARRISON EC

1 cup salt
16 cups ground pears
8 cups chopped onions
14 bell peppers, seeded and chopped
8 hot peppers, seeded and chopped
6 cups vinegar
4 cups sugar
2 tablespoons ground turmeric
2 tablespoons mustard seed
2 tablespoons celery seed

In a bowl, pour salt over pears, onion and peppers, and let stand several hours. Drain juice using a colander. In a pot, boil vinegar, sugar and spices 5 minutes. Mix pear mixture with spiced vinegar solution and boil 5 minutes. Place in jars and process for canning or refrigerate.

Cranberry-Orange Chutney

MRS. J.E. GIBBONS | SHERMAN, GRAYSON-COLLIN EC

1 cup fresh orange sections
¼ cup orange juice
4 cups cranberries
2 cups sugar
1 cup chopped, unpeeled apple
½ cup raisins
¼ cup chopped walnuts or pecans
1 tablespoon vinegar
½ teaspoon ground ginger
½ teaspoon cinnamon

Combine all ingredients in a large saucepan and bring to a boil. Reduce heat and simmer 5 minutes or until berries begin to burst. Chill until ready to serve.

Grandma's Pear Relish

MRS. GARLAND CARROLL | CLEBURNE, JOHNSON COUNTY EC

15 large pears
6–10 sweet peppers (green and red)
6 or more hot peppers
1 cup prepared mustard
2 cups vinegar
3 cups sugar
2 tablespoons salt
12 medium onions

Grind pears and peppers. Place in a large pot with rest of ingredients. Bring to boil and boil 20 minutes. Place in jars and process for canning, or refrigerate.

Bread and Butter Pickles

MRS. THOMAS G. NEWMAN | LUBBOCK, COMANCHE COUNTY EC

6 medium onions, sliced
24 cups sliced cucumbers
Salt
5 cups sugar
1 tablespoon celery seed
1½ tablespoons ground turmeric
½ cup mustard seed
5 cups cider vinegar
Red peppers (optional)

In a large bowl, combine onions and cucumbers. Salt heavily and let stand 3 hours. Drain. Place sugar, spices and vinegar into a large pot. If desired, add a little red pepper, cut finely. Bring to a boil. Add the cucumber mixture. Allow to heat but not boil. Put in jars and process for canning or refrigerate.

COOK'S NOTE: If you do not want to can the spices, put them in a cloth sack and allow to boil in vinegar and sugar, then remove sack before canning.

Never-Fail Crisp Pickles

MRS. CAL LUEDKE | MART, LIMESTONE COUNTY EC

16 cups sliced cucumbers
6 medium white onions, sliced
1 sweet green pepper, cut into strips
⅓ cup salt
3 cups distilled white vinegar
5 cups sugar
1½ teaspoons ground turmeric
1½ teaspoons celery seed
2 tablespoons mustard seed

Put cucumbers, onions, pepper and salt in a large container. Cover with cracked ice. Mix thoroughly. Let stand for 3 hours. Drain. Place in a large pot. Combine remaining ingredients and pour over cucumber mixture. Heat to boiling. Place in jars and process for canning or refrigerate. Makes 8 pints.

Home-Style Kosher Dill Pickles

MRS. O.M. SANDERS | VALLEY MILLS, MCLENNAN EC

Fresh dill
Garlic cloves
Pepper
1 small green or red pepper, diced (optional)
Cucumbers, fresh and firm
8 cups water
4 cups vinegar
1 cup kosher salt (non-iodized)

To each quart jar, add 1 head fresh dill, 1 clove garlic and a pinch of pepper. Wash cucumbers and pack in jars. Bring water, vinegar and salt to boil. Pour over cucumbers and seal. Process for canning or refrigerate. Pickles are ready after 3–4 weeks.

Green Cherry Tomato Pickles

MRS. R.T. LOVELADY | SNYDER, MIDWEST EC

2 pounds hard green tomatoes
2 red peppers
2 garlic cloves
2 tablespoons chopped dill
2 teaspoons mustard seed
2 teaspoons mixed pickling spice
1 cup water
1 cup white vinegar
1 teaspoon salt

Wash and dry tomatoes. Pack them in quart jars along with 1 each pepper and garlic clove, plus 1 tablespoon dill and 1 teaspoon each mustard seed and pickling spice. Bring water, white vinegar and salt to a boil. Pour over tomatoes; seal immediately. Process for canning or refrigerate. Makes 2 quarts.

Pickled Okra

MRS. HOUSTON BARTLETT | BOVINA, DEAF SMITH EC

3 pounds okra
5 garlic cloves
5 hot peppers
4 cups vinegar
½ cup water
6 tablespoons salt
6 tablespoons celery seed
6 tablespoons mustard seed

Pack small okra in clean pint jars. Add a clove of garlic and a pepper to each jar. Boil the other ingredients and pour over okra. Seal jars. Process for canning or refrigerate. Let set for 2 weeks. Makes 5–6 jars.

Pickled Dilly Beans

MOLLIE L. GARDNER | HAMILTON, HAMILTON COUNTY EC

2 pounds fresh green snap beans
4 small garlic cloves
4 heads fresh dill or 4 teaspoons dill seed
½ teaspoon red pepper flakes
2½ cups white vinegar
2½ cups water
4 tablespoons kosher salt

Wash beans and break off stems. In each of 4 sterilized pint jars, put 1 clove garlic, 1 head dill or 1 teaspoon of dill seeds, and ¼ teaspoon red pepper flakes. Fit beans in jars, allowing ½-inch headroom at the top of each jar. Trim beans, if necessary. Bring vinegar, water and salt to a boil. Pour over beans, filling to within ¼ inch of the rim. Fasten jar tops and process for canning or refrigerate.

COOK'S NOTE: Uniformly sized, straight beans are the most attractive choice. This is a delicious and nutritious snack. Let mellow for a few weeks before serving.

Pickled Cauliflower

FLO CONNER | SCHULENBURG, FAYETTE EC

1 head cauliflower, broken into flowerets
Salt
Water
1 cup vegetable oil
½ cup cider vinegar
1 rib celery, including top, thinly sliced
1 small onion, chopped
1 thick lemon slice
1 clove garlic, minced
¼ teaspoon peppercorns
¼ teaspoon mustard seed
1 bay leaf
⅓ cup chopped pimientos

Cook cauliflower in ½ inch boiling, salted water 10 minutes, or until tender when poked with a fork; drain and set aside. In a saucepan, boil remaining ingredients except pimiento; pour over cauliflower. Gently stir in pimiento. Cover and chill. Makes 1½ quarts.

Bar-B-Q Sauce

MRS. GEORGE R. ALEXANDER | LONGVIEW, UPSHUR RURAL EC

1 cup ketchup
½ cup water
1 teaspoon prepared mustard
2 tablespoons brown sugar
2 tablespoons Worcestershire sauce
2 tablespoons vinegar
Juice of 1 lemon
Hot sauce, to taste
Salt and pepper, to taste
1 small onion
1 teaspoon shortening

Combine all ingredients except onion and shortening. Sauté onion in shortening over low heat. Add sauce mixture and cook about 10 minutes over low heat.

Barbecue Sauce

AUGUST BARTOSH | ARLINGTON, MCLENNAN COUNTY EC

1 cup maple syrup
1 cup ketchup
¼ cup vinegar
2 tablespoons Worcestershire sauce
4 teaspoons onion salt
2 teaspoons chili powder
2 teaspoons dry mustard

Blend all ingredients and mix well. Let stand in refrigerator for a day before using. Sauce can be stored for months in refrigerator.

Chef's Cheese Sauce

MRS. PAT ADCOX | SNYDER, MIDWEST EC

½ cup sour cream
4 tablespoons butter or margarine, softened
1 cup shredded sharp American cheese
4 tablespoons chopped green onion
    or 2 tablespoons chives

Bring sour cream, butter and cheese to room temperature; add onions. With electric mixer, beat together until light and fluffy.

COOK'S NOTE: Great on baked potatoes.

Jezebel Sauce

LAVONNE DROEMER | GIDDINGS, BLUEBONNET EC

1 jar (16 ounces) apple jelly
1 jar (16 ounces) peach jelly
3 tablespoons dry mustard
1 tablespoon ground black pepper
½ cup plus 2 tablespoons horseradish

Mix together all ingredients. Chill. Serve over a large block of soft cream cheese with crackers. Makes 1 quart and keeps for weeks.

COOK'S NOTE: This is "sweet hot" and very good! This is a great gift.

Plum Sauce

MRS. JAMES A. NOEL | BAY CITY, JACKSON EC

2 large cans (15 ounces each) purple plums
   in heavy syrup
1 apple, diced
¾ cup crushed pineapple, drained
½ cup white vinegar
½ cup sugar
¼ teaspoon salt
1 small jar (4 ounces) drained pimientos

Drain plums, reserving 1 cup syrup. Remove seeds
and put fruit with reserved syrup in saucepan. Add
remaining ingredients and simmer 1 hour. Force
through a coarse sieve or food mill. Makes 2 cups
and keeps just like jam in refrigerator.

   COOK'S NOTE: Serve with meat, duck, goose or
wild game.

Tartar Sauce

MRS. HARRIETT E. HUDSON | BAY CITY, JACKSON EC

1 cup mayonnaise
1 tablespoon grated onion
4 tablespoons grated dill pickle
1 tablespoon capers, mashed
¼ cup lemon juice
½ teaspoon salt
Dash black pepper

Mix well and chill before serving.

Shrimp Cocktail Sauce

ELDA HUSE | WEST, HILL COUNTY EC

2 cups ketchup
2 cups chili sauce
¼ cup vinegar
6 drops hot sauce
¼ cup finely minced onion
¼ cup finely minced celery
2 teaspoons Worcestershire sauce

Combine all ingredients and mix well. Keep in jars
in refrigerator.

Damma Hot

MRS. ERNEST LOCKLAR | MIDLAND, CAP ROCK EC

4 cups coarsely chopped green tomatoes
4 cups chopped onions
4 cups chopped hot peppers
4 cups vinegar
2 cups sugar
1 cup prepared mustard

In a large pot, boil all ingredients 10 minutes and
put in jars. Process for canning or refrigerate.
Makes about 7½ pints.

   COOK'S NOTE: If hot peppers are extra hot, sweet
peppers may be substituted.

One-Minute French Dressing

WILMA STARK | CANTON, NEW ERA EC

2 teaspoons salt
1 teaspoon sugar
½ teaspoon pepper
1 teaspoon paprika
½ cup vinegar
1½ cups vegetable oil

Combine and shake in covered jar. Makes 2 cups.

   COOK'S NOTE: As a variation, add 2 teaspoons
crumbled blue cheese per ½ cup of dressing.

Pepper-Cream Salad Dressing

LAVONNE DROEMER | GIDDINGS, BLUEBONNET EC

½ cup mayonnaise
¼ cup sour cream
⅓ cup grated Parmesan cheese
1 tablespoon lemon juice
⅛ teaspoon hot sauce
1 teaspoon cracked black pepper, or to taste

Combine all ingredients and chill. Serve over crisp
salad greens. Makes 1 cup.

Dressing for Cabbage Slaw
MRS. EDWIN BERTSCH | PLUM, BLUEBONNET EC

3 tablespoons sugar
1 teaspoon dry mustard
3 tablespoons flour
1 teaspoon salt
¼ teaspoon black pepper
1 cup vinegar
1 cup buttermilk
3 egg yolks, well beaten
2 tablespoons butter

Into a pot, sift together sugar, mustard, flour, salt and pepper. Add remaining ingredients except butter and cook over low heat until thick, stirring constantly. When thick, stir in butter. Makes 1 pint.

COOK'S NOTE: This recipe is at least 100 years old. The slaw can be stored in the refrigerator in a covered jar or dish, and it will keep for several weeks. It is very good with beef, pork or navy beans.

Cranberry Honey
MRS. R.T. LOVELADY | SNYDER, MIDWEST EC

2 cups cranberry cocktail
3 cups sugar
1 teaspoon grated orange zest
1 cup honey
½ bottle fruit pectin (3 ounces total)

In a saucepan, bring first 3 ingredients to a boil; simmer 10 minutes. Add honey. Bring to a rapid boil; boil 1 minute. Remove from heat. Add pectin; skim. Pour into jelly jars and process for canning or refrigerate. Makes 5 6-ounce jars.

Heavenly Jam
MICHELLE ADAMS | POTEET, KARNES EC

3 pounds ripe peaches, mashed
3 pounds sugar
1 large jar (16 ounces) maraschino cherries with juice
Grated zest of 1 orange
Pulp of 2 oranges

Combine peaches and sugar and let stand overnight. Chop cherries, reserving juice. Add cherries, juice, orange zest and pulp to a saucepan; cook 1 hour. Pack in jars and process for canning or refrigerate.

Fig Preserves
MRS. HOWARD B. SARGENT | TOLAR, ERATH COUNTY EC

3 cups figs, cut-up or ground
3 cups sugar
2 small boxes (3.4 ounces each) strawberry Jell-O

Combine figs, sugar and Jell-O. Let set until watery. In a large saucepan, cook until thick, approximately 30 minutes. Pour in jars and process for canning or refrigerate.

Hot Pepper Jelly
AUDIE NEWTON | NEWTON, JASPER-NEWTON EC

¼ cup hot peppers
¾ cup bell pepper
6½ cups sugar
1½ cups cider vinegar
1 bottle (6 ounces) pectin

Seed and finely grind peppers in a blender. Mix peppers, sugar and vinegar. In a pot, bring to a rolling boil that cannot be stirred down. Remove from heat and cool 5 minutes. Add pectin; mix thoroughly. Pour in jars and process for canning or refrigerate.

Greek Seasoning

MRS. ALBERT YOUNG | AXTELL, NAVASOTA VALLEY EC

2 tablespoons salt
1 teaspoon black pepper
2 tablespoons parsley
1 tablespoon dill weed
1 teaspoon tarragon
1 teaspoon thyme
1 teaspoon rosemary
2 teaspoons garlic powder
1 tablespoon oregano

Put ingredients in a blender; whirl until pulverized.

COOK'S NOTE: Serve with salads; sprinkle on fish or chicken before baking or broiling; or use as seasoning for dips.

Poultry Seasoning Blend

MRS. LUTHER BLEZINGER | NEW ULM, SAN BERNARD EC

1½ tablespoons rubbed sage
1½ tablespoons onion powder
1½ tablespoons pepper
1½ tablespoons celery seed
1½ tablespoons dried thyme
1½ tablespoons dried marjoram
2¼ teaspoons dried rosemary
2¼ teaspoons garlic powder

Combine all ingredients in a bowl, stirring well. Store in an airtight container in a cool, dry place. Makes ½ cup.

No-Salt Seasoning

JO DIEGEL | LEAKEY, BANDERA EC

5 teaspoons onion powder
1 tablespoon garlic powder
1 tablespoon paprika
1 tablespoon dry mustard
1 tablespoon thyme
½ teaspoon pepper
½ teaspoon celery seed

Mix all ingredients thoroughly. Makes ¼ cup seasoning.

Marinade

LINDA MARTIN BEACH | GAINESVILLE, COOKE COUNTY EC

1½ cups vegetable oil
¾ cup soy sauce
¼ cup Worcestershire sauce
2 tablespoons dry mustard
2½ teaspoons salt
1½ teaspoons parsley flakes
1 tablespoon pepper
½ cup red wine vinegar
1 clove garlic, crushed
⅓ cup lemon juice

Blend all ingredients in blender 30–40 seconds, or shake vigorously in a shaker. Store covered in refrigerator until ready to use. Let meat soak 3–8 hours, depending on cut; cook as usual.

COOK'S NOTE: This marinade has made the cheapest cut of roasts or steaks very tender. While living on base at Camp Pendleton, California, we military wives exchanged a lot of recipes. This one was a real find, and before we ever grilled, we marinated first, because it made any cut of meat so tender.

Marinade for Venison or Cabrito

MARTHALYN SMITH | PALESTINE, NEW ERA EC

2 cups white vinegar
2 cups Burgundy or vermouth
1 onion, sliced
2 tablespoons black pepper
2 tablespoons salt
1 tablespoon tarragon
2 garlic cloves

Mix all ingredients together. Marinate meat 24 hours.

Meat Marinade

BELINDA VINKLAREK | FLATONIA, FAYETTE EC

½ cup pineapple juice
1 cup soy sauce
½ cup vinegar
1 cup brown sugar
1 teaspoon garlic powder (optional)

Mix all ingredients in saucepan. Allow to simmer, stirring frequently, until it begins to boil. Remove promptly. Allow mixture to cool. Place meat in marinade and refrigerate until ready to cook, at least 30 minutes.

COOK'S NOTE: This is delicious with pork and chicken cuts, and can also be used with beef and seafood.

Homemade Wine Sauce

MRS. ANTON A. BUJNOCH SR. | HALLETTSVILLE, GUADALUPE VALLEY EC

2 tablespoons cornstarch
Water
1 cup homemade wine (or your favorite)
½ cup sugar
½ cinnamon stick

Mix cornstarch with a little water and set aside. In a saucepan, bring wine, sugar and cinnamon stick to a boil; remove from heat. Add cornstarch mixture, stirring constantly. Cook 1 minute longer.

COOK'S NOTE: Delicious on pancakes.

Old-Fashioned Apple Butter

DORIS ROBERSON | PLAINVIEW, SWISHER EC

16 large tart apples
½ cup water
½ teaspoon cinnamon
¾ teaspoon ground allspice
¾ teaspoon ground cloves
1 cup sugar

Core apples and cut into thick slices. Place apples in a heavy, covered saucepan with water. Heat and simmer until tender. Place cooked apples in a food processor. Using a chopping blade, process apples into a slightly coarse sauce. Place 1 quart applesauce in a 2-quart, microwave-safe bowl. Add spices to the sugar and mix well. Add sugar mixture to applesauce and blend. Place bowl in microwave; heat on high 5 minutes. Mix and turn bowl; continue heating until hot and bubbling, or sugar is dissolved. Cool and store in airtight container in the refrigerator. Serve on hot biscuits.

COOK'S NOTE: There are several apple orchards in our West Texas community, making apples in abundance. We wanted to can apple butter but could not find a recipe. My daughter and I began to experiment, and we devised this recipe.

Ice Cream Sauce

RITCHIE SCHROEDER | LITTLEFIELD, LAMB COUNTY EC

1½ cups sugar
1 cup evaporated milk
¼ cup butter
¼ cup light corn syrup
Dash of salt
½ cup toffee bits (Heath Bits'o Brickle preferred)

Combine sugar, milk, butter, syrup and salt. Bring to boil over low heat. Boil 1 minute. Remove from heat. Cool slightly before adding toffee bits. Cool, stirring occasionally, then chill. To serve, stir sauce and spoon over ice cream or pie. Refrigerate sauce in tightly covered container. Serves 8.

Lemon Sauce

MRS. A.C. MINZENMAYER | WINTERS, COLEMAN COUNTY EC

½ cup sugar
2 tablespoons flour
¾ cup cold water
2 tablespoons butter
Grated zest and juice of 1 lemon
1 egg yolk

In a saucepan, mix sugar and flour. Add water and stir until smooth; add butter and lemon zest. Boil 5 minutes, stirring constantly, until thick. Add lemon juice and slightly beaten egg yolk. Cook 2 minutes longer, stirring constantly. Use warm or cold. Makes 1 cup.

COOK'S NOTE: Good on bread pudding.

Brandied Peaches a la Mode

MARGARET J. MCKENZIE | KENEDY, KARNES EC

1 cup peach juice
1 teaspoon cinnamon
½ teaspoon ground nutmeg
8 canned peach halves
¼ cup brandy
Vanilla ice cream

Combine juice and spices in saucepan; bring to boil. Simmer 10–15 minutes. Add peach halves and heat until warm. Remove from heat and stir in brandy. Place peach halves in individual serving dishes with a scoop of ice cream. Spoon sauce over top. Serve with plain cookies or pound cake, if desired. Yields 8 servings.

Cream Sauce for Bread Pudding

MRS. ROY MASHBURN | MERKEL, TAYLOR EC

1 cup sugar
1 tablespoon flour
2 egg yolks, beaten
2 cups milk
2 tablespoons vanilla extract
1 teaspoon butter

Blend first 4 ingredients and cook in saucepan over low heat, stirring constantly. Mix in vanilla and butter. Pour over pudding when serving.

Peach Honey

GRADY TAYLOR | POST, LYNTEGAR EC

6–7 cups chopped peaches
5 cups sugar

Blend in blender. Cook in a saucepan, 5 minutes at a rolling boil. Refrigerate.

Strawberry-Cranberry Sauce

MRS. HARRY A. TUBBS | POST, LYNTEGAR EC

2 packages (10 ounces each) frozen sliced
    strawberries, thawed
½ cup sugar
¼ cup water
1 package (12 ounces) cranberries
¼ cup thinly sliced crystalized ginger
Rind from ½ large orange, cut into julienne strips
2 cinnamon sticks

Drain liquid from strawberries into a 3-quart saucepan. Add sugar and water to strawberry liquid. Bring to a boil, stirring to dissolve sugar. Add cranberries, ginger, orange rind and cinnamon. Return to boil, reduce heat; simmer 10 minutes or until cranberries pop. Stir in strawberries. Remove from heat and cool. Refrigerate.

COOK'S NOTE: This sauce can be kept several weeks in refrigerator and improves with age.

INDEX

Cream Cheese Icing 145
Fluffy White Frosting 146
Good Quick Frosting 145
Lemon Icing 146
Marshmallow Icing 146
Seven-Minute Icing 146
Shiny Chocolate Glaze 145

GRAPES
Green Grape Pie 175
Grape Salad 52

HAM
See "Pork"

ICE CREAMS
Apricot Ice Cream 206
Fried Ice Cream 205
Grandmother Hunter's Ice Cream 206
Lemon-Orange Sherbet 206
Tutti Fruiti Ice Cream 206
Voluptuous Butterfinger Ice Cream 205

JAMS & JELLIES
Fig Preserves 215
Heavenly Jam 215
Hot Pepper Jelly 215
Old-Fashioned Apple Butter 217

LAMB
Mexican Lamb Chops 113
Persian Cabbage Dolma 105
Roasted Leg of Lamb 112

LEMON
Cold Lemon Souffle 204
Easy-Cheesy Lemon Bars 152
French Lemon Pie 182
Lemon Angel Dessert 202
Lemon Chess Pie 181
Lemon Chiffon Pie 182
Lemon Dainty 202
Lemon Pecan Pie (With Cream Cheese Pastry) 185
Lemon Sauce 218
Lemon Sour Cream Pie 182
Lemon Squares 151
Lemon-Banana Pie 183
Pink Lemonade Pie 182

MAIN DISHES
Almond Chicken 80
Apple Baked Pork Chops 107
Arroz Con Pollo (Rice with Chicken) 79
Baked Deviled Egg Casserole 112
Baked Trout or Bass 114
Bar-B-Q Chicken in the Oven 76
Bar-B-Qued Meatballs 99
Bass Casserole 115
Bavarian Steak Rolls 91
Bazziola 92
Beef Pot Pie 100
Beef Roast With Gravy 91
Beef Sour Cream Enchiladas 90
Beef Stroganoff 90
Beefy Mexican Lasagna 93
Black-Eyed Pea Cornbread 95
Brazos Quiche 109
Breakfast Trash 111
Buttermilk Baked Chicken 77
Cabbage Roll 105
Calabacita (Squash Casserole) 106
Chalupa (Pork Roast With Pinto Beans) 107
Chalupa Loaf 89
Cheese Enchiladas 110
Cheesy Bacon Spaghetti 108
Cheesy Chicken Tortilla Stack 85
Cheesy Ham and Broccoli Bake 112
Chicken and Cheese Lasagna 77
Chicken and Dressing 82
Chicken and Dressing Casserole 82
Chicken Caruso 82
Chicken Casserole 84
Chicken Cherokee 82
Chicken Enchilada Casserole 76
Chicken Enchiladas 85
Chicken Flautas 84
Chicken Fritters 78
Chicken Paprika 78
Chicken Pie 81
Chicken Taco Casserole 84
Chiles Rellenos 110
Chuckwagon Casserole 88
Coke Steak 94
Cornbread Meatloaf 102
Country-Fried Catfish 114
Cowboy Casserole 93
Creole Pork Chops 108
Dad's Day Off Bar-B-Que 88

MUFFINS

WILD GAME

MY FAVORITES

MY FAVORITES

MY FAVORITES

MY FAVORITES

MY FAVORITES

MY FAVORITES

MY FAVORITES

MY FAVORITES

MY FAVORITES

MY FAVORITES

MY FAVORITES

MY FAVORITES

MY FAVORITES

MY FAVORITES

MY FAVORITES

MY FAVORITES

MY FAVORITES

MY FAVORITES

MY FAVORITES